AF902212

Studies in the History of Law and Justice

Volume 32

Series Editors

Mortimer Sellers, University of Baltimore, Baltimore, USA
Georges Martyn, Law Faculty, University of Ghent, Ghent, Belgium

Editorial Board Members

António Pedro Barbas Homem, Faculty of Law, Universidade de Lisboa, Lisbon, Portugal

Emmanuele Conte, Facolta di Giurisprudenza, Università degli Studi Roma Tre, Roma, Italy

Maria Gigliola di Renzo Villata, Law & Legal History, Università degli Studi di Milano, Milano, Italy

Markus Dirk Dubber, Faculty of Law, University of Toronto, Toronto, Canada

William Ewald, University of Pennsylvania Law School, Philadelphia, USA

Igor Filippov, Faculty of History, Moscow State University, Moscow, Russia

Amalia Kessler, Stanford Law School Crown Quad, Stanford University, Stanford, USA

Mia Korpiola, Helsinki Collegium for Advanced Studies, Helsinki, Finland

Aniceto Masferrer, Faculty of Law, Universidad de Valencia, Valencia, Spain

Yasutomo Morigiwa, Nagoya University Graduate School of Law, Tokyo, Japan

Ulrike Müßig, Universität Passau, Passau, Germany

Sylvain Soleil, Faculté de Droit et de Science Politique, Université de Rennes, Rennes, France

James Q. Whitman, Yale Law School, New Haven, USA

The purpose of this book series is to publish high quality volumes on the history of law and justice. Legal history can be a deeply provocative and influential field, as illustrated by the growth of the European universities and the *Ius Commune*, the French Revolution, the American Revolution, and indeed all the great movements for national liberation through law. The study of history gives scholars and reformers the models and courage to question entrenched injustices, by demonstrating the contingency of law and other social arrangements. Yet legal history today finds itself diminished in the universities and legal academy. Too often scholarship betrays no knowledge of what went before, or why legal institutions took the shape that they did.This series seeks to remedy that deficiency.

Studies in the History of Law and Justice will be theoretical and reflective. Volumes will address the history of law and justice from a critical and comparative viewpoint. The studies in this series will be strong bold narratives of the development of law and justice. Some will be suitable for a very broad readership.

Contributions to this series will come from scholars on every continent and in every legal system. Volumes will promote international comparisons and dialogue. The purpose will be to provide the next generation of lawyers with the models and narratives needed to understand and improve the law and justice of their own era. The series includes monographs focusing on a specific topic, as well as collections of articles covering a theme or collections of article by one author.

Ioanna Pervou

Protecting Nationals Abroad and the Reconceptualization of Sovereignty

Springer

Ioanna Pervou
Law Faculty
Democritus University of Thrace
Komotini, Greece

ISSN 2198-9842 ISSN 2198-9850 (electronic)
Studies in the History of Law and Justice
ISBN 978-3-032-05230-8 ISBN 978-3-032-05231-5 (eBook)
https://doi.org/10.1007/978-3-032-05231-5

© The Editor(s) (if applicable) and The Author(s), under exclusive license to Springer Nature Switzerland AG 2025

This work is subject to copyright. All rights are solely and exclusively licensed by the Publisher, whether the whole or part of the material is concerned, specifically the rights of translation, reprinting, reuse of illustrations, recitation, broadcasting, reproduction on microfilms or in any other physical way, and transmission or information storage and retrieval, electronic adaptation, computer software, or by similar or dissimilar methodology now known or hereafter developed.
The use of general descriptive names, registered names, trademarks, service marks, etc. in this publication does not imply, even in the absence of a specific statement, that such names are exempt from the relevant protective laws and regulations and therefore free for general use.
The publisher, the authors and the editors are safe to assume that the advice and information in this book are believed to be true and accurate at the date of publication. Neither the publisher nor the authors or the editors give a warranty, expressed or implied, with respect to the material contained herein or for any errors or omissions that may have been made. The publisher remains neutral with regard to jurisdictional claims in published maps and institutional affiliations.

This Springer imprint is published by the registered company Springer Nature Switzerland AG
The registered company address is: Gewerbestrasse 11, 6330 Cham, Switzerland

If disposing of this product, please recycle the paper.

as ever, to my parents, Yannis and Areti

Preface

This book explores the forcible protection of nationals abroad (forcible PNA) doctrine, which occupies legal theory for quite a long time. This doctrine is fairly considered dubious, or simply dangerous, for the structure of the international community, as it tests the limits and resilience of the principle of state sovereignty.

Having this key observation in mind, this book examines the evolution of the doctrine in the course of time. The first chapter emphasizes the doctrine's invocation in the pre-Charter era. This historical analysis is crucial, in order to understand how the doctrine emerged and what it meant initially. The examination of certain incidents demonstrates how states understood forcible PNA, as part of their exercise of sovereign rights. In addition, this pre-Charter analysis of the doctrine helps to better understand the post-Charter approach towards it, by way of juxtaposition.

The second chapter is an in-depth analysis of the doctrine in relation to the UN Charter. It explores how the UN system and the general prohibition of recourse to force affected the doctrine's legality. Although this analysis is thought to be redundant or obsolete, it is necessary to better understand the fluctuations in the doctrine's legal acceptance. The chapter's startpoint is that the doctrine has a negative connotation. Based on this proposition, it examines its similarities and differences compared to other doctrines, introducing an exception to the threat or use of force. This chapter offers a brief overview of the doctrine in the post-war legal reality. Although the prevailing view suggests that the doctrine does not fit into the logic of the UN Charter, it survived in the rhetoric of states, thus proving its necessity.

In the same course, the third chapter further analyzes how the post-Charter state practice on forcible PNA was shaped. This chapter demonstrates the occasions on which states invoked the doctrine and marks the key elements of their legal justification. It sheds light on the differentiation between theory and practice. The first three chapters are indispensable to the topic's better understanding. Although there are already such analyses in international literature, these chapters offer the requisite historical and legal foundations to better comprehend when the doctrine came up in the course of time and how it is employed by states.

The fourth chapter is a detailed analysis of the recent Russian discourse regarding forcible PNA and how its invocation was a Trojan Horse, hiding its territorial claims. The chapter is illuminating as it proves how state policy may turn this doctrine into a manipulative tool. The Russian discourse is thoroughly examined not only with regard to the recent hostilities against Ukraine; rather, it also analyzes how the invasion of Georgia has shaped the Russian line of argumentation, also serving as a test for the international community's acceptance of the doctrine's invocation. In this framework, it explores how international judicial bodies have assessed the doctrine's invocation so far.

Finally, the final chapter explores whether there is a human dimension and if PNA is a matter that would be better addressed through human rights institutions. The association between forcible PNA and human rights is not anew, and many authors have pointed to the nexus between the two. Forcible PNA puts nationals in the epicenter, like human rights protection. However, the connection between these two legal domains (use of force and human rights) is a perennially difficult undertaking, usually treated with distrust. However, this book proposes that there is no ground to attempt reading the doctrine through the lens of human rights, due to the reconceptualization of state sovereignty.

Throughout all chapters the concept of state sovereignty is central, and it turns out that the doctrine's perception relies on our understanding of the principle. This correlation gave rise to the book's key idea that state sovereignty has been considered for quite some through the lens of territoriality, or better that it was equated with territorial integrity. It is this interpretation of sovereignty that outlaws at once forcible PNA. However, this perspective disregards that forcible PNA keeps coming in state discourse and that the occasions which require recourse to force to rescue a state's nationals residing abroad are increasing, as a direct result of globalization. In this sense, the book aims to demonstrate how state sovereignty needs to be seen from a human-centric angle.

Forcible PNA, although a doctrine for the use of force, puts nationals at its epicenter and brings back the idea that nationality is an equally important pillar of state sovereignty. This proposal is becoming increasingly important due to the new conditions brought about by globalization. Although territoriality is well established and the inviolability of borders is a major requirement of the international legal order, globalization has given rise to human mobility. This fluidity reshapes the concept of nationality and thus makes it clear that the state sovereignty concept evolves. A more human-centric approach to it, due to globalization, may as well mark a shift to the way we observe the reasons to recourse to force. Therefore, the absolute distinction between legal fields is an obstacle to the better understanding of state sovereignty. In this context, the forcible PNA doctrine offers an opportunity to understand its change. As such, it is suggested that the doctrine will keep coming up in states' discourse in the future and play a central role in their practice.

Komotini, Greece Ioanna Pervou

Acknowledgments

Throughout this course I was lucky enough to have the support and advice of many people. I would first like to thank Prof. Constantine Antonopoulos for sharing valuable thoughts on the book's topic. The idea of this project has long been discussed among peers and colleagues. I sincerely would like to thank Francesco Messineo, Efthymios Papastavridis, Kelly Pisimisi, Ilias Plakokefalos, and Maria Spyridaki for their comments on the book's drafts. Finally, I would not be able to accomplish this project without the unquestioning support of my family and friends. My immense thanks to Yannis, Areti, Yannis, Kostis and Sofia, who put up with me in my everyday life and have stood by me since day one of this project.

Competing Interests The author has no competing interests to declare that are relevant to the content of this manuscript.

Contents

Abbreviations

ARSIWA	Articles on Responsibility of States for Internationally Wrongful Acts
Art.	Article
ECtHR	European Court of Human Rights
ECOWAS	Economic Community of West African States
EU	European Union
Forcible PNA	Forcible Protection of Nationals Abroad
IAPF	Inter-American Peace Force
ICISS	International Commission on Intervention and State Sovereignty
ICJ	International Court of Justice
IIFFMCG	Independent International Fact-Finding Mission on the Conflict in Georgia
NATO	North Atlantic Treaty Organization
NEOCG	Non-Combatant Evacuation Operation Coordination Group
NEOs	Non-Combatant Evacuation Operations
OAS	Organization of American States
OECS	Organization of Eastern Caribbean States
OSCE	Organization for Security and Cooperation in Europe
PACE	Parliamentary Assembly of the Council of Europe
PCIJ	Permanent Court of International Justice
R2P	Responsibility to Protect
R2Pn	Responsibility to Protect nationals
RUF	Revolutionary United Front
UDHR	Universal Declaration of Human Rights
UK	United Kingdom
UN	United Nations
UNCh	United Nations Charter
UNCLOS	United Nations Convention on the Law of the Sea
UNEF	United Nations Emergency Force (Palestine Dispute)
UNGA	United Nations General Assembly
UNOC	United Nations Operation Congo

UNOMIC	United Nations Observer Mission in Georgia
UNSC	United Nations Security Council
US	United States of America
USSR	Union of Soviet Socialist Republics
VCLT	Vienna Convention on the Law of Treaties
WWI	First World War
WWII	Second World War

Chapter 1
Protection of Nationals Abroad in the Pre-Charter Era

1.1 Vattel's Extraterritoriality of Sovereignty as the Doctrine's Matrix

Recourse to force to protect one's nationals abroad is an institution which is assumed to have emerged either during the Renaissance, or more precisely at the aftermath of the French Revolution,[1] based on Grotius' guardianship theory, which led the foundations for decentralized humanitarian military intervention.[2] More precisely, it was the outcome of the asymmetric commercial relationships between Western European countries and the rest. PNA is tiny part of Europe's extraterritorial imperialism, according to which citizens of European great powers at the time were accorded preferential treatment when being abroad.[3] If the established privileges were deemed inadequate for their protection, or in case they faced imminent danger, then forcible PNA was part of their states of origin protection spectrum of options.

The doctrine's legal foundation is located in the now well-known standpoint of Emmerich de Vattel, according to whom

> [w]however ill-treats a citizen indirectly injures the state, which must protect that citizen. The sovereign of the injured citizen must avenge the deed and, if possible, force the aggressor to give full satisfaction or punish him, since otherwise the citizen will not obtain the chief end of civil society, which is protection.[4]

According to the most prominent interpretation of this excerpt, a state's jurisdiction is not confined within its borders. On the contrary, it extends to any place where a

[1] Borchard (1934), p. 361.

[2] Criddle (2015), p. 307.

[3] Todd (2018), p. 111.

[4] de Vattel (1916), p. 136.

© The Author(s), under exclusive license to Springer Nature Switzerland AG 2025

I. Pervou, *Protecting Nationals Abroad and the Reconceptualization of Sovereignty*, Studies in the History of Law and Justice 32,
https://doi.org/10.1007/978-3-032-05231-5_1

state's nationals are and guarantees their protection against any threat or injury. More specifically, a state has

> the exclusive power among other internal authorities to represent and rule its people within the territory, but it also has the exclusive power among other public authorities outside (that is, other States) to represent and rule its people within the said territory.[5]

Vattel's teachings were the impetus for long and fruitful debates pertaining to the concept of sovereignty *per se*, the means a state may employ to safeguard its sovereign rights and finally the international legal organization.

To better comprehend Vattel's dictum one needs to first consider the historical context in which it emerged. Vattel's perception of sovereignty and its limits were formulated during the late eighteenth century. During that period the concept of sovereign states as we currently perceive it was not yet cemented. Except for colonial powers, empires still existed, albeit the institution was in decline. In this sense, the international community consisted of far less subjects: there were fewer states and institutionalized international cooperation scarcely existed. International relations were based mostly on bilateral agreements between sovereigns, and their terms reflected the dynamics of power between them. In plain terms, the notion of 'sovereign equality' was out of sight. More precisely, the concept of sovereign equality expanded only to European states, that were considered "civilized", irrespective of their political power, prosperity, or influence in international relations. Although Vattel explains in Droit des Gens that a dwarf is no less human than a giant, to illustrate how states are equal, this metaphor applies only to the European states, which formed at a time a distinct "political system, an integral body".[6] Except for this sort of equality between states, the concept was deemed inapplicable to any other entity. In other words, "it was the community of *civilized* states that mattered for the purposes of international law".[7]

Vattel's taking on the concept of sovereignty is usually thought to echo the interests of colonial powers of the time, attempting to establish a classification scheme among nations based on whether they were considered civilized or not, by the ones which perceived that role for themselves. However, a non-sporadic study of his teachings reveals that Vattel's understanding of international law was the combination of positivist dictums and pragmatistic observations. Thus, PNA as part of extraterritorial sovereignty was plain truth at that time. A practice so often employed by states, that could not be disregarded by theory.[8] Thereat, the subjects of international law at the time kept for themselves the role of active protectors for their citizens and international stability in turn, establishing for themselves an "international right to security".[9]

[5] Beaulac (2003), p. 262.

[6] Koskenniemi and Kari (2020), p. 170.

[7] Tzouvala (2019), p. 86.

[8] Cavallar (2008), p. 207.

[9] Kalmanovitz (2018), p. 222.

From this viewpoint, it becomes clear that Vattel's perception was quite far from the concept of sovereign states as they now exist. Sovereignty was a well-established institution, but it was not necessarily defined in terms of territoriality; rather, sovereignty was the archetypical manifestation of state power.[10] According to this understanding of sovereignty, recourse to force for the protection of nationals abroad is a sign of solidarity and the evolution of civil society. As Edwin Borchard observes, protection of citizens abroad is "a primitive form of clan organization and of an early social institution which deemed an injury to a member of the clan as an injury to the clan itself, justifying collective revenge".[11] In this sense, one may well suggest that up till the early modern period, "the scope of political power and responsibility and thus also authority and legitimacy was defined by the relationship between a polity and its people, not by territory".[12] Taking these into account, it follows that sovereignty was closely intertwined with nationality rather than territoriality; a condition which was reversed at the emergence of nation-states.

The second issue of concern regarding Vattel's perception is the means that states are entitled to use, in order to effectively protect their citizens abroad. At this point, two considerations come up. PNA is not confined to the strict limits of the use of force, in the first place. Strong nationality ties also meant the exercise of protection and the pursuit of national interests through peaceful means. This view remained almost unchanged over time and survived the UN Charter. For example, Hersch Lauterpacht upheld that alien residents in a foreign country continue "to owe allegiance to the sovereign of [their] own state [and] that allegiance expresses itself in [their] continued subjection to the laws of [their] own country".[13] Two conclusions are drawn from this proposition. First, that national jurisdiction was not fully established during that time, thus allowing for nationals abroad to be excluded from the jurisdiction of their state of residence. Second, this perception allows for the differentiated treatment of people due to their nationality. Aliens were exempted from a state's authority, for better or worse.

Diplomatic protection, the legal correlation of the forcible PNA, was a well-founded institution during the previous centuries, yet not consolidated. Vattel's same writings are considered as the ones which shape diplomatic protection in the form it has today. Therefore, Vattel's theory comprises both peaceful and forcible means for the protection of a state's citizens abroad. It is, therefore, proposed that

> [t]he modern approach to diplomatic protection took shape in the 18th century, and is reflect in the writing of Vattel, who expressed it as an obligation of the sending State to protect its citizens when they are injured abroad [...] In this formulation, the view that is was the duty of the sending State to protect its citizens injured abroad was joined to the view that the sending State was thereby vindicating its own rights.[14]

---

[10] Mueser (2018), p. 141.

[11] Borchard (1929), p. 121.

[12] Leira and Græger (2020), p. 4.

[13] Lauterpacht (1947), p. 335.

[14] Crawford (2017), p. 137.

Thus, there can be no doubt that Vattel's perception of sovereign protection included both diplomatic and forcible means. This observation allows for a better understanding of Vattel's teachings. Not only, they were not promoting PNA and forcible interventionism in general; to the contrary, they promoted "peaceful imperialism" when possible. Such an interpretation of Vattel's teaching was employed by Lin Tse-hsu to criticize British intervention in the opium wars.[15] For example, jurisdictional or judicial supremacy of the civilized nations and the imposition of their legal norms on other subjects, was considered a much better option.[16]

Finally, it is estimated that Vattel's teachings had a significant impact on states' foreign policy for many years. In this sense, this theory was modified according to emerging needs and the challenges posed each time. The start of the nineteenth century signified the creation of nation-states and the fall of empires. Although colonialism remained a strong institution, this development led to Vattel's re-reading. From that time onwards, PNA became a synonym for the use of force, while diplomatic protection gained ground in the international sphere and became a distinct form of protection. During the nineteenth century, they were both deemed valuable tools, available to powerful states. Super-powers of the nineteenth century considered that the use of force to protect their nationals abroad was a prerogative recognized as part of their external sovereignty.[17] That is, although territoriality was prioritized over nationality, powerful states continued favoring the use of this doctrine. Both the institution of diplomatic protection, as well as recourse to force for the protection of nationals abroad progressed, as they formed distinct part of state policy. They had a parallel course; the gradual consolidation of diplomatic protection did not lessen interventions in the name of nationals, as some would probably have expected.[18]

Vattel's position is also consistent with the fundamental core of international law, that does not recognize individuals as subjects of it. As a result, states bear responsibility to protect them and "avenge the deed". Therefore,

> Vattel's thesis not only asserted the right of the national state of the alien to protect its national, but implied that there was an obligation resting upon the alien's national state to protect him. It is clear that Vattel conceived the right of protection as inhering in the national state [...] the injury done to the alien was regarded as being a violation of an obligation owed by the host state to the alien's national state. Formally, this explanation was the result of the theory that the individual had no rights at international law.[19]

In this sense, both diplomatic and forcible protection emanated from states' responsibilities vis-à-vis their nationals and other nation-states.[20] It is a primitive way of conceptualizing state responsibility. This idea is reaffirmed in jurisprudence too.

---

[15] Cavallar (2008), p. 209.

[16] Zurbuchen (2010), p. 81.

[17] Caflisch (2011), p. 266.

[18] Borchard (1915).

[19] Amerasinghe (2004), p. 44.

[20] Dunn (1941), p. 15.

For example, the Vattelian perception of states' responsibility to protect their nationals is reflected in the *Mavrommatis Palestine Concessions* case before the PCIJ, where it was stated that

> [b]y taking up the case of one of its subjects and by resorting to diplomatic action or international judicial proceedings on his behalf, a State is in reality asserting its own rights – its right to ensure, in the person of its subjects, respect for the rules of international law. The question, therefore, whether the present dispute originates in an injury to a private interest, which in point of fact is the case in many international disputes, is irrelevant from this standpoint. Once a State has taken up a case on behalf of one of its subjects before an international tribunal, in the eyes of the latter the State is the sole claimant.[21]

Vattel's theory gave a strong nuance of how the international community would serve civil society. If this theory is read out of its historical context it is a projection of the international community's desirable integration.

It is aptly pointed that PNA, in all its forms—peaceful or forcible—has been one of the first expressions of human rights protection. Although problematic and imperfect it signified states' interests to guarantee their nationals rights or claims.[22] However, in the pre-Charter era it legalized forcible intervention by powerful states, affirming the saying that might is right. On most occasions, states possessing economic and military power vacillated between diplomatic, judicial and forcible protection, usually combining aspects of them all. The *Costa Rica Packet* case is a typical example in this regard, as the UK intervened and demanded damages for the arrest and detention of the whaling-ship's captain by Holland. The UK was dissatisfied with the decision of the Dutch judiciary and requested an arbitral award.[23] The case is exemplary as it demonstrates how PNA is invoked to question another legal system's validity. Although, both the UK and the Netherlands were robust colonial powers at the end of the nineteenth century, the formed did not hesitate to doubt the latter's national legal order and demand the issuance of an arbitral award. What is more, it is interesting to notice that the UK decided to exercise pressure to achieve the captain's protection, who was a naturalized British subject, and obtain compensation for his unlawful detention and loss of the whaling period.[24] In this sense, the *Costa Rica Packet* case demonstrates that PNA was mostly a matter of choice: a practice employed by colonial powers to consolidate their primacy among equals and show strength to the weak.

A small group of states reserved for themselves the privilege to recourse to force or proceed with coercive and punitive measures and exert their power over other countries, more simply a way to export their law.[25] This supremacy was established

---

[21] *Mavrommatis Palestine Concessions* case, judgment of 30 August 1924, PCIJ, Ser. A, No. 2, p. 12.

[22] Mégret (2020), p. 455; Περγαντής (2017), pp. 150–152.

[23] Oppenheim (2005), p. 254; Mullins (2001), pp. 267–285.

[24] Second report on State Responsibility by Mr. Gaetano Arangio-Ruiz, Special Rapporteur, UN Doc A/CN.4/425 & Corr. 1 and Add.1 & Corr. 1, para 48.

[25] Green (1975), p. 234.

on the level of their legal civilization, and they so distinguished between civilized, semi-civilized and barbarous States. Thereat, it has been contended that

> [a]mong nations possessing a higher standard of civilization there are recognized methods of obtaining redress, varying in the degree of coercion brought to bear as they approach hostilities. [...] In cases like those above mentioned, a State has the right and duty of demanding redress or restitution, and of exacting guarantees against renewal. Should diplomacy fail, even when supported by threats of further action, it must materialize those threats and take one of two courses, either measures more or less pacific in character, yet strongly coercive, or the final arbitrament of war. It has the right intervene and prevent the continuance of the offence.[26]

Two conclusions can be directly inferred from the above. First, recourse to force was considered the last resort for the protection of a state's nationals abroad. A wide range of actions were recognized in case an offense occurred. From diplomatic means, or arbitration, to coercive measures and military action. It is worth noticing that diplomatic protection was not necessarily a better alternative compared to the forcible PNA. The institution acquired an imperialistic character: superpowers recourse to diplomatic protection if the decisions of domestic courts against their nationals did not satisfy their interests. In that case, they intervened on behalf of their citizens and requested arbitration. On some occasions they did not even wait for the exhaustion of domestic legal remedies. Diplomatic protection took the form of diplomatic intervention, even with the aid of armed forces.[27] The institution's misinterpretation resulted in the formation of the Calvo clause, which provided that recourse to diplomatic protection would take place after the dispute was dealt with by national judiciaries, to secure that weaker states would not suffer continuous interventions in their national legal order.[28] Although the clause referred to the equal treatment of investors and was fell part of insolvency law, it gradually became a synonym to jurisdictional equality. That is, aliens were not entitled to a higher degree of protection compared to a state's citizens. They had first to submit their claims to local courts, before turning to their state of nationality.[29] It was initially a clause against judicial and financial suppression of the weak.

Second, states' display of power was justified on their legal civilization. This differentiation between civilized, semi-civilized and barbarous states was a hint of the severity of measures the civilized would employ against the rest. In this regard, intervention to prevent intolerance and anarchy and to enforce reparation for injury to life and property was considered legitimate in the pre-Charter era. According to Lingelbach, forcible intervention in response to injury of life and property of nationals abroad was an action dictated by civilized states' responsibilities vis-à-vis their subjects and by the need to preserve international stability, given that "anarchy leads to insecurity of life and property and jeopardizes the interests of other nations".[30]

---

26 Brook (1905), p. 177.

27 Carstén (1962), p. 40.

28 Shan (2007), pp. 123–163; Feller (1933), pp. 461–468.

29 Garcia-Mora (1950), p. 206.

30 Lingelbach (1900), p. 21.

1.2 Forcible Interventions in the Name of Nationals' Rights Abroad

During the 19th and early twentieth century forcible interventions for the protection of a state's nationals abroad have been numerous. Among them, the Don Pacifico affair is an incident which has historically attracted attention.

David Pacifico was a Jew born in Gibraltar in 1784. From 1837 on he was residing in Athens, at the beginning appointed as consul of Portugal in Greece, and after resignation he remained in the Greek capital and worked as a private merchant. The incident which triggered the conflict took place in 1847 in Athens, when civilians approached Pacifico's residence to complain about suspending the local custom of burning the effigy of Judas Iscariot on Easter morning. It is reported that civilians falsely believed that this suspension was instigated by Pacifico, because he was a Jew. Their protest resulted in the violent trespassing of Pacifico's residence, destruction and the loss of valuables. At the aftermath of this incident, Pacifico invoked his allegiance to Great Britain to request protection and compensation from the Greek government. In his correspondence with the British ambassador in Athens he enumerated in detail his losses by the "barbarians".[31] The UK demanded compensation by the Greek state to restore Pacifico's damage. After long discussions no agreement was reached, and diplomatic means seemed ineffective. The UK's Ministry of Foreign Affairs decided to proceed with coercive measures against Greece, to satisfy its claims. In effect, on January 22, 1850, all vessels of the Greek government had been seized by the British fleet. The blockade lasted approximately for 2 months and the Pacifico crisis ended when the Greek government agreed to compensation.

Overall, the affair was the climax of the deteriorating bilateral relations between the UK and Greece. More specifically, the relations between Greece and the UK were already troubled. The main source of disputes was the protectorate exercised by Britain over the Ionian islands and their policy respectively. In addition, other minor incidents created a climate of disharmony: restitution and apologies for the alleged mistreatment of the sailors from the British ship, the Fantôme, as well as compensation demanded by a British historian, George Finlay.[32] Apart from a sentiment of humiliation of the Greek state and people, the Pacifico affair affected the relations between the UK, France and Russia who were jointly protecting Greece after it gained its independence. The bold stance held by the British Ministry of Foreign Affairs met the sharp confrontation from the opposition. The UK's naval blockade was considered a pretext and a means of pressure to Greece with a view to satisfy Britain's interests.

Nevertheless, apart from disagreement on the effectiveness of the British foreign policy, opposition did not challenge the UK's right to forcibly protect its subjects abroad. Even though, few parliamentarians sympathized with Pacifico himself, protection of nationals' interests abroad rested within the executive's implementation

[31] Whitten (1986), p. 256.

[32] Hicks (2004), p. 518.

of the "civis Romanus sum" principle.[33] The debate in the House of Commons is laminating in this regard, as it was stated that

> while the House fully recognizes the right and duty of the Government to secure to Her Majesty's subjects residing in foreign States the full protection of the laws of those States, it regrets to find, by the correspondence recently laid upon the table by Her Majesty's command, that various claims against the Greek Government, doubtful in point of justice or exaggerated in amount, have been enforced by coercive measures directed against the commerce and people of Greece, and calculated to endanger the continuance of our friendly relations with other Powers.[34]

The Don Pacifico affair is an example of the so-called "gunboat diplomacy,"[35] and what Brownlie called the "kind-hearted gunmen".[36] In plain terms, states' willingness to "employ some degree of naval force [...] in time of peace".[37] Civilized states of the time, did not hesitate to recourse to force whenever they considered the interests of their nationals residing abroad had been violated. These interventions were in sheer contrast with any understanding of territoriality; they were authorized on the grounds that nationals' mistreatment could be the result of the inability of semi-civilized or barbaric states to familiarize with the rule of law and implement it. It turns out that forcible PNA occurred even when there was no peril for people's lives and well-being. In many cases, it was a matter of financial disputes and claims of satisfaction.[38]

The British empire favored this doctrine; the Pacifico affair was just but an example of its consolidated foreign policy. Likewise, recourse to force was authorized whenever the UK felt that its hegemony was endangered, like in the *Costa Rica packet* affair. Another example arose in 1904, when the Nicaraguan government confiscated the property of British turtle fishers. The UK responded by sending a gunboat to reverse injustice.[39] The same policy was embraced by other powerful states at the time. For example, the US Court of Appeals adjudicated *In re Neagle* that the use of armed forces abroad to protect a state's nationals is not subject to statutory authorization, but it forms part of the presidential powers.[40] Considering such precedents, it comes as no surprise that the US officially adopted in 1948 the state's rightful recourse to force to protect its nationals' lives and property abroad against arbitrary violence. Although this legislative provision was consistent with the American practice in the preceding years, it entered into force right after the adoption of the UN Charter, where the US vehemently denied unilateral recourse to

[33] Brown (2002), p. 12.

[34] House of Lords. (17 June 1850). Affairs of Greece – Lord Stanley. HL Deb vol 111 cc1293-404, para 1332. Retrieved February 22, 2025, from https://api.parliament.uk/historic-hansard/lords/1850/jun/17/affairs-of-greece

[35] Murfett (1999), pp. 81–93.

[36] Brownlie (1973), pp. 139–148.

[37] Cable (1981), p. 23.

[38] Miles (2018), p. 158.

[39] Brook (1905), pp. 177–178.

[40] *In re Neagle*, US Circuit Court, N.D. California. (September 16, 1889) 39 F. 833 (N.D.Cal. 1889).

force, proposing the absolute character of the prohibition of the use of force.[41] A form of 'jurisdictional imperialism' that survived the post–1945 hegemonic period.[42]

During the second half of the nineteenth century, powerful states did not hesitate to intervene in other states' domestic affairs, to suppress uprisings and rebellions. The presence of naval forces on the coasts of those states was a constant reminder that force could be used at any point. The threat of military intervention is intended to safeguard their economic and political interests and rescue their nationals if needed. However, most such incidents did not reach the level of military intervention, and thus forcible PNA did not take place. There are a few such examples reaffirming this pattern. This was the case of the Mejba Revolt in Tunisia in 1864,[43] and similarly the Mokrani Revolt in Algeria in 1871.[44] Although military intervention was avoided, the display of power by states whose interests would be affected were a catalytic factor in easing tensions and restoring the favored regimes in these states' governance. These examples are commonly brought up as forcible PNA, however the argument of subjects' protection was a minor one.[45] After all, in both cases the states in turmoil were either protectorates, or former colonies of the intervening ones. Therefore, interference in their domestic affairs was expected, or even instigated by their governors.[46]

Finally, a culminating point for the doctrine of forcible PNA in the pre-Charter era was the Boxer rebellion in China. This insurgency was soon transformed into war and provoked multinational counterinsurgency, largely resembling today's military evacuation operations. More specifically, the rebels were a secret society who called themselves "The Righteous and Harmonious Fists". However, western states codenamed them "boxers" because they practiced martial arts. The rebels protested the Chinese dynasty's failure to deal extreme poverty, as well as its loose policy vis-à-vis western powers. They gradually gained support by the general population with the motto "Support the Qing, Extinguish the Foreigners". In 1900, insurgency escalated, and violence intensified. The Boxers burned churches, targeted foreigners and Christians. Afterwards, they surrounded the building blocks where Western countries' embassies were located. The dynasty sided with the rebels. These

[41] Art. 614 entitled "Use of Force Against a Friendly State" provides that "1. The use of force by United States naval personnel against a friendly foreign state, or against anyone within the territories thereof, is illegal. 2. The right of self-preservation, however, is a right which belongs to states as well as to individuals, and in the case of states it includes the protection of the state, its honor, and its possessions, and the lives and property of its citizens against arbitrary violence, actual or impending, whereby the state or its citizens may suffer irreparable injury. The conditions calling for the application of the right of self-preservation cannot be defined beforehand but must left to the sound judgment of responsible officers, who are to perform their duties in this respect with all possible care and forebearance. In no case shall force be exercised in time of peace otherwise than as an application of the right of self-preservation as above defined". Navy Department (1948), p. 73.

[42] Margolies (2011), p. 576.

[43] Moore (1965), pp. 13–14.

[44] Vince (2020), p. 70.

[45] Ronzitti (2019), p. 435.

[46] Wood Renton (1933), p. 222.

developments prompted the response of western countries, mostly European joined by others,[47] who sought the relief of their nationals, facing immediate peril. Eleven states (including the US, the UK, France, Russia, Italy and Germany) sent troops to protect their nationals trapped in Beijing.[48] The situation worsened when the Western forces bombarded Chinese forts and China officially declared war against them. Western forces allied and outnumbered the Chinese; as a result, China declared an armistice and the conflict soon ended. In 1901 the conflicting parties signed a protocol which provided China ought to compensate the western powers. The Boxer rebellion was a bloodshed, given the large number of casualties. It is estimated that around 20,000–30,000 Chinese Christians lost their lives, alongside 2000 Chinese soldiers and 1000 Western troops.[49]

Western forcible intervention to suppress the Boxer rebellion is the epitome of the PNA doctrine. The allied western forces rushed to help their nationals, whose lives were in actual and imminent peril. In this regard, the military invasion of China was not a shield to promote their national interests. The multinational counterinsurgency operation would qualify even according to the criteria set nowadays by the UNCh for the lawful use of force. What is more, it is reasonably considered the predecessor of military alliances and such coalitions.[50] It is also a unique occasion, since so many great powers of the time united and proceeded with a military operation in defense of their nationals.

Forcible PNA was well established by the time the Boxer rebellion occurred. This incident was certainly not an exception to the rule, since the practice endured changes in international relations and was a common feature of some states' policies. PNA was one of the major arguments Japan brought forward to justify its invasion in China's Manchuria in 1931. Respectively, it was reported that

> Japan complains of innumerable insults and irritating actions against her nationals, of the issuance of secret instructions to local Chinese government officials to ignore Japanese rights, to foster anti-Japanese education among Chinese school children, and to obstruct Japanese residence and travel in Manchuria.[51]

Japan's foreign policy was anticipated, considering the long-lasting character of the conflict in Manchuria. There are two points though, which differentiate this case from the rest. First, one needs to consider that neither Japan nor China were included in the small club of the self-proclaimed "civilized nations". In this sense, forcible PNA did not signify Japan's attempt to export legal civilization, nor the dynamics between the two states looked like a Goliath and David contest. Up till then, the doctrine was employed by "strong States [which] were inclined to intervene with weaker ones, financially as well as forcible, to protect the interests of their

[47] Zhao and Pasture (2022), p. 86.

[48] Ouellet (2009), p. 515.

[49] Shichor (2016), pp. 101–103.

[50] Otsuka (2018), pp. 111–130; Bradley (2019), p. 755.

[51] Mallory (1932), p. 223.

nationals".[52] Second and most important, Japan officially proclaimed that its conventional obligations stemming from the Kellogg-Briand pact, and the Nine-Power treaty[53] were not violated, although both legal documents provided that the contracting parties renounced war as an instrument of national policy.[54] However, it was generally perceived by third parties that outlawing war in the pact did not affect Japan's claim to guarantee its nationals safety since the Chinese were unable and unwilling to do so;[55] rather it meant that no territorial gains from such military actions would be recognized.[56]

The 1931 Manchurian incident seems to have established a more concise concept of what forcible PNA involves. Recourse to force in the name of one's nationals does not contravene peace agreements, and it is permitted for so long as it does not entail territorial claims, leading to annexation.[57] Third states' reaction to the Japanese intervention favored the argument that using force to safeguard the rights of one's nationals abroad was considered legitimate in principle. To this direction, the words of the US Secretary of State, Henry Stimson are a typical mark of the prevailing view then. According to him, "a nation which sought to mask imperialistic policy under the guise of defense of its nationals would soon be unmasked".[58] This view was later upheld by the Lytton report and subsequently adopted by the League of Nations.[59] Overall, forcible PNA was accepted by the international legal order, and it was the Japanese imperialistic practice which turned the doctrine's invocation to an unaccepted aggression.[60]

There are three major observations to be inferred from the preceding analysis and examples. First, the conjunction between sovereignty and extraterritoriality. Unlike the post-Charter era, sovereignty was not a synonym to territoriality and had a certain external value. In this sense, states were justified to exert influence and pressure with all available means at their disposition. In this regard, the term "intervention" refers to every possible way a state may interfere with another state's internal affairs and does not necessarily imply the use of force. Forcible PNA was just but an option for the states that could afford it and support it militarily. The second remark refers to who was considered a national.

The above examples demonstrate the low standards employed by the intervening states regarding the concept of a "national". Protection was not afforded only on a subject that could claim nationality by birth or blood, but to anyone who had strong

[52] State Practice during the Pre-United Nations Period (2002), p. 30.

[53] Treaty Between the Nine Powers Concerning the Chinese Customs Tariff (Nine-Power Treaty). (Washington, 6 February 1922). Retrieved, February 22, 2025 from https://worldjpn.net/documents/texts/pw/19220206.T3E.html

[54] Cherrington (1928), p. 13.

[55] Pemberton (2019), p. 460; Takaki (1932), p. 952.

[56] Cherrington (1928), p. 13; Jessup (1935), pp. 110–116.

[57] Wright (1932), p. 64.

[58] The Far Eastern Problem: Official Texts and Summary of the Lytton Report (1933), p. 38.

[59] See, Hudson (1933).

[60] Wetzler (2020), p. 142.

ties with a state or served a country by promoting its interests abroad. In this sense, anyone who had some sort of allegiance to a state could receive protection in case of peril or injury, even if this entailed the use of force.[61] Third, PNA, either diplomatic or forcible, was not a settled doctrine; rather it emerged and was shaped through state practice. The normative foundations of the doctrine were few. This is why PNA could possibly take any form, from a long-standing naval blockade, to demanding arbitration, or implementing punitive measures. The doctrine took a more concise form at the start of the twentieth century, when states distinguished PNA from self-defense, and seemed to have exempted it from any international obligation prohibiting the unilateral use of force. Apart from the operation addressing the Boxer rebellion, and the invasion of Manchuria, the incidents where states recourse to force to rescue their nationals abroad proliferated in the wake of the twentieth century.[62]

1.3 The Doctrine's Application and the League of Nations Scheme

Exploring the doctrine's application during the pre-Charter era cannot but examine whether it survived the League of Nations scheme. The answer to this question would be expected to be straightforward, given that the League's Covenant provided an elaborate set of provisions establishing a centralized system for recourse to war.[63] Yet, the Covenant is limited only to war, and it did not contain provisions regarding forcible measures short of war.[64] This was the source of ambiguity and led to opposite legal interpretations.[65]

On one hand, many writers proposed that the legal scheme under the Covenant outlawed war and thus forcible PNA could not be tolerated. This argument followed a line of thinking *a majori ad minus*: if war and acts of aggression were totally disavowed, then no room was left for such occasions, as it would lead to "a world of violence and conquest".[66] At the same time, it was fortified by the fact that the Covenant was the outcome of states' admission that the Great War was the outcome of unilateral actions and recourse to self-help, coupled with the absence of

[61] See, Gosewinkel (2021), pp. 1–59.

[62] Ronzitti (1985), p. 22.

[63] Clark Arendt and Beck (1993), pp. 19–20.

[64] Kolb (2018).

[65] According to Art. 10 of the League of Nations Covenant "The Members of the League undertake to respect and preserve as against external aggression the territorial integrity and existing political independence of all Members of the League. In case of any such aggression or in case of any threat or danger of such aggression the Council shall advice upon the means by which this obligation shall be fulfilled." Covenant of the League of Nations, 28th June 1919 (108 LNTS 188, UKTS 4, 225 CTS 195).

[66] Pemberton (2019), p. 471.

international regulation thereto.[67] In this sense, recourse to force in the name of one's nationals abroad was incompatible with the League of Nations' system, as it would give states a great deal of leeway, undermining the League's centralized philosophy.[68] On the other hand, it was proposed that rescue operations, or small-scale interventions to protect people and property in peril did not fall under the general prohibition of unilateral use of force introduced by the Covenant.[69]

According to this rationale, forcible PNA military operations fell short of the Covenant's prohibition, as they aimed at rescuing nationals, leaving territorial claims out of their scope. Therefore, they could neither be prohibited, nor ruled out as a possibility. This course of thinking found resonance among states, in an attempt to explain how their state practice was consistent with their obligations emanating from their League membership. Forcible PNA was not considered a form of self-defense, or an act of aggression; rather, it was a means of protection that could not be forbidden in the framework of assuming obligations by virtue of membership in an international organization. Examples vary from the Greco-Turkish war (1920–1922) and the Greek invasion of Turkey in the name of its nationals and the attempt to create the Greater Greece, or the Corfu incident of 1923, when Mussolini's Italy proceeded with the naval bombardment of Corfu after Italians who formed part of an international boundary delegation were murdered on Greek soil. On both occasions the League tolerated military interventions, as it was unwilling or unable to halt them. The Western Powers of the time held conferences to resolve these issues, bypassing the League of Nations system.[70] Forcible PNA and retaliation were the doctrinal legal bases for such actions.[71] This view highlighted the inherent bond between states and their nationals, while it shaped the form forcible PNA could acquire. Indeed, during the League's existence, forcible PNA incidents did not cease; they were standardized. Military interventions by stronger states against weaker ones in the name of their nationals' interests.[72]

The two interpretations above balance between the Covenant's idealistic reading and a more pragmatic approach.[73] Yet, they cannot offer the full picture regarding the doctrine's application. The League's approach towards states' nationals residing abroad was different. First, there was no doubt that there were many territorial claims and border conflicts that needed be resolved at that time, not only because of WWI, but mainly because the formation of states and the reshaping of the international community were central features of that period.[74] Second, the fact that large

---

[67] Arendt and Beck (1993), p. 19.

[68] Steiner (1993), p. 41.

[69] Keen (1919), p. 103.

[70] Jensen (1979), p. 558

[71] See, Travlos (2020); Questions Resulting from the Corfu Incident Submitted September 28, 1923 by the Council of the League of Nations to the Special Commission of Jurists and the Replies of That Commission (1924), pp. 155–161.

[72] Hudson (1923), p. 176.

[73] Beneš (1932), p. 68.

[74] Stavenhagen (1996), pp. 2–3.

groups resided permanently outside the borders of their state of nationality was an indisputable reality. Acknowledging these, the League of Nations took significant steps to protect ethnic or national groups residing outside their state of origin. For the League, PNA does not fall into the area of use of force, but it relates to human rights protection. The League of Nations had a totally different perspective than the one of states. PNA could be achieved by imposing certain obligations to states to respect and protect the rights of aliens.[75] In this framework, one could include its laborious efforts to promote and protect legal safeguards for minorities,[76] as well as the initiatives took towards a clearer international legal framework regarding nationality and freedom of movement.[77] This view is reaffirmed by the fact that in 1930 the League of Nations attempted to draft a convention on State Responsibility for Injuries to aliens.[78] As was asserted, the PNA doctrine was a subject not ripe for codification.[79]

Forcible PNA and unilateral actions could be averted if certain legal standards were put in place for the protection of certain groups abroad. Although the remaining question is whether a state is still entitled to use force in the name of its nationals abroad, when the impugned states disregard the obligations, they undertook. Then again, forcible PNA is put forward as an inherent and inalienable state prerogative, rendering all efforts made by the League of Nations useless. After all, this was the reality the international community confronted during the interwar period: collective security and a centralized system regulating force was an official commitment of the League's members, but it was either repeatedly disrespected, or a reason to abandon the League, as did Japan due to the organization's position regarding the invasion of Manchuria.[80]

Except for the Manchurian incidents, other occasions demonstrated that forcible PNA was deemed a legal option by states, even when they had undertaken obligations providing otherwise. Therefore, the view that the doctrine survived by the Covenant is not unfounded.

1.4 Forcible PNA: The Existence of a Customary Norm

This brief overview of the theoretical and practical aspects of the doctrine in the pre-Charter era leaves no doubt that states' recourse to force to protect their nationals' lives and interests abroad was a conscious choice that shaped their foreign

[75] Saar Basin, Protection Abroad of the Interests of the Saar Inhabitants (1923), pp. 412–425; Free City of Danzig (1924), pp. 890–891.

[76] Rosting (1923), p. 645.

[77] Reale (1931), pp. 506–509; Spiro (2021), pp. 573–576.

[78] Berkes (1920), p. 338.

[79] Lillich and Neff (1978), p. 99.

[80] Brown (1933). Retrieved, February 22, 2025 from https://www.upi.com/Archives/1933/02/24/Japan-stuns-world-withdraws-from-league/2231840119817/

policy. Records from official debates and correspondence demonstrate that those states employing the doctrine did so with the firm belief that it was a legitimate option, emanating from their sovereignty. In other words, state practice was coupled with *opinio juris* and the forcible PNA was perceived as an inherent right of states. Or, it is suggested that in the absence of a customary rule prohibiting the threat or use of force in the pre-Charter era, there was no norm precluding states from forcible PNA.[81]

Capitalizing on Vattel's teaching, those states interested in establishing the legitimacy of forcible PNA followed a course of thinking according to which

> [i]t cannot be denied that a certain point the interest of a State in exercising protection over its nationals and their property can take precedence over territorial sovereignty, despite the absence of any conventional provisions. The right of intervention has been claimed by all states; only its limits are disputed.[82]

From this perspective, there is an alleged customary norm permitting states to recourse to force in the name of their nationals abroad. Taking this for granted, there are two questions that need to be answered. First, which is the content of such a customary rule, and second if this rule was accepted and endorsed by all states, thus indicating the existence of an international norm. As far as the first point of discussion is concerned, the constitutive elements of this customary norm remained purposely vague. States supporting the existence of custom on this field of law did not connect forcible PNA with self-defense. As a result, such military interventions were not bound by the prerequisites of self-defense.[83] Although they referred to the inherency of their ability to protect their nationals abroad, their argumentation focused on extra-territoriality and the existence of nationality ties, or allegiance. Foreign lives, or even property, precede over the principle of the inviolability of borders.[84]

The normative understanding of the rule was nebulous, as the intervening states did not offer extensive justification as to the reasons which drove their decisions. The conceptualization of customary norms is an innate problem to this source of law. Custom is certainly dependent on the historical context, which may well overwhelm the sources of international law.[85] In this regard, the test put forward by judge Humphrey Waldock is broadly considered as delineating the content of the customary norm of recourse to force for PNA. According to it, there must be and imminent threat of injury to nationals (1), a failure or inability on the part of the territorial sovereign to protect them (2), and the measures of protection are strictly confined to the object of protecting them against injury (3).[86] The Waldock test on the customary criteria for recourse to force to protect nationals abroad resembles a

[81] Pobjie (2024), p. 22.

[82] Anglo-Spanish Arbitrations, Beni-Madan, Rzini Claim (1925) UNRIAA, Vol. II, 616.

[83] Fonteyne (1973), p. 251.

[84] Bowett (1958), p. 104.

[85] Warbrick (2000), p. 633.

[86] Waldock (1952), pp. 466–467.

lot the criteria that shall be met for the legitimate invocation of Art. 51 UNCh. Waldock's imminent threat of injury to nationals refers directly to imminence, the territorial sovereign's inability, or failure to protect foreigners is what renders recourse to force necessary, whilst the last criterion on the strict confinement of force to the object of protection from injury is directly linked to proportionality. This reading of the customary norm on forcible PNA is much stricter than the actual state practice that preceded the UNCh. From this viewpoint, the Waldock test excludes the concept of self-help and countermeasures from the legal framework. As such, the Pacifico affair would not fit the doctrine, while operations like the ones addressing the Boxer rebellion would suffice.

The second point of concern on the acceptance of such a norm is a riddle which has not been satisfactorily solved till today. For the establishment of a customary rule apart from the elements of state practice and *opinio juris*, one needs to further delve into the norm's acceptance, that is the states that practice it and defend its legality. Forcible PNA during the 18th, 19th and early twentieth century rested fundamentally on the proposition that semi-civilized and barbaric states were either unwilling, or unable to protect foreign subjects residing in their territory.[87] They were considered states with primitive legal systems unable to implement the rule of law or simply lands of corruption. In this respect, civilized states bore the duty to protect their subjects, and at the same time deemed intervention a measure of instruction to uncivilized states on the rules of international law.[88] A way of introducing to them the "common international standard of justice" and succeeding in the "gradual reduction of the local prejudices and misunderstandings".[89] Evidently, forcible intervention indicates the imperialistic, or hegemonic perception of international law at the time.[90]

Further, international law in the examined time period had a totally different frame: fewer states existed, the institutions of colonization and protectorates were still on the rise, whereas those states that had recently gained their independence were too weak to take a more active role in the formation of international law rules.[91] Latin American states attempted to express their disagreement on diplomatic and military interventions on behalf of foreign nationals by formulating the Calvo and alike doctrines (like the Hull formula).[92] It is even suggested that these doctrines form altogether customary protective rules for the land of weaker states and properties of their nationals.[93] Thereat, the legitimacy of state practice was doubted. As it is nowadays asserted, for customary rules to evolve,

[87] Corten (2006), pp. 810–811.
[88] Heraclides and Dialla (2015), p. 49.
[89] Root (1910), p. 528.
[90] von Bernstorff (2018), p. 249.
[91] Linklater (2021), p. 144.
[92] Thomas (1959), pp. 427–431.
[93] See, Babu (2020).

> an acceptance on the part of the whole of states is needed, which entails a criteria that is both quantitative (a very large majority is required) and qualitative (this majority must include states with different political systems and values belonging to all regions of the world).[94]

After all, it has been asserted several years later that civilized states have often abused their power and violated the principles of rational law in relation to nations of different cultures.[95] It is not without problems to ascertain the existence of a customary norm permitting the forcible PNA. There is consistent and repetitive state practice, coupled with *opinio juris*, resulting from official conversations; yet it seems that this rule was the result of a very narrow interpretation of law practiced by a closed club of states that reserved for themselves a superior position in the international plane. Of course, it is also asserted that this course of evolution determined the formation of international law in general, and so it is a historical condition that cannot be overlooked.[96] In addition, states falling under the categories of semi-civilized or semi-barbarian ones embraced the doctrine and applied it to conflicts where they had the financial and military power to support it. Thus, the doctrine expanded its field of application when the circumstances permitted so.

A customary norm either for the civilized ones, or for those which were capable of planning and executing military rescue operations remains a matter of concern.[97] To substantiate this view, it is underlined that customary norms are not universal. To the contrary, customary rules may well be regional,[98] or bilateral,[99] or meet the opposition by a significant number of international law subjects. Its existence is not synonymous with its ambit. Thus, the doctrine's customary value is not dependent on the limited number of states which practiced forcible PNA. The ethical question of whether it promoted a hegemonic philosophy over international law receives nowadays a straightforward answer. It certainly did as historical evidence shows.[100] Yet, the course of history cannot be overlooked. This is also why both states and eminent publicists proposed criteria and described thoroughly what the norm entailed. By clarifying its content, ambiguity over the value of such a customary rule would be limited. Therefore, even if forcible PNA was a customary rule among, and for, the "civilized" ones (a usage among civilized nations),[101] this historical truth cannot be undone.[102] After all, states have time and again preserved "a decisive

---

[94] Corten (2005), p. 140.

[95] Orakhelashvili (2006), p. 324.

[96] Weiler (2004), p. 550.

[97] Wood (2019), p. 323.

[98] *Haya de la Torre Case*, Judgment of June 13th, 1951: ICJ Rep 1951, pp. 71, 81.

[99] *Case Concerning Right of Passage over Indian Territory (Merits)*, Judgment of 12 April 1960: ICJ Rep 1960, pp. 6, 41.

[100] von Bernstorff (2018), p. 240.

[101] Sir Michael Wood, 'First Report on Formation and Evidence of Customary International Law' (17 May 2013) UN Doc A/CN.4/663, 136.

[102] Fonteyne (1974) p. 251: Marcelo Vázquez–Bermúdez, 'First Report on General Principles of Law' (5 April 2019) UN Doc A/CN.4/732, 8.

role in determining whether a rule of international law has come into existence and whether certain interests will be protected and in what way".[103] Therefore, forcible PNA as law introduced by the powerful ones, was neither anew, nor an exception to the rule. In general terms, international customary rules are not assessed based on their moral value. Their existence and validity rely on states' *opinio juris*, which encompasses moral parameters. The course of history proves that even states which were once considered semi-civilized, or barbaric included the doctrine in their discourse when their political power and financial status made it possible. The examples of states adopting imperialistic discourse during the course of their history are more than a few. This customary norm's acceptance is more a matter of power dynamics than a moral question.[104] Finally, if one is to support the existence of such a customary rule, there is always the possibility to consider those states discarding it as persistent objectors.

All in all, even if these assertions are taken for granted, there is no certainty whether forcible PNA could and has survived the UN regime without changes. An *ad hoc* evaluation of each incident is inevitable and shows the broad span of occasions the doctrine was evoked. Institutional attempts for codification failed miserably, demonstrating states' hesitance to be bound by conventionally. The Charter's entry into force and the new era it signified for state relations and international law have certainly affected the doctrine's content, application and re-raised questions as to its customary value.

1.5 Conclusions

The doctrine's development in the pre-Charter era had several fluctuations, following the transformations the concept of a state. Its theoretical underpinnings are precarious, as they were based on the subjective and fragmented interpretation of the teachings of eminent publicists of the time. PNA took several forms during the eighteenth and nineteenth centuries, signifying a wide range of actions for the state invoking the doctrine. The common element of state practice during that time is states' assertion that sovereignty is detached from territoriality, and thus there was no legal fault in intervening in the interior of other states for the sake of nationals. In the rise of the twentieth century, the doctrine has taken a more concise form. PNA became a synonym to forcible measures, and it was fully dissociated from the institution of diplomatic protection. The twentieth century state practice demonstrated that forcible PNA was distinct from a state's right to self-defence, although the two were closed. In the pre-Charter era, the doctrine was a synonym to power, used on occasion to bring weaker states to the "right path".

[103] Gaja (2011), p. 45.

[104] Murphy (2014), p. 137.

The doctrine's innate hegemonic character raised several doubts on its legal validity, especially after the creation of the League of Nations. The creation of an international organization to safeguard international peace and security was a turn for the international legal order. Institutionalization came as a counterweight to states' self-regulation. However, recourse to force in the name of a state's nationals was not heavily affected by the League of Nations system. Although the League formally disapproved of unilateral actions and recourse to self-help, it remained inactive on certain occasions, which was perceived as a sign of toleration. State practice proves how states considered forcible PNA a legitimate option, that did not contravene their obligations for the maintenance of peace and security after WWI. For this reason, the argument that forcible PNA was a customary norm found supportive ears, despite opposite legal argumentation.

Forcible PNA in the pre-Charter era follows the transformations of the concept of sovereignty. Before the consolidation of nation-states, it was a fluid concept, testing the limits of territoriality and nationality. Sovereign interests largely determined the dynamic between the two limps of sovereignty. Neither territoriality, nor nationality were fixed terms. Although extraterritoriality is considered a condition cementing the notion of territoriality, it has a corrosive function too, since it does not guarantee the inviolability of borders. Thus, the feature of territoriality was not well-established in the pre-Charter era.[105] In addition, the extraterritorial character of sovereignty was intentionally confused and identified with states' extraterritorial jurisdiction. This equation currently makes sense, due to the clear demarcation between territoriality and extraterritoriality, where the last is the exception to the former. At that time though, extraterritorial sovereignty was a sign of inequality between states, separating the strong from the week. The same rationale is mutatis mutandis applicable to the notion of nationality. Although nationality and the criteria of its attribution were way clearer and more specified, states applying the forcible PNA doctrine opted for a more elastic interpretation, favoring their interests. It was not only the nationality of individuals that mattered, but also that of property. This is why the doctrine is not only associated with the development of the use of force rules, but it has been central to international investment law too. Forcible PNA has been a catalyst in the formation of property rules too. Given the ambiguity surrounding the characteristics of sovereignty, it is no surprise that forcible PNA had a negative meaning in the post-Charter era. Consolidating the institution of sovereignty implied outlawing doctrines such as forcible PNA.

[105] Lythgoe (2024), p. 32

References

Books

Amerasinghe CF (2004) Local remedies in international law, 2nd edn. Cambridge University Press
Arendt AC, Beck RJ (1993) International law and the use of force. Routledge
Borchard E (1915) The diplomatic protection of citizens abroad: or, the law of international claims. Banks Law Publishing Company
Bowett DW (1958) Self-defense in international law. Frederick A. Praeger
Brown D (2002) Palmerston and the politics of foreign policy 1846–55. Manchester University Press
Cable J (1981) Gunboat diplomacy, 1919–1979, political applications of limited naval force, 2nd edn. Palgrave Macmillan
de Vattel E (1916) The law of nations, or, the principles of the law of nature applied to the conduct and affairs of nations and sovereigns (Charles G. Fenwick trans.), 3rd edn. Carnegie Institution
Gosewinkel D (2021) Struggles for belonging, citizenship in Europe, 1900–2020. Oxford University Press
Heraclides A, Dialla A (2015) Humanitarian intervention in the long nineteenth century, setting the precedent. Manchester University Press
Hudson MO (1933) The verdict of the league: China and Japan in Manchuria. The official documents with notes and introduction. World Peace Foundation
Jessup PC (1935) International security: the American role in collective action for peace. Council on Foreign Relations
Kolb R (2018) International law on the maintenance of peace, Jus Contra Bellum. Edward Elgar
Lingelbach WE (1900) The doctrine and practice of intervention in Europe. American Academy of Political and Social Science
Linklater A (2021) The idea of civilization and the making of the global order. Bristol University Press
Lythgoe G (2024) The rebirth of territory. Cambridge University Press
Moore CH (1965) Tunisia since independence. The dynamics of one-party government. University of California Press
Murphy JB (2014) The philosophy of customary law. Oxford University Press
Navy Department (1948) United States navy regulations. United States Printing Office
Oppenheim L (2005) In: Roxburgh RF (ed) International law, a treatise, Vol. I – Peace, 3rd edn. The Lawbook Exchange Ltd.
Pemberton J-A (2019) The story of international relations, cold-blooded idealists. Palgrave Macmillan
Pobjie E (2024) Prohibited force. The meaning of 'use of force' in international law. Cambridge University Press
Ronzitti N (1985) Rescuing nationals abroad through military coercion and intervention on grounds of humanity. Martinus Nijhoff Publishers
Stavenhagen R (1996) Ethnic conflicts and the nation-state. Palgrave Macmillan
Travlos K (2020) Salvation and catastrophe: the Greek-Turkish War, 1919–1922. Lexington Books
Vince N (2020) The Algerian war. The Algerian revolution. Palgrave Macmillan
Wetzler P (2020) Imperial Japan and defeat in the Second World War: the collapse of an empire. Bloomsbury Academic
Περγαντής Β (2017) Η Ανθρώπινη Διάσταση της Διπλωματικής Προστασίας, Φύση και οριοθέτηση του Θεσμού. Εκδόσεις Σάκκουλα

Articles

– (1923). Saar Basin, Protection Abroad of the Interests of the Saar Inhabitants. League Nations Off J 4(4):412–425
– (1924). Free city of Danzig. League Nations Off J 5(6):890–891
– (1924). Questions resulting from the Corfu Incident Submitted September 28, 1923 by the Council of the League of Nations to the Special Commission of Jurists and the Replies of That Commission. Int Conciliation 10:155–161
– (1933). The far eastern problem: official texts and summary of the Lytton report. Int Conciliation, 15, 1–92
– (2002) State practice during the pre-United Nations period. Int Law Stud Ser US Naval War Coll 77, 25–40
Beaulac S (2003) Emer de Vattel and the Externalization of Sovereignty. J Hist Int Law 5(2):237–292
Beneš E (1932) The league of nations: successes and failures. Foreign Aff 11(1):66–80
Berkes A (1920) The league of nations and the international law of state responsibility. Int Commun Law Rev 22(3–4):331–362
Borchard EM (1929) The protection of citizens abroad by armed forces. Ann Am Acad Polit Soc Sci 144:121–127
Borchard EM (1934) The protection of citizens abroad and change of original nationality. Yale Law J 43(4):359–392
Brook FB (1905) State protection of subjects abroad. Law Mag Rev Q Rev Juris 30(2):157–181
Carstén EJS (1962) Some considerations upon the conception, development, and importance of diplomatic protection. Germ Yearb Int Law 11:37–48
Cavallar G (2008) Vitoria, Grotius Pufendorf, Wolff and Vattel: accomplices of European colonialism and exploitation of true cosmopolitans. J Hist Int Law 10(2):181–210
Cherrington BM (1928) The Kellogg Pact – a contrast in legal and moral interpretations. Denver Bar Assoc Rec 5(10):13–16
Corten O (2006) The controversies over the customary prohibition on the use of force: a methodological debate. Eur J Int Law 16(5):803–822
Criddle EJ (2015) Standing for human rights abroad. Cornell Law Rev 100(2):269–334
Dunn FS (1941) The international rights of individuals. Proc Am Soc Int Law Annual Meet 35:14–22
Feller AH (1933) Some observations on the Calvo Clause. Am J Int Law 27(3):461–468
Fonteyne J-PL (1973) The customary international law doctrine of humanitarian intervention: its current validity under the U.N. Charter. Calif West Int Law J 4(2):203–270
Fonteyne J-PL (1974) The customary international law doctrine of humanitarian intervention: its current validity under the U.N. Charter. Calif West Int Law J 4(2):203–270
Gaja G (2011) The protection of general interests in the international community. Recueil des Cours 364:9–185
Garcia-Mora MR (1950) The Calvo Clause in Latin American Constitutions and International Law. Marquette Law Rev 33(4):205–218
Green LC (1975) Civilized law and primitive peoples. Osgoode Hall Law J 13(1):233–250
Hicks G (2004) Don Pacifico, democracy, and danger: the protectionist party critique of British Foreign Policy, 1850-1852. Int Hist Rev 26(3):515–540
Hudson MO (1923) How the league of nations met the Corfu Crisis. World Peace Found Pamphlet Ser 1923:176–198
Jensen PK (1979) The Greco-Turkish War, 1920–1922. Int J Middle East Stud 10(4):553–565
Kalmanovitz P (2018) Sovereignty, pluralism, and regular war: Wolff and Vattel's englightment critique of just war. Political Theory 46(2):218–241
Keen FN (1919) Revision of the league of nations covenant. Trans Grotius Soc 5:95–108
Lauterpacht H (1947) Allegiance, diplomatic protection and criminal jurisdiction over aliens. Camb Law J 9(3):330–348

Lillich RB, Neff SC (1978) The treatment of aliens and international human rights norms: overlooked developments at the UN. Germ Yearb Int Law 21:97–118
Mallory WH (1932) The permanent conflict in Manchuria. Foreign Aff 10(2):220–230
Margolies DS (2011) The ill-defined fiction of extraterritoriality and sovereignty exception in the late nineteenth U.S. Foreign Relations. Southwest Law Rev 40(4):575–604
Mégret F (2020) The changing face of protection of the state's nationals abroad. Melb J Int Law 21(2):450–468
Mueser B (2018) The nation and property in Vattel's theory of territory. Glob Intellect Hist 3(2):137–155
Mullins S (2001) The Costa Rica packet affair: colonial entanglements and tests of empire in pre-federation New South Wales. J R Aust Hist Soc 87(2):267–285
Orakhelashvili A (2006) The idea of European international law. Eur J Int Law 17(2):315–347
Otsuka U (2018) Coalition coordination during the boxer rebellion: how twenty-seven "councils of senior naval commanders" contributed to the conduct of operations. Naval War Coll Rev 71(4):111–130
Ouellet E (2009) Multinational counterinsurgency: the western intervention in the boxer rebellion 1900-1901. Small Wars Insur 20(3–4):507–527
Reale E (1931) The passport question. Foreign Aff 9(3):506–509
Ronzitti N (2019) Rescuing nationals abroad revisited. J Conflict Secur Law 24(3):431–448
Root E (1910) Basis of protection to citizens residing abroad. Am J Int Law 4(3):517–528
Rosting H (1923) Protection of minorities by the league of nations. Am J Int Law 17(4):641–660
Shan W (2007) Is Calvo dead? Am J Comp Law 55(1):123–163
Spiro PJ (2021) Nationals abroad: globalization, individual rights, and the making of modern international law. Am J Int Law 115(3):573–576
Takaki Y (1932) World peace machinery and the Asia Monroe Doctrine. Pac Aff 5(11):941–953
Thomas AJ (1959) Protection of property of citizens abroad. Proc Inst Priv Invest Abroad 1959:417–448
Todd D (2018) Beneath sovereignty: extraterritoriality and imperial internationalism in nineteenth century Egypt. Law Hist Rev 36(1):105–138
von Bernstorff J (2018) The use of force in international law before World War I: on imperial ordering and the ontology of nation-state. Eur J Int Law 29(1):233–260
Waldock H (1952) The regulation of the use of force by individual states in international law. Recueil des Cours 81(II):455
Warbrick C (2000) Brownlie's principles of public international law: an assessment. Eur J Int Law 11(3):621–636
Weiler JHH (2004) The geology of international law – governance, democracy and legitimacy. Zeitschrift für ausländisches öffentliches Recht und Völkerrecht 64(3):547–562
Whitten D (1986) The Don Pacifico affair. Historian 48(2):255–267
Wood M (2019) Customary international law and the general principles of law recognized by civilized nations. Int Commun Law Rev 21(3–4):307–324
Wood Renton A (1933) The revolt against the capitulatory system. J Comp Leg Int Law 15(1&4):212–231
Wright Q (1932) The Manchurian crisis. Am Polit Sci Rev 26(1):45–76
Zhao X, Pature P (2022) The 'European' in the boxer movement. Int Hist Rev 45(1):81–94
Zurbuchen S (2010) Vattel's law of nations and the principle of non-intervention. Grotiana 31:69–84

Book Chapters

Babu RR (2020) Standard of compensation for expropriation of foreign investment. In: Chaisse J et al (eds) Handbook of international investment law and policy. Springer, pp 1–18

Bradley CA (2019) U.S. war powers and the potential benefits of comparativism. In: Bradley CA (ed) The Oxford handbook of comparative foreign relations law. Oxford University Press, pp 753–770

Brownlie I (1973) Thoughts on kind-hearted Gunmen. In: Lillich RB (ed) Intervention and the United Nations. University Press of Virginia, pp 139–148

Caflisch L (2011) Chapter X: Vattel and the peaceful settlement of international disputes. In: Chetail V, Haggenmacher P (eds) Vattel's international law in a XXIst century perspective. Martinus Nijhoff, pp 257–266

Corten O (2005) Breach and evolution of customary international law and the use of force. In: Cannizzaro E, Palchetti P (eds) Customary international law on the use of force. Koninklijke Brill NV, pp 119–144

Crawford J (2017) The International Law Commission's articles on diplomatic protection revisited. In: Maluwa T et al (eds) The pursuit of a brave new world in international law, essays in Honour of John Dugard. Nijhoff, pp 135–171

Koskenniemi M, Kari V (2020) State sovereignty. In: Viñuales JE (ed) The UN friendly relations declaration at 50, an assessment of the fundamental principles of international law. Cambridge University Press, pp 166–188

Leira H, Græger N (2020) Introduction: the duty of care in international relations. In: Græger N, Leira H (eds) The duty of care in international relations: protecting citizens beyond the border. Routledge, pp 1–17

Miles K (2018) History and international law: method and mechanism – empire and 'usual' rupture. In: Schill SW et al (eds) International investment law and history. Edward Elgar, pp 136–163

Murfett MH (1999) Gunboat diplomacy: outmoded or back in vogue? In: Dorman A et al (eds) The changing face of maritime power. Macmillan Press Ltd, pp 81–93

Shichor Y (2016) Crackdown: insurgency, potential insurgency and counterinsurgency in modern China. In: Heuser B, Shamir E (eds) Insurgencies and counterinsurgencies, national styles and strategic cultures. Cambridge University Press, pp 95–112

Steiner Z (1993) The league of nations and the quest for security. In: Ahmann R et al (eds) The quest for stability: problems of West European Security 1918–1957. Oxford University Press, pp 35–70

Tzouvala N (2019) Civilization. In: d' Aspremont J, Singh S (eds) Concepts for international law, contributions to disciplinary thought. Edward Elgar, pp 83–104

Jurisprudence

PCIJ

Mavrommatis Palestine Concessions case, judgment of 30 August 1924, PCIJ, Ser. A, No. 2, p. 12

ICJ

Case Concerning Right of Passage over Indian Territory (Merits), Judgment of 12 April 1960: ICJ Rep 1960, p. 6
Haya de la Torre Case, Judgment of June 13th, 1951: ICJ Rep 1951, p. 71

Arbitral Awards

Anglo-Spanish Arbitrations, Beni-Madan, Rzini Claim (1925) UNRIAA, Vol. II, 616

National Jurisprudence

In re Neagle, US Circuit Court, N.D. California. (September 16, 1889) 39 F. 833 (N.D.Cal. 1889)

UN Documentation

Marcelo Vázquez-Bermúdez, 'First Report on General Principles of Law' (5 April 2019) UN Doc A/CN.4/732, 8
Second report on State Responsibility by Mr. Gaetano Arangio-Ruiz, Special Rapporteur, UN Doc A/CN.4/425 & Corr. 1 and Add.1 & Corr. 1, para 48
Sir Michael Wood, 'First Report on Formation and Evidence of Customary International Law' (17 May 2013) UN Doc A/CN.4/663, 136

Online Material

Brown, S. (24 February 1933). Japan Stuns World, Withdraws from League. Retrieved, February 22, 2025 from https://www.upi.com/Archives/1933/02/24/Japan-stuns-world-withdraws-from-league/2231840119817/
House of Lords. (17 June 1850). Affairs of Greece – Lord Stanley. HL Deb vol 111 cc1293-404, para 1332. Retrieved February 22, 2025, from https://api.parliament.uk/historic-hansard/lords/1850/jun/17/affairs-of-greece
Treaty Between the Nine Powers Concerning the Chinese Customs Tariff (Nine-Power Treaty). (Washington, 6 February 1922). Retrieved, February 22, 2025 from https://worldjpn.net/documents/texts/pw/19220206.T3E.html

Miscellaneous

Covenant of the League of Nations, 28th June 1919 (108 LNTS 188, UKTS 4, 225 CTS 195)

Chapter 2
Protection of Nationals Abroad Under the UN Charter

2.1 PNA and the Prohibition of the Use of Force

Forcible PNA through military operations, or smaller-scale rescue missions is *prima facie* contrary to the spirit of 2(4). However, this proposition is not that self-evident, taking into account that the doctrine's supporters argue that PNA is not putting a state's territorial integrity or political independence at risk as Art.2(4) requires. The doctrine is by definition aiming at the protection of nationals only, and as such it does not contravene the protective scope of the use of force prohibition. This debate echoes the two major lines of argumentation over the interpretation of Art. 2(4): on one hand, the more restrictive reading of the prohibition of the use of force, according to which the UN Charter's provision aims at limiting use of force by effective legal regulation.[1] On the other hand, it is proposed that Art. 2(4), alongside 51 too, leave the pre-existing customary norms untouched. In turn, this means that states' customary right to self-help is permitted.[2] This normative debate over Art. 2(4) extended to the forcible PNA doctrine as well. After the Charter's entry into force, it remained a question whether forcible PNA is an admissible state practice.

2.1.1 The Restrictive Interpretation of Permission to Use Force

The interpretation of the prohibition to use force and the right to self-defense has been a major issue of concern at the aftermath of the UN Charter's entry into force. Although forcible PNA was not considered up till WWII as part of state's right to

[1] Brownlie (1959), p. 717.

[2] Gordon (1985), p. 277.

© The Author(s), under exclusive license to Springer Nature Switzerland AG 2025

I. Pervou, *Protecting Nationals Abroad and the Reconceptualization of Sovereignty*, Studies in the History of Law and Justice 32,
https://doi.org/10.1007/978-3-032-05231-5_2

self-defense, this became part of the debate in the post-Charter era since self-defense is the only permissible exception to the use of force prohibition provided by the Charter. Therefore, most of the discussion turned on whether forcible PNA is an aspect of the state's right to self-defense.

Theory did not produce a unified view on the prohibition's definite content, while ordinary interpretation tools did not apply for two reasons. First, because the general interpretative methods, as enshrined in Art. 31 VCLT,[3] were not codified yet, and second due to the norm's immeasurable quality. More specifically, it is aptly pointed out that Art. 2(4) was meant to develop a 'predictive quality" and influence state practice, instead of setting a restrictive norm.[4] From this viewpoint, the prohibition to use force in the UN Charter cannot be separated from its historic context and the international community's attempt to centralize and coordinate the use of force.

The interpretation of Art. 2(4) over the ensuing decades in the adoption of the Charter revolved around the dilemma concerning whether the provision introduced a restrictive rule governing states' practice, or if the prohibition was self-restricting by making reference to territorial integrity and political independence, or to consistency with the purposes of the UN, further restricting its scope of application. Thus, the term "restrictive" was found at the heart of the debate concerning those cases where states' resorting to force was permitted by the UN Charter. At the time, the doctrine of protecting nationals abroad was commonplace for colonial powers, and as such it occupied much of this debate.

According to theorists who consider that Art. 2(4) shall receive broad interpretation, and therefore the wider possible scope of application, forcible PNA is an "intervention almost certainly illegal in the modern law",[5] leaving no room for its invocation by states. More specifically, this line of argumentation adheres to the Lauterpachtian principle that "there shall be no violence"[6] and outlaws any legal justification for resorting to force. This course of thinking narrows considerably the limits of the right to self-defense, and any such doctrine falling under its scope of application. Overall, this interpretation takes into account the Charter's historical context by sticking to the presumption that the maintenance of world peace excludes any unilateral act, except for in very few cases which qualify as self-defense. In this context, two observations are made. First, it is upheld that no matter the reasons for recourse to force, the magnitude of a state's actions always impairs another state's territorial integrity and political independence.[7] In this sense, these additions to Art. 2(4) guarantee that there will be no legal vacuum. According to the American delegate at the San Francisco conference who analyzed the American view, the drafters' intention was

---

[3] UN, *Vienna Convention on the Law of Treaties*, UNTS Vol. 1155, p. 331 (23 May 1969), Art. 31(1).

[4] Gordon (1985), 273.

[5] Brownlie (1961), p. 184.

[6] Lauterpacht (1955), pp. 306, 309.

[7] Brownlie (1967), pp. 265–269.

> de declarer, dans les termes les plus généraux, une interdiction absolue et sans restriction. [Le phrase] ou de toute autre manière [signifiait] qu' il n' y aurait pas de lacunes.[8]

The second observation relates to the fact that according this argumentation, protecting nationals abroad does not qualify as self-defense; ergo, it constitutes a source of turbulence in the Charter's regime.[9] Unlike the League of Nations, the UN Charter provided for a more flexible system of collective security, which sought to minimize unilateral forcible operations. Nevertheless, there seem to be different readings of the Charter, supporting that the UN scheme excludes any unilateral action not qualifying as self-defense. Hence the relationship between Arts 2(4) and 51 is not an absolute dipole.

If forcible protection of nationals in the territory of a third state is deemed to be totally ruled out by the Charter, not fitting its regime not even exceptionally,[10] then such a view would overlook state practice before the Charter's entry into force, according to which forcible PNA fell short of war and was considered by most states as a measure of self-help. What is more, this viewpoint is overwhelmed by the Charter's historical mission and cannot reconcile with doctrines which emerged during the UN's course. That is, it does not coincide with the humanitarian intervention and responsibility to protect doctrines. Finally, it is suggested that forcible PNA is a pretext to intervention, clothing states' geopolitical interests.[11] This point of view bears aspects of reality. Forcible PNA has long been used by states as an excuse for territorial claims and historical examples affirm the wide range of occasions it has been invoked. Thus, an interpretation totally outlawing any alike doctrines would be idealistic, far from unremitting state practice.

These views received particular attention from 1945 until the early 90s before the international environment allowed the UN to activate to the fullest its collective security mechanisms. During this period, when Chapter VII lay dormant, the view that Art. 2(4) was impervious prevailed.[12] In the meantime, this restrictive interpretation of the permission to use force did not only cover the PNA doctrine, but also intervention on the basis of regional arrangements, intervention to assist national liberation movements, and use force after the territorial sovereign's consent was secured.[13] The paradox is that these four cases reflected states' policy from 1945 till the early 90s; as such, these four cases have survived the absolute prohibition set by 2(4), in a period when collective security was at a standstill. Bearing this in mind, these four cases, which were upheld as reasonable justifications to use force, were not sources of turbulence, but evince how the UN's regime evolved. Although it is held that very few states continue claiming the existence of a self-standing right to protect their nationals abroad, post-1945 state practice points to the opposite.

---

[8] Wehberg (1951), p. 62.

[9] Brownlie (2002), pp. 1, 9.

[10] Randelzhofer (2002), p. 117

[11] Gray (2018), pp. 88, 159–160.

[12] Murphy (1994), p. 201.

[13] Brownlie (2002), p. 9.

All in all, this interpretation opts for "the progressive exclusion of traditionally accepted exceptions to the ban on the use of force"[14] and turns Art. 2(4) into a norm which cannot be bypassed in any event.[15]

2.1.2 PNA under the Restrictive Interpretation of Art. 2(4)

Contrary to the above, a more restrictive reading of Art. 2(4) shapes the claim that the UN Charter does not prohibit the use of force by states to protect their nationals abroad. This line of thinking is based on two distinct points. This narrow interpretation of the prohibition instituted in Art. 2(4) allows the Charter's conciliation with pre-existing customary norms, while it is in alignment with subsequent legal practice, including judicial decisions, or soft law instruments.

More specifically, this approach lies in the fact that the prohibition is not a general but a qualified one and applies only when force targets another state's territorial integrity, or political independence. This argument relies mostly on the Charter's travaux préparatoires, when states struggled in the United Nations Conference on International Organization (UNCIO) in San Francisco to conclude to the Charter's body. It is recorded, that the proposal for principle 2(4) in Dumbarton Oaks was quite different, as it provided that "All members of the Organization shall refrain in their international relations from the threat or use of force in any manner inconsistent with the purposes of the Organization". It is further noted that states which contented the addition of the phrase "territorial integrity and political independence" considered it as "awkward" or "illogical, because it comprises two negations", stating that the Dumbarton Oaks was perfect, with no exception to the use of force.[16] Since this view did not prevail during negotiations for the Charter's adoption, the inclusion of the terms "territorial integrity" and "political independence" is not part of the principle's linguistic completion. As a result, this phrase is considered a restriction to the prohibition according to this point of view.

It is claimed that otherwise Art. 2(4)'s second clause would have no practical use or legal implication. This argument has been criticized as circuitous, as it allows states to justify their recourse to force through an effects-based approach: that is, where use of force has endangered a state's integrity or independence. In this regard, it misses the point that the Charter prohibits the use of force as a means to be employed by states, irrespective of its magnitude or other characteristics. That would lead to an *ad hoc*, or exhaustive evaluation of each military operation *ex post*

[14] Tams (2009), p. 351.

[15] Jiuyong (2018), p. 4.

[16] Documents of the United Nations Conference on International Organization (1945). San Francisco, 1945 Vol VI, Commission I, General Provisions. United Nations Information Organizations, p. 68.

facto. As a result, it would relativize the prohibition's content, rendering the rule without practical value.[17]

This idea that force is permissible as long as it is not perilous to the invaded state's integrity or territorial status was first expressed at the *Corfu Channel* oral pleadings on behalf of the United Kingdom, where the applicant held that use of force to guarantee a state's right to innocent passage is not in contravention of the international legal scheme.[18] The concept that the forcible PNA does not fall under the restrictive scope of the UN Charter has been developed by way of analogy.

From this perspective, Art. 2(4) does not affect states' pre-existing customary right to forcibly protect their nationals abroad.[19] Bowett suggests that protecting nationals with the use of force is a self-standing right which was neither abrogated by the UN Charter in general incompatible with Article 2(4). What is more, he underlines that there is no reference in the PNA doctrine to soft law documents, which were intended to function interpretatively in relation to the prohibition on the use of force, such as the UN Declaration 2625 (XXV) on Friendly Relations.[20] This rationale is based on the key principle of international law that anything not explicitly prohibited is permitted, further underlining that neither states nor the UN were ready to renounce the formers' right to forcibly protect their nationals abroad.[21]

However, the value of this reading relies on the fact that it offers a temporal bridging between pre-Charter practice and Art. 2(4). Yet, there have been two major points of concern about this theory: that this view overestimates the value of states' customary right to protect their nationals abroad, while at the same time it abandons the existence of the customary prohibition to use force. In this sense, it does not achieve a fair balance between the prohibition and its pre-Charter exceptions. Moreover, critics mention that if this natural / realistic approach were to prevail then it would set the foundations for the extensive use of force by states, particularly by colonial powers who wish to prolong their influence over their former colonies under the pretext of protecting their nationals.[22]

These two diametrically opposed readings of Art. 2(4) demonstrate how difficult it is to justify the legality of a state's recourse to force to protect their nationals abroad, while they also encapsulate the theoretical debate over the prohibiting of force. The fact that two completely opposite theories came forward evinces the doctrinal bewilderment regarding forcible PNA.[23] Finally, a third, intermediate view was framed regarding the doctrine's legality under Art. 2(4). A few scholars accepted

---

[17] Boer (2015), p. 15

[18] ICJ, *The Corfu Channel Case*, Oral Proceedings (Second Part), Reply by Sir Eric Beckett (UK) 19 I 49 555–567.

[19] Bowett (1957), pp. 112–114.

[20] UNGA, Declaration on Principles of International Law concerning Friendly Relations and Cooperation among States in accordance with the Charter of the United Nations (24 October 1970) A/RES/2625(XXV).

[21] Bowett (1986), p. 40.

[22] Corten (2005), pp. 804, 809.

[23] Raby (1989), p. 470.

that Art. 2(4) does not absolutely prohibit the use of force, but they figured the protection of nationals abroad doctrine as "inconsistent with the purposes of the United Nations". This is because unilaterally resorting to force to protect one's nationals would contravene the Charter's major tenet: to centralize the use of force so as to guarantee the maintenance of peace and security.[24] This view prioritizes territoriality over nationality. These two figures of sovereignty coexist, but a conflicting relationship often develops between them.[25] By trespassing a state's borders to rescue nationals, territorial integrity is violated even if there are no territorial claims following the PNA doctrine. A state's nationals facing perils abroad is an issue falling under the scope and powers of the UN system. Thus, it is not easy to characterize such an occasion as part of a state's domestic affairs, irrespective of the definite bonds between nationals abroad in peril and their country of nationality, or origin. Therefore, if force is to be used this is a decision to be made by the UN's organs, taking unilateral actions out of the question.

This debate did not last long, given that theory uncovered the problem that the justification of recourse to force due to nationality bonds would not be an easy task under the very prohibition on unilateral force. Therefore, it was soon proposed that the legality of forcibly protecting a state's nationals abroad should be considered as a facet of the right to self-defense. The state invading in order to protect its nationals does not resort to force due to its aggressive policy; on the contrary, it is defending its nationals, extending a protective shield over them.

2.2 Forcible PNA and the Right to Self-defense

In spite of these critical remarks, several authors endorsed the view that the doctrine's legality was not jeopardized by the UN Charter's adoption of it. They further elaborated on the relation between the two and pointed out the need for a holistic approach towards the UN Charter, not focusing solely on the prohibiting of force.

The key pillars of the UN on which the Charter is founded, as well as the organization's function itself, are on the one hand the maintenance of international peace and security and on the other the protection of human rights. From this standpoint it is argued that forcible protection of nationals abroad falls within the ambit of a series of legally justified reasons to resort to force unilaterally. The doctrine is directly linked to states' right to forcible self-help, either when their nationals residing abroad are injured, or when they are mistreated by the government of the invaded state.[26]

Therefore, it is suggested that use of force to protect one's nationals abroad is an expression of states' inherent right to self-defense, which predates the Charter and

---

[24] Jessup (1946), p. 93.

[25] Parrish (2009), p. 826.

[26] Lillich (1969), pp. 207–211; Lillich (1968), p. 331.

exists customarily. The link between forcible PNA and the right to self-defense came due to their customary character. It was suggested that the inherent character of self-defense that was asserted in the Charter encompassed all pre-existing customs related one way or another to the use of force. What is more, the doctrine's legality is not a matter of customary law only, and it may well be applied through the Charter's regime. As a result, it cannot be considered a sheer violation of Art. 2(4) of the UN Charter, since it serves its scopes and triggers Art. 51.

The view that a state holds a right to protect its nationals abroad as an act of self-defense is in full alignment with the concept of "external territoriality" introduced by Vattel.[27] This close nexus between a state and its nationals either residing in, or happening to be under, the jurisdiction of a third state constituted a strong cause in the pre-Charter era, and it has also been reiterated by several states and scholars over the last years. This strong nexus between a state and its nationals is currently reinforced and has been reshaped so that it does not constitute a peril to another state's sovereign rights. The following statement of Greenwood that "since population is one of the attributes of statehood, an attack upon a state's population would seem to be just as much an attack upon that state as would an attack upon its territory" is revealing.[28]

This inextricable link between a state and its nationals has a twofold meaning when it comes to the forcible protection of the latter. The first is that it narrows the limits of a state's right to use force in the name of its nationals. It is not a self-standing right; rather, it comes as an act of defense. In turn, this signifies the prerequisites for its enactment: use of force to protect a state's nationals needs to fulfill the requirements of self-defense, either in its customary form, or under Art. 51 of the Charter.

2.2.1 *The Doctrine and States' Inherent Right to Self-defense*

The customary value of the right to self-defense is uncontested: even the drafters of the Charter mentioned the right's inherent character in Art. 51. The Article's wording does not leave space for ambiguity; it is widely accepted that the pre-existing customary right to self-defense exists alongside the Charter's provisions. If this proposition is taken for granted, then the forcible PNA doctrine is legally founded on states' right to self-defense and continues to exist alongside the Charter's regime.[29]

In this context, two questions arise: how Chapter's Art. 51 has influenced the content of the customary norm for recourse to force for self-defense, and how this

---

[27] See Chap. 1.

[28] Greenwood (1987), p. 941.

[29] Shiryaev (2007–2008), p. 86.

interrelation has affected the doctrine's content.[30] By founding the doctrine's legality on the customary right to self-defense, one reaffirms the existence of *opinio juris* on the matter, a subtle agreement between states to use force against other states in the name of their nationals. The perennial question when it comes to customary norms and natural law, though, concerns the particular content of the norm and how it may be defined, given that it relies exclusively on state practice, which may vary occasionally. As far as the customary rule on forcible PNA is concerned, apart from potential variations in state practice, a major problem over the existence of *opinio juris* emerges. During the 19th and 20th centuries, when military operations in the name of nationals abroad took place, the existing *opinio juris* at the time was shared between few states, which were either colonial or superpowers. For this reason, the doctrine gradually attained a negative connotation as it was applied for hegemonic and imperialistic reasons. In the post-Charter era, though, due to the radical changes in the international spectrum and the rebranding of the sovereign state, this hegemonic attitude cannot stand. However, one needs to admit that, although the doctrine echoed imperialistic trends, it spread and was adopted by states once considered weak, or unable to employ military force for the protection of their nationals abroad.

Consequently, it would not be easy to argue that the customary value of forcible PNA remains intact, primarily due to decolonization. The tremendous shifts the international community went through after WWII, and the need to guarantee that no hegemonic views will jeopardize international peace and security, have prevailed and been explicitly expressed through the Charter's adoption. In other words, the new reality launched by the UNCh safeguarded international law so that it would not serve as a tool for a handful of states that could use it to their advantage. The UNCh set limits to the exertion of power by former hegemonies over newly created member-states. In this sense, if the doctrine is to be tolerated under Art. 51, then it must meet its prerequisites, and reliance on the customary rule of self-defense does not suffice. This approach aims to rationalize the doctrine's application by states, as the Charter both defines and limits the exercise of the right to self-defense.[31]

The above observations echo an idealistic perception of the Charter and depart from its functional reality. Compared to the Covenant, the Charter introduced a more balanced system to safeguard international peace and security. Great powers remained at the forefront of the international legal system, holding for themselves a crucial role in deciding when an action is perilous for the maintenance of peace and security or not. Superpowers not only have a central role in the activation of the collective security system, but they also contribute to the evaluation of self-defense claims.[32] Since the United Nations' Security Council (UNSC) is vested with the power to determine which actions constitute a threat to international peace and security, military interventions that are not characterized as such, gain political support and points of legitimacy.

---

[30] Magenis (2002), p. 429.

[31] Schachter (1986), pp. 132–133; Schachter (1984–1985), p. 291.

[32] Kelly (2020), p. 115; Moeckli and Fasel (2017), pp. 70–71.

Although decolonization marked the UN's course, it cannot be easily asserted that "hegemonies" as far as peace and security are concerned, ceased to exist. Even if the UNSC is seen as a "bastion of strong leadership in an unstable world […] its composition, mandate and lack of constitutional limits to its power" show towards the direction of modern hegemonies.[33] The UNSC's practice, tallied with those of its permanent member-states, demonstrates a shift in the customary rule regarding self-defense and forcible PNA, that most certainly does not point towards a more peaceful direction. Recourse to force in the post-Charter era is regulated but not diminished, and states' references on their customary right to self-defense, or forcible PNA multiplied.[34]

As mentioned above, states with the necessary resources and organization used forcible PNA to justify their military interventions through time. Therefore, it is not a matter of a hegemonical attitude demonstrated by superpowers against the rest only. Instead, it is about the realistic reading of international relations, determining which states assume the stronger and the weaker roles respectively in foreign affairs, according to their military power.[35] This view coincides with state practice during the first decades of the twentieth century, when forcible PNA was invoked by states which had the means to support military operations, irrespective of any other particularity. State practice in the Charter era does not disavow forcible PNA, states rather tailored it to the Charter's prerequisites.

If this view is adopted, then it could be either proposed that customary law survived the Charter, although its content was restricted, or that a new customary norm emerged after the Charter's entry into force. If the Charter is not reflective of customary law permitting forcible PNA, then the argument that a new norm emerged, reconciling the Charter's obligations and states' practice.[36] Both scenarios converge, as they suggest that forcible PNA is subsumed by the right to self-defense and thus states shall fulfill its prerequisites. In this context, many governments support that forcible PNA is part of their right to self-defense. This view has gained ground over the years, and it proves that

> reliance on self-defense as a legal ground for protecting nationals in emergency situations of peril probably reflects a reluctance to rely solely on the argument of humanitarian intervention as an exception to article 2(4), or on the related point that such intervention is not "against the territorial integrity or political independence" of the territorial state and not inconsistent with the Charter.[37]

This view demonstrates that nationality ties are a strong reason to employ force against another state. If a state's nationals are in peril, there are grounds for their rescuing, and this could be seen as a form of self-defense. In this regard, forcible

---

[33] Roele (2020), p. 122; Tzanakopoulos (2011), p. 99.

[34] Franck (1970), p. 811.

[35] Wingfield (2000), p. 467.

[36] Milanovic (2021), p. 1336.

[37] Schachter (1984), p. 1632.

PNA as part of states' right to self-defense is a stronger claim than humanitarian intervention.

2.2.2 *The Doctrine and the Criteria Set by UNCh Art. 51*

UNCh Art. 51 has undergone extensive theoretical elaboration, whilst states have further contributed to its interpretation. Bringing the doctrine under the regulatory field of Art. 51 has reduced the number of cases where states may invoke PNA, for they need to prove that abuses suffered by their nationals are equal to an armed attack against their territory. In this regard, Art. 51 turns forcible PNA into a refined version of humanitarian intervention, where existing nationality ties make the case for states resorting to force. Scholars have boldly asserted that the application of Art. 51's prerequisites to the doctrine is a positive step[38] for two reasons: first, it does not expand the provision's scope but reduces the cases where states may invoke Art. 51; second, it brings states' practice under the Charter's scrutiny. As such, it does not thwart the Charter's systemic interpretation.[39]

Yet the doctrinal application of Art. 51 to validate a state's use of force to protect its nationals against another sovereign state is not a convenient path to follow either. Art. 51 requires the occurrence of an armed attack for its activation. Therefore, it propounds a flexible interpretation of Art. 51, equating the offences committed against nationals abroad with an armed attack against the state's territory.[40] In this respect, the prerequisites of necessity, imminence and proportionality need be redefined, by stretching their ordinary meaning.

2.2.2.1 Necessity

An armed attack is necessary to precipitate the right to self-defense. It has been confirmed time and again that

> Article 51 of the Charter may justify a use of force in self-defence only within the strict confines there laid down. It does not allow the use of force by a State to protect perceived security interests beyond these parameters".[41]

In this regard, there is consistency over the view that there is a relationship of action and response between an armed attack and the right to self-defense. Conversely, self-defense cannot be invoked without prior armed attack attributed to the state

---

[38] Schachter (1989), p. 272.

[39] Higgins (1994), p. 246.

[40] Franck (2002), p. 77; Linnan (1991), p. 121; cf. Alexandrov (1996), p. 203.

[41] ICJ, *Case Concerning Armed Activities on the Territory of the Congo (Democratic Republic of Congo v. Uganda)*, Judgment, ICJ Rep 2005, p. 168, para 148.

against which defense is organized.[42] Given that an armed attack is a necessary precondition for exercising self-defense, the question which remains is whether an attack against nationals is equal to an armed attack against a state. In order for such a prerequisite to be fulfilled, the attack against individuals abroad shall be of sufficient gravity as to qualify as an armed attack.[43]

From this perspective, it is underlined that

> [t]he state on whose territory foreign nationals are facing an extreme danger [may not have] committed an international delict [either because] the offensive acts are not attributable to it [or because] it has respected its obligation of due diligence in protecting the life and liberty of aliens.[44]

The mere occurrence of an armed attack does not necessarily grant the right to exercise self-defense. On the contrary, it shall be attributed to the state against which defense is exercised, and if self-defense involves the doctrine then the attack shall be targeted, or at least endanger the defending state's nationals abroad.[45] This stringent scheme is founded on the most strict and grammatical interpretation of Art. 51. It leaves the door open for the doctrine's application only if the nationals of a state abroad are under a systematic attack which imperils their existence as a group, or if the state of their residence is party to a conflict.

A more progressive interpretation of the necessity requirement and of armed attack in turn is demanded for the functional coexistence of the doctrine with Art. 51. In this sense, it is suggested that necessity is nothing but the certainty of the threat of irreparable harm to nationals in addition to the lack of non-forceful options for preventing harm from coming to them.[46] This twofold reading of necessity cements the lawfulness of recourse to force to protect nationals abroad as it renders it the last option available, following the Charter's overall philosophy on the centralization of the use of force. In this sense, there is a turning point in a state's decision to forcefully protect its nationals abroad, i.e., when all alternative means to achieve this have been exhausted.[47]

Nonetheless, this view bears difficulties too, as defending states shall prove their certainty regarding their nationals' perilous situation, and additionally demonstrate that they have made every effort to avoid recourse to force. Such efforts vary from issuing guidance to their nationals for the evasion of a state which is amidst turbulence to offering them consular assistance in leaving their place of residence. This twofold reading of necessity is no less clear-cut than the traditional one, also limiting states' ability to lawfully invoke the doctrine. Yet it has been endorsed particularly

---

[42] ICJ, *Case Concerning Military and Paramilitary Activities in and against Nicaragua (Nicaragua v. United States of America)*, Judgment, ICJ Rep 1986, p. 103, para 194.

[43] UNGA, 'Definition of Aggression' (14 December 1974) UN Doc. A/Res/3314, Art. 2.

[44] Raby (1988), p. 256.

[45] Dreyfuss (2012), p. 260.

[46] Eichensehr (2008), p. 470.

[47] Mignot-Mahdavi (2021), p. 164.

for operations aiming to release a state's nationals held captive abroad.[48] As far as hostages are concerned, theory and state practice converge. The element of captivity and subsequent effective control over hostages, as compared to a general threat against a state's nationals, makes equating hostage-taking to an armed attack an easier task. As a result, holding another state's nationals captive is definitely a means of coercion which triggers self-defense. As long as captivity endures, the state of hostages' nationality activates the right to exercise self-defense in their name. The case of hostages is easier to justify since there is definite and insurmountable causal link between nationals' danger and the wrongfulness of the state who holds them in captivity.[49]

This proposition is best illustrated by the case of the Tehran hostages in the American embassy. In that case, a series of measures, including the exercise of self-defense to protect interests from imminent substantial deprivations by the target state, were broadly discussed. The differentiating element was that the embassy premises and its personnel were seized, and there was a "symbolic identification of those persons with their state" compared to the fifty American tourists that would have been held captives.[50] This incident demonstrates how the particularities of captivity render equating it to an actual armed attack against the defending state's sovereignty almost self-evident.[51]

The same rationale was pretty much followed with respect to the Entebbe incident too. The international community's tolerance regarding the Israeli intervention stemmed from the necessity to rescue their nationals. Military necessity was evident since there were no other means to offer them protection. On a second reading, its legitimacy was found on its proportionate character.[52] The Entebbe incident has received thorough analysis, and it is suggested that it is a turning point for the doctrine's course.[53] The incident's factual background does not allow for multiple legal interpretations and thus straightforward answers are provided. The vexed question which comes next is whether forcible PNA could justify Israel's action during the 2023–2024 ongoing Gaza war. There are two major features which distinguish the two, leaving aside the territorial status of the strip.[54] First, nationals' captivity is attributed to a non-state actor and not a state. It is not doubted that Hamas organized and designed the abduction and captivity plan of Israeli nationals, bearing responsibility for it. This brings forth an issue which occupies international law for quite a long time. That is whether recourse to self-defense, and forcible PNA by extension,

---

48 Galani (2021), p. 115.

49 Schweisfurth (1980), p. 179; O'Connell (2002), p. 894.

50 Williams Jr. (1980), p. 34.

51 D'Angelo (1981), p. 509.

52 Gordon (1977), p. 134; Margo (1977), p. 321.A

53 See Chap. 3.

54 *Legal Consequences of the Construction of a Wall in the Occupied Palestinian Territory*, Advisory Opinion, ICJ Reports 2004, p. 136, p. 194, para 138 et seq: *Legal Consequences Arising from the Policies and Practices of Israel in the Occupied Palestinian Territory, Including East Jerusalem*, Advisory Opinion, ICJ, 19 July 2024.

is justified against non-state actors. Second, it is by now doubted whether the Israeli response to the incident of 7th October 2023 is proportionate, taking into account that the war lasted for more than a year and the Gaza strip suffered thousands of victims, most of whom civilians.[55]

On the question of legitimate self-defense against non-state actors, theory does not stumble on the Charter's traditional interpretation which permits self-defense against states only. After the 9/11 attacks, it is widely accepted that self-defense is permissible against the territory of nonconsenting states, if they former were attacked by non-state actors located in the soil of the latter.[56] It is also asserted that self-defense against non-state actors in occupied territories is permitted as well.[57]

The second issue regarding the magnitude of the Israeli response to the incident of 7th October 2023 is mostly a matter of proportionality.[58] However, if one is to interpret the conflict from the lens of forcible PNA, then it may be argued that the use of force is justified for so long as the hostage rescue operation lasts. Therefore, hostage rescue necessitates recourse to force, and proportionality shall be measured on these terms.[59] This "ends-means proportionality" notion prioritizes hostage rescue and use of force is permitted if it is necessary.[60] If forcible PNA is not accepted as a states' right in the context of defense, then in this case Israel could not have taken any action to rescue its hostages. Similarly, there are occasions where states opted for patient diplomacy[61] and did not recourse to force for the release of their nationals in captivity. Yet, diplomatic success is not taken for granted and presupposes the existence of minimum dialogue between captors and the kinstate. Such an example took place in 2007 when fifteen British Royal Navy Personnel were taken captives by the Iranian naval forces. Their captivity lasted approximately twenty days, and their release was the outcome of diplomatic pressure by the UK.[62]

This analysis falls short of many aspects regarding the Gaza conflict, yet it underlines how a state's duty vis-à-vis its nationals cannot be neglected. Legal discourse has focused mostly on the territorial status of the strip, the prerequisites of self-defense, and the use of force's consequences. Although hostages' captivity has attracted attention, it did not top legal discussion, and thus forcible PNA has not been considered a legitimate basis for Israel's actions. This happened mostly because only three hostages were rescued in the first phase of the military operations. Thus, it comes as a reasonable result that hostage rescue is of extraordinary

---

[55] HRC (25 March 2024). Report of the Special Rapporteur on the situation of human rights in the Palestinian territories occupied since 1967, Francesca Albanese. UN Doc A/HRC/55/73, para 72.

[56] Henderson (2020), p. 811.

[57] Milanovic (2023). Retrieved, February 22, 2025 from https://www.ejiltalk.org/does-israel-have-the-right-to-defend-itself/

[58] Dannenbaum and Dill (2024), p. 663.

[59] McMahan (2024), pp. 405 et seq.

[60] ibid.

[61] Kralev (2024), p. 35.

[62] Eldred (2008), pp. 251–252.

difficulty.[63] In this sense, it may well be argued that military operations served as a means of pressure for the release of hostages.

This analysis demonstrates that when the peril faced by a state's nationals is so grave, like in cases of captivity, then the prerequisite of necessity is met. Otherwise, a state would be deprived of any means to rescue its nationals, but the diplomatic ones.

2.2.2.2 Imminence

The second requirement of imminence traditionally relates to the time frame in which an armed attack occurs, which renders self-defense an inescapable response to it.[64] Although imminence is a feature not directly provided for by the Charter, it is widely accepted that it can be deduced from the use of simple present in the phrase "an armed attack occurs", with the further claim that this choice made by the drafters excludes anticipatory or preemptive self-defense from the arc of legality. As such, imminence is also referred to as immediacy[65] or proximity.[66] This view prevails as it is in accordance with the customary norm of self-defense, also known as the *Caroline formula*. According to the Caroline formula the necessity for self-defense must be imminent and extreme.[67]

The Caroline formula serves as an argument in favor of the forcible PNA doctrine, given that it echoes nineteenth-century international law when self-defense was considered an attribute of state sovereignty.[68] All in all, although the formula echoes a pre-Charter viewpoint on the use of force, imminence is a feature that further narrows down legitimate use of force to protect one's nationals abroad. This element further decreases the doctrine's ambit under the Charter's centralized system.[69] More specifically, to validate forcible PNA under the cover of self-defense, an imminent threat of injury or death has to exist and put a state's nationals in peril.[70] There is wide acceptance over a strict interpretation of this requisite, for otherwise states would raise claims of forcible protection abroad indiscriminately and without any temporal limit, further jeopardizing the preservation of international peace and security. By adjusting the doctrine to the requirements of Art. 51 UNCh one excludes the time lapse between the occurrence of a peril to a national or their property abroad and the measures taken to ensure their protection. In this sense, the Pacifico affair, when there was an eight-year time span between the alleged attack

[63] Byman (2024), p. 70.

[64] Alexandrov (1996), pp. 149–165.

[65] Gill (2006), pp. 361–369.

[66] Zedalis (1987), pp. 129–175.

[67] Green (2006), p. 469.

[68] Antonopoulos (1999), p. 126.

[69] Waldock (1952), p. 467.

[70] Ronzitti (1985), p. 57.

and the measures taken to ensure the subject's protection,[71] would not be tolerated under the UNCh.

Although imminence plays a crucial role in shaping the modern norm of self-defense, there are still occasions which cannot be easily addressed. For example, imminence cannot provide a clear and precise answer to cases of repeated human rights violations over time, whose accumulation attains the threshold of an armed attack. This jigsaw puzzle is difficult to solve even when territorial claims are involved.[72] *A fortiori*, it cannot be certain when the systematic violation or downgrading of aliens' vital rights by a state in its territory prompts a legitimate claim of self-defense by the state of their nationality. Imminence is the criterion which offers a necessary degree of probability whereby the right to self-defense is exercised by a state. In cases of the systematic downgrading of an alien group's rights in a state's territory, the doctrine has rarely been raised and other bases for intervention have been preferred by the protecting states. Although there are quite a few states which have introduced in their legislation provisions regarding protection of their diasporas from mistreatment,[73] a peril which triggers forcible PNA needs be more tangible. Such an example is Russia; according to federal legislation "compatriot descendants" are people of Russian origin residing in other states. Russia as the kinstate provides for a preferential treatment for them, even though these populations are not characterized as national minorities.[74] National legislation varies regarding protection of states' diasporas; nevertheless, it is not implied that a state's enhanced interest in those groups is an active entitlement for the use of force.

Forcible PNA as a facet of self-defense requires imminence; in this regard, the doctrine is put forward mostly in the following scenarios: (a) evacuation efforts of a state's nationals are found amidst an armed conflict or unrest, (b) a clear obstruction by the host state materializes that impels the use of force by the state of nationality, or (c) rescue operations are performed on particular occasions like hostage-taking.[75] The above confirm how imminence has shaped the concept of "peril" and the doctrine's application in turn. Such forcible interventions meet the criterion of imminence only when "nationals are in immediate danger of losing their lives or are threatened with serious injury".[76] Forcible PNA requires tangible forms of threat, thus minimizing the number of occasions which excuse self-defense.

---

[71] Casey (2020), pp. 18–19.

[72] *Case Concerning Armed Activities on the Territory of the Congo* (2005) para 146.

[73] Piccoli (2020), p. 352; Ragazzi (2014), p. 79; Kalm (2013), p. 385; Yorke (2012), p. 87

[74] Federal'nyj zakon ot 24/5/1999 N 99-FZ "O gosudarstvennoj politike Rossijskoj Federacii otnošeenii sootečestvennikov za rebežom" [Federal Law on the State Policy of the Russian Federation in Respect of the Compatriots Abroad of 24 May 1999, No. 99-FZ].

[75] Kreß and Nußberger (2018), p. 226.

[76] Barrie (1999), p. 800.

2.2.2.3 Proportionality

Proportionality is the final requirement of Art. 51 UNCh and there is doctrinal debate over its meaning. The three most significant interpretations of proportionality are that the defending state may use no more force than necessary (a), that the defensive action must be quantitatively "commensurate" (b), or that the damage inflicted in self-defense shall not be disproportionate in comparison with the pursued objective.[77] From the doctrine's perspective, proportionality focuses primarily on the pursued objective; that is to save a state's nationals in peril. As such, defensive acts should have at their epicenter the rescue of nationals and must not expand against the territorial integrity or political independence of the third state. In this context, proportionate self-defense to protect one's nationals is not a matter of necessity (a), nor is it a matter of quantitative evaluation (b) but shall have nationals' protection as its sole target, pointing to the third interpretation as the most suitable.

Thus, proportionality is considered as "the least amount necessary [quantum of force] to secure the nationals' freedom and [it shall] be used for the sole purpose of securing the nationals' freedom".[78] This analysis has two prongs: proportionality is a matter of the magnitude of force employed by the defending state, and at the same time it bears the qualitative feature that it shall be employed only for the salvaging of the nationals at stake. These two elements are interrelated, although they do not necessarily coincide. More specifically, although the magnitude of the necessary use of force is commensurate with defense of the nationals' population, this does not automatically ensure that the defending state's operational planning and its initial incentive to resort to self-defense are only driven by their nationals' security. Such a proportionality analysis evidently carries a biased position towards the doctrine and its compatibility with the UNCh, anticipating states' potential will to shield under such operations military actions that are employed to impose and secure their interests. This view seems to take into consideration the historical aspect of the doctrine and to account for its political sensitivity as well.[79]

This reading of proportionality on forcible PNA is useful primarily to avert territorial claims by the intervening state. Although forcible PNA is technically a breach of sovereignty, it is an acceptable exception to the use of force prohibition on the condition it does not threaten a state's territorial integrity. Yet, this restrictive version of proportionality does not fully take into account both operational parameters, and the need to provide nationals abroad with sufficient protection. On the operational aspect of such missions, there is general agreement that successful raids, like the Entebbe model, are not always an option. Even rescue and evacuation operations are military in character and the use of force varies according to the level of hostility expected. Securing protection for nationals, alongside military personnel, may well require force exceeding narrow limits. Location, the number of

[77] Akande and Liefländer (2013), p. 566; Johansen (2019), pp. 255–270.

[78] Eichensehr (2008), p. 476.

[79] Græger and Lindgren (2018), pp. 188–210.

nationals in peril, as well as the type of risk they confront are factors affecting a mission's operational design, and in effect the levels of proportionality. For example, on several occasions the kinstate does not have sufficient information as to the exact location and status of their nationals, nor is there certainty regarding the type of peril confronted by the captives.

In this event, forcible PNA is founded on the presumption that captivity itself is an act indicating hostility and danger. Thus, military operations are not deployed based on hard evidence; rather, peril is the result of uncertainty over nationals' well-being. This broad understanding of what peril consists of directly affects proportionality. For example, the Mayaguez incident of 1975 is a disputed case of forcible PNA.[80] The US military operation for the rescue of the crew and recovery of the ship was the outcome of short unsuccessful attempts to establish diplomatic dialogue. Yet, the legality of forcible PNA is doubted, on the grounds that there was no evidence, but mere suspicion, that the American naval personnel was life-threatened. Previous seizures of other vessels ended up soon, and the crew was released unharmed. If this course of thinking is accepted, then the American operation had an offensive character, and no justification under the Charter's Article 51.[81]

What is more, apart from the use of force and the existence of nationals residing abroad, the doctrine also involves the concept of protection. If recourse to force is the last resort for a state, then protection shall be guaranteed. Investing financial and human resources in such missions is quite a burden for the intervening state. Forcible PNA does not involve civilian protection only; operations need also to safeguard that there are no military losses and minimize the perils of enemy captivity for soldiers.[82] Therefore, certainty that these operations will be successful is a primary concern. If they take the form of an evacuation operation, then protection has a simple definition: to move people out of an area. The same does not apply to all other occasions though. That is, a hostage rescue operation is much more dangerous.[83] Captivity either by state forces, non-state actors, or terrorist groups implies that nationals are a target for their captors, a parameter which affects the character of the operation. Captors' unpredictable reactions during rescue missions are an extra risk to the welfare of hostages, forcing the kinstate to take additional measures to ensure the mission's accomplishment, redefining the concept of proportionality in effect.[84] Additionally, it is anticipated that a state engaging in such a mission wishes to eliminate the source of peril. It would not be wise to opt for the release of hostages without exterminating the actor responsible for captivity. These parameters require a different reading of protection and proportionality, extending their limits to the destruction of any prospective peril for the rescued.

---

80 Hann (1977), p. 550; Simmons (1978), p. 43.

81 Paust (1976), p. 800; Sadoff (2009), p. 463.

82 Bohrer and Osiel (2013), p. 638; Bohrer (2016), p. 191.

83 Charters (1980), p. 27.

84 Galani (2016), p. 88.

Overall, it is asserted that Art. 51 "demands reciprocal limitation on the scope, duration, and intensity of the protective response".[85] However, to evaluate if invoking and applying the forcible PNA doctrine is within the boundaries of legality, one needs to look beyond the ordinary interpretation of self-defense requirements. Necessity, imminence and proportionality make sense only through the lens of peril and protection. These two are necessary parameters to consider, in order to sketch the limits of forcible PNA as a form of self-defense. The source and type of peril faced by nationals determine how protection will be accomplished, further shaping the details of every mission. Therefore, a narrow or restrictive understanding of proportionality cannot be the standard regarding forcible PNA; or the term's content shall be redefined respectively. Proportionality limits are hard to tell apart; the only clear line discerning legality from illegality is for the intervening state not to raise territorial claims, rendering the operation and offensive one.

2.2.2.4 PNA and Non-combatant Evacuation Operations

Forcible PNA is significantly limited under the discourse of Art. 51. Theory points to the fact that the requirements of necessity, immediacy and proportionality, when read together, allow only for rescue operations, or so-called "non-combatant evacuation operations" (NEO). This view is the predominant approach within the doctrinal debate, as it builds up a more comprehensive argumentation, underlying the idea that since states are bound by the restrictions of Art. 51, use of force shall be limited to minimum-scale rescue or evacuation operations. In this framework, the kinstate breaches a third state's sovereignty through forceless operations which aim at the rescue of their nationals alone.[86] These military operations are defensive in nature, and the defending states involve their armies only to guarantee the security of their citizens during the attempt to relocate them to a safe haven. This is an operational terminology which has been instituted primarily by the armed forces of the US, the UK and Canada to point at the need for such missions in cases of turmoil.[87] Although this reading of the doctrine seems to have found a fine balance between the requirements of Art. 51 and the heightened cases of crises involving nationals abroad, it has not escaped criticism as well. Critics have underlined that states which introduced the terminology have attempted to legitimize small-scale military operations via the back door, soon attracting support from other states too, such as India[88] and China.[89]

NEOs have mostly been performed during the last two decades, and more specifically in regions which faced turmoil due to the "Arab spring". Although evacuation of a state's citizens abroad is the sole purpose of NEOs, still it is considered

[85] Wingfield (2000), p. 465.

[86] Thomson (2012), p. 656.

[87] ibid.

[88] Raina (2019), pp. 120–137.

[89] Duchâtel et al. (2014), p. 47.

"a tangible demonstration of state-provided security and an illustration of national prestige" given that "not all states possess the means to project hard power beyond their borders".[90] This new turn in the forcible PNA doctrine brings forth four distinct comments. First, it confirms the need of states to protect their citizens when found caught up in armed conflicts or crises abroad. Evacuation or rescue operations are a sign of some states' perception that their nationals abroad form part of a broader political community under the shield of central government. Second, although NEOs are not necessarily forcible operations, they still are considered a demonstration of hard power, taking the place of diplomatic means to resolve such delicate cases. Third, NEOs are the result of a hard equation between a state's resources and its capabilities to execute such a mission on the one hand, and the particularities of each case on the other, including the number of nationals in peril, their eligibility to be relocated etc. In this regard, NEOs are a significant development in the protection of nationals abroad saga, but they do not solve the puzzle when it comes to mass evacuations that shall take place,[91] nor do they remove political nuances from such operations. Few mass non-combatant evacuation operations have taken place over the last few years. Cooperation among states was the element which made such operations feasible, as in the case of Lebanon in 2006. It is always in the kin-state's discretion to deploy a NEO or not, after evaluation of its interests. In this sense, forcible PNA always involves a heavy political choice before an operation is executed. Finally, non-combatant evacuation operations usually pertain to cases when a state's nationals are trapped in a crisis and are not part of it. If the host state is hostile against another state's nationals abroad then NEOs are not an option.

States' growing acceptance of taking recourse in NEOs or acquiescing to such operations poses the question about the existence of a customary rule with this particular content. It is proposed that NEOs form a customary norm in *statu nascendi*, since they are favored by state practice, while they are covered by *opinio juris* due to their non-direct opposition to the UNCh's principles.[92] If such a customary rule is in formation, then one needs to clarify whether NEOs substitute for the Doctrine's pre-Charter understanding, further transforming forcible PNA according to the existing order of things (a), or if this is a new norm existing alongside the older one (b).[93] Both legal constructs can be equally well established, depending on which reading of the UNCh one decides to apply. If the UN is considered to have built the international regime for the use of force from scratch, then a customary rule permitting NEOs is a novelty that emerged from the Charter's teleological interpretation coupled with states' practice. In this scheme, NEOs are an exception to the prohibition on the use of force for the protection of nationals abroad. In contrast, if NEOs coexist with norms previously established, such as states' right to forcible self-help, then these operations shall be considered a modification of the pre-existing norms.

---

[90] Bond (2016), pp. 28–29.

[91] Condon (2007), p. 68.

[92] Randelzhofer (2002), p. 133.

[93] ICJ, *North Sea Continental Shelf*, Judgment, ICJ Reports 1969, p. 3, para 63.

In this second scenario, though, one needs to further clarify if state practice, both within the UN or beyond the organization's ambit, fits with this reading. This is certainly a dilemma. There are few cases when states put forward their position either in support of or against NEOs' legality in their statements within the UN, and it comes out that they clearly rely upon pre-Charter norms.[94] This approach, together with the absence of a positive acceptance of NEOs by UN organs, alludes to their doctrinal establishment regarding the customary right to self-defense.

The NEO concept originated from the operational need of states to evacuate and repatriate their nationals residing in places where turmoil escalated, thereby posing a threat to their life or to their physical integrity. Thus, these operations are explicitly provided for in some states' operational manuals, further verifying the existence of *opinio juris* regarding their legitimacy. In addition, the NEO discourse has been further elaborated to an outstanding level. At least sixteen states have agreed to cooperate on the execution of NEOs, as partners with a view to successfully evacuating eligible persons in case of threat. This informal coalition is the NEO Coordination Group (NEOCG), whose foundation involves asset and information sharing during evacuation operations.[95] The rationale behind this coalition is to determine how nationals of more states can be safely transferred from dangerous zones. This new doctrine falls between collective self-defense and reciprocal assistance, given that information and asset sharing is considered the most notable benefit of NEOCG. Thus, NEOCG is a unique coalition lying between the traditional notion of collective self-defense and a state's legal right to self-help. It could be characterized as "collective self-help", since states share the same understanding of self-defense and act collectively in its name, although not under the UN's collective security rules.[96]

Yet the development of NEO remains controversial; given the concept's functional origin, there are still contentions over its legality. First, such operations may well involve military force to guarantee the evacuees' safety. Therefore, their design is superficially similar, but essentially different, from rescue operations. Due to their operational character, noncombatant evacuation missions are accepted to be military assisted in areas where the political environment is hostile, or even uncertain, even if there is authorization by the host state's government.[97] In addition, the initial design of NEOs provided for small-scale operations, which minimized in turn the possibility of recourse to force. Over time, though, all those states espousing the use of NEOs have authorized the launch of ever larger operations, introducing the concept of mass-NEOs.[98] Evacuation operations of larger groups of nationals,

[94] Day (1992), p. 50.

[95] Director Development (March 2021), p. 39. Retrieved February 22, 2025, from https://assets.publishing.service.gov.uk/government/uploads/system/uploads/attachment_data/file/979907/20210412-JDP_3_51_NEO_web_V2-O_1_.pdf

[96] Alcala and Nasu (2023), p. 10.

[97] Clark Jr. (1995). p. 2. Retrieved February 22, 2025 from https://apps.dtic.mil/sti/pdfs/ADA293291.pdf accessed 26 July 2024.

[98] Dixon (2017), p. 53.

presumably of different nationalities, have increased the probability of military engagement, and thus NEOs have departed from their initial defensive character. Moreover, mass-NEOs magnify, as a matter of fact, the presence of the operating state in the host territory. In this sense, some have suggested that NEOs, in their contemporary form, fall under the wide spectrum of "stability operations",[99] as they form an amorphous form of warfare, the so-called "small wars".[100]

In this context, mass NEOs in the 2006 Israel-Lebanon conflict did not attract negative criticism regarding their legality. More specifically, "nations, particularly those with close ties to Israel and sophisticated resources that could be activated quickly in the region, acted relatively promptly"[101] to evacuate their expatriates. For example, Australia launched "Operation Ramp" and evacuated approximately 5000 Australians and 1350 "approved foreign nationals;[102] France proceeded with "Operation Baliste" to safe transfer around 14,500 nationals;[103] India established "Operation Sukoon" and evacuated at least 1800 Indian nationals; the United Kingdom launched "Operation Highbrow" and rescued almost 4500 individuals,[104] while Canada's operation was called "Operation Lion" and the Canadian forces evacuated 14,000 Canadians.[105] Other states launched similar smaller scale operations too.

However, on a doctrinal level such operations are outside the UN scheme and Chapter VII in particular. It appears that NEOCG is a contested formulation which has created a doctrinal side-system to the UN's collective security.[106] The discrepancy between NEO legality in international law and their international recognition as necessary missions stems from the rapidly changing international spectrum. That is, although they are not technically self-defense acts, nor do they follow the UNCh standards, their scope is not contested primarily because they are not viewed as attempts to intervene in another state's internal affairs. In this sense, their operational orientation denudes them from political confrontations. As such, they are not perceived as political choices, although they are found on them. NEOs signify the deteriorating relations between the intervening state and the one considered perilous for the evacuees, while consent is not taken for granted. In this sense, there is controversy over the compatibility of such operations with the strict conditions set by the UNCh.[107]

---

[99] Headquarters, Department of the Army (31 July 2019). Retrieved February 22, 2025 https://armypubs.army.mil/epubs/DR_pubs/DR_a/pdf/web/ARN18011_ADP%203-07%20FINAL%20WEB.pdf

[100] Turns (2009), p. 397.

[101] Jureidini (2011), pp. 199–203.

[102] Dudgeon (2006), p. 22.

[103] France – Royaume-Uni (2007), p. 8.

[104] Massey (2007). Retrieved February 22, 2025 from https://assets.publishing.service.gov.uk/media/5a78f0d840f0b62b22cbe023/lebanon-op-highbrow-debrief.pdf

[105] The Standing Senate Committee on Foreign Affairs and International Trade (2007), p. 13.

[106] Hammerstad (2014), p. 247.

[107] Day (1992), p. 64.

All in all, NEOs have gained the growing support of states, while in many cases public opinion sides with them because of their necessity, as they are the sign of the dynamic and time-sensitive environment that characterizes turmoiled states. The recent example of the evacuation of approximately 124,000 people from Afghanistan's Kabul, through airlift, has been widely considered as a legitimate operation.[108] This evacuation operation has attracted wide interest in the media due to images of Afghans hanging onto American airplanes and flee Afghanistan.[109] To the contrary, less attention is given so far in legal discourse. The 2021 evacuation operation signified the end of almost twenty years of American presence in Afghani soil, after the 9/11 terrorist attacks. As soon as the Biden administration decided to withdraw from Afghanistan, the Taliban regime returned to power causing doubts among Afghans on the regime they would establish. Withdrawal of the American forces from Afghanistan is not the common type of evacuation operations. Although it falls under the NEO definition, since it was a non-offensive operation, aiming at the safe return of American nationals to their homeland, this operation differs in many terms.[110] First, the evacuees did not face peril during their residence abroad, nor was the state unwilling or unable to protect them. American withdrawal was a political decision which did not meet opposition by the Afghani authorities. As a result, safe evacuation met some minimum standards and guarantees, since it meant the end of American military presence in Afghanistan. The Afghan authorities not only consented to this operation, but it also welcomed it. The crucial point though, does not relate to the safe withdrawal of Americans; rather it relates to the evacuation of Afghan nationals, who had been assisting the American forces and favored their presence on their state's soil. Their condition was considered critical after the Talibans regained control, and they faced danger of mistreatment, or life. In this regard, Operation Allies Welcome was a sophisticated operation which provided for the evacuation of Afghans, after they had completed certain steps for their migration in the US.[111] Initially, Afghan airports were used for their evacuation, and after the Taliban took power over the country, there were stopover flights from Qatar and Kuwait. This process was covered positively by the media, and there were even voices asking for a more massive NEO of Afghan nationals, an option which was rejected as it was thought to aggravate interstate relations.[112]

---

[108] Kitfield (2022). Retrieved February 22, 2025 from https://www.airandspaceforces.com/remembering-the-largest-non-combatant-evacuation-operation-allies-refuge-in-u-s-history%EF%BF%BC/

[109] Levi et al., (2021), p. 37; Administration of Joseph R. Biden, Jr., 2021 Remarks on United States Evacuation Efforts in Afghanistan and an Exchange with Reports (2021), pp. 1–9.

[110] Klein (2024), p. 71.

[111] US Department of Homeland Security (2021). Retrieved February 22, 2025 from https://www.dhs.gov/archive/publication/fact-sheet-operation-allies-welcome

[112] Nagler (2021), p. 511; Joint Declaration between the Islamic Republic of Afghanistan and the United States of America for Bringing Peace to Afghanistan. Retrieved February 22, 2025 from https://www.state.gov/wp-content/uploads/2020/02/02.29.20-US-Afghanistan-Joint-Declaration.pdf

NEOs do not identify with the forcible PNA doctrine entirely. Operation Allies Welcome proves—among others—that NEOs are not strictly determined by the nationality of the evacuees; rather they extend to people considered allies, based on their nationality. Coordination between allies for the evacuation of their nationals, or even of third country citizens, takes place more and more often.[113] This feature differentiates NEOs from the traditional understanding of forcible PNA. NEOs carry equal elements of self-defense, forcible PNA and humanitarian intervention. Association with the right to self-defense rests on the fact that such operations are defensive in nature. Accordingly, its relationship with forcible PNA arises from the need to rescue nationals residing in a state weak or unwilling to ensure their protection; while relevance to humanitarian intervention results from the widening of the number of people whose rescue is attempted, in which case the nationality criterion is bypassed. Thus, there are humanitarian grounds for their rescue. NEOs combine aspects of all three doctrines justifying recourse to force. As such, they are not an advanced form of forcible PNA, but a hybrid form of the use of force resulting from operational necessity.

2.2.3 The Doctrine's Modification According to UN Requirements

The doctrine has gone through many phases from 1945 onwards. The theory of self-defense has gradually gained ground as the most solid foundation for the forcible PNA under the UNCh. The debate over the doctrine's attachment to Art. 2(4) was soon abandoned in an attempt to minimize states' opportunity to take recourse in the forcible PNA, and to secure the prohibition's absolute character by cementing its central role in the Charter's regime. As a result, self-defense has been a catalyst for the doctrine's use in the post-Charter era, and contemporary state practice relies almost exclusively on it.[114]

The strict interpretation of Art. 51's criteria is dictated by the right's exceptional character in the UNCh system. This reading strives to outlaw indiscriminate use of force under the pretext of protecting one's nationals abroad, further questioning the legality of the use of force for humanitarian purposes, or "rectification".[115] The requirements of necessity, imminence and proportionality seem to have shaped state practice pointing at the doctrine's modification to NEO and rescue operations. From a *jus ad bellum* perspective, forcible protection of nationals abroad is an exception to the prohibition on force rule, and if it does not meet the standards of the right to self-defense it constitutes a potential threat to international peace and security.

However, protecting one's nationals abroad is not only a matter of *jus ad bellum.*

[113] Whittemore (2008), p. 402; Biermann (1999), p. 199.

[114] cf. Ronzitti (2006), p. 354.

[115] State Responsibility, State Self-Help and Problems of Public International Law (1980), p. 30.

Moreover, its conception as a threat to international peace and security is misleading as it incorporates pre-Charter aspects of state practice, by which force is not centrally regulated or under international scrutiny. All in all, there are several questions that *jus ad bellum* cannot effectively address,[116] including the doctrine's innate connection with the principle of humanity, or the expectation that nationality ties predetermine some kind of protective action, whether forcible or not. The most crucial aspect of the doctrine which remains unaddressed, though, is if the systematic downgrading of a population with which the kin-state has national ties legitimizes self-defense actions against the host state. This scenario has brought forward an extensive theoretical discussion which exceeds the forcible PNA doctrine, further pointing to the fact that such acts of intervention are not only a matter of *jus ad bellum*.

2.3 PNA as an Act of Aggression

Although forcible PNA finds no solid, or at least obvious, basis in the UNCh, thus keeping the doctrinal debate alive, there are no implications that it is connected to the notion of aggression. The term has been the source of endless controversy both in the fields of the use of force and in criminal justice. Generally speaking, "aggression" stands for an armed attack (*aggression armée*), although there are linguistic distinctions. According to the UN definition

> aggression is the use of armed force by a State against the sovereignty, territorial integrity or political independence of another State, or in any other manner inconsistent with the Charter of the United Nations, as set out in this Definition.[117]

The nexus between aggression and the prohibition on using force is obvious, as the former is a grammatical reflection of the latter. It emerges that aggression is defined as the profound and direct violation of Art. 2(4). From a historical perspective, defining aggression has engaged the international community in a fruitful debate.[118] The primary scope of this debate was, according to the Union of Soviet Socialist Republics, "to define the concept of aggression as accurately as possible", which in turn would determine the duties of states in the event of the outbreak of hostilities.[119] Defining aggression was an additional legal safety valve sought by states during the Cold War to avert the use of force. A close look at the state proposals and negotiation

---

[116] Zedalis (1990), p. 235.

[117] UN Doc. A/Res/3314, Art. 1.

[118] Wilmshurst (2008), p. 2. Retrieved February 22, 2025 from https://legal.un.org/avl/pdf/ha/da/da_e.pdf

[119] Report of the International Law Commission on its Third Session (16 May to 27 July) *Official Records of the General Assembly, Sixth Session, Supplement No. 9* (A/1858, reproduced in *Yearbook of the International Law Commission 1951*, vol. II, 123–144), 131, para 35. See also, UNGA, Report of the Special Committee on the Question of Defining Aggression (25 April–30 May 1973). 28th Session. UN Doc. Supp. No. 19 (A/9019).

records aptly demonstrates that states attempted to enhance the absolute character of the prohibition on the use of force. Thereat, explicit reference to sovereignty in the definition of aggression was expected to leave no doubt as to what constitutes a violation under Art. 2(4).[120]

After a contextual reading of aggression, it could be contended that the use of force to protect nationals abroad would be outlawed. By way of simplification, one could possibly argue that if protection of nationals abroad is not permitted under UNCh Art. 2(4), then it constitutes an act of aggression. Or, conversely, that the 3314/74 definition of aggression introduces a stricter prohibition than that of Art. 2(4), therefore rendering the forcible protection of nationals abroad illegal. However, this proposition is false, primarily for two reasons. First, forcible PNA is defensive in principle.[121] The doctrine is based on the concept that a state's nationals abroad are confronting imminent danger, and that action is taken so as to alleviate their harmful condition. Counter to this, aggression signifies a state's intent to wage a war and violate another state's sovereignty, territorial integrity or political independence. Second, position statements in the long debate before the definition's adoption did not make any connection between the doctrine and aggression. In particular, the Union of Soviet Socialist Republics, which vehemently proposed a strong definition of aggression, excluded from its scope of application the forcible PNA.[122] There were states though, like Belgium and the UK, strongly opposing to this view, and further suggesting that "by mistreating foreigners in its own territory a state commit[s] an act of aggression against the country of which the foreigners were nationals".[123]

Overall, recourse to force to protect nationals abroad is currently not considered an act of aggression, at least in principle. In this regard, the doctrine is not linked to the concept of aggression by definition, even though its legality under the UNCh is disputed. Negotiations over aggression did not proved relevant to the doctrine's legality, mainly due to aggression's innate conceptual difficulty. This proposition was illustrated in the statement of the special rapporteur on the draft code of offences against the peace and security of mankind, Mr. Spiropoulos, who mentioned that

> whenever governments are called upon to decide on the existence or non-existence of 'aggression under international law', they base their judgment on criteria derived from the 'natural', so to speak, notion of aggression ... and not on legal constructions. [This] natural notion [of aggression] is a concept per se, [which] is not susceptible of definition. A 'legal' definition of aggression would be an artificial construction, which could never be comprehensive enough to comprise all imaginable cases of aggression, since the methods of aggression are in a constant process of evolution.[124]

---

[120] Raby (1989), p. 450.

[121] Stone (1977), p. 227.

[122] Ronzitti (1985), pp. 11, 50.

[123] Krylov (1995), p. 379.

[124] Report of the International Law Commission on its Third Session (1951) 131, para 39.

This statement highlights that recourse to force follows certain legal delimitations, but the assessment of its legality is of a circumstantial nature. Thus, it remains ambivalent whether forcible PNA survives because of its defensive character, or because of the standing legal right of states vis-à-vis its nationals.

This analysis pertains to the doctrinal coexistence of the UNCh regime and the discourse of the forcible PNA. This analysis, though, is circumscribed by the historical perspective of the Cold War period, the political positions of the states involved and the subsequent legal interpretations the above imposed. The end of the Cold War gave rise to doctrinal evolution and a less stringent interpretation of the UNCh. States' policy towards recourse to the use of force was largely reversed. It is proposed that a post-Cold War reading of Art. 2(4) prioritized the idea of a qualified prohibition, instead of a general one.[125] Legal alterations as a result of the brand new political scenery did not leave untouched the PNA rationale, further necessitating researching it in conjunction with the concepts of humanitarian intervention and R2P.

2.4 PNA and Humanitarian Intervention

Humanitarian intervention is a much-discussed concept, primarily because it is associated with the functional revival of the UNSC after the end of the Cold War. The term generally refers to "coercive intervention by states, singly or collectively, through economic sanctions or by use of military force, in response to gross violations of human rights",[126] or as "the use of military instrument by one or more states in the territory of another state for the purpose of ensuring compliance with a minimum international standards of human rights".[127] Humanitarian intervention is fairly considered a breakthrough, as it shifted international attention away from the inviolability of state sovereignty to the protection against gross human rights violations. Thereat, the concept points at the significance of human rights protection for the maintenance of international peace and security. To many, humanitarian intervention was much anticipated as it managed to bring together two central pillars of the international community, amending the view that the grammatical neglect of human rights by the UNCh further entailed the UN's indifference to them. In effect, it demonstrated the UN's embracing of humanitarian values.[128] This doctrinal approach was strengthened and further boosted by historical conjuncture, and in particular the atrocities that took place in Iraq, the former Yugoslavia, Sudan and Rwanda.[129]

[125] Mrazek (1989), p. 109.

[126] Henkin (1994), p. 383.

[127] Chilstrom (1974), p. 95.

[128] Donnelly (1993), p. 638.

[129] O'Donoghue (2005), p. 167; Antonopoulos (1999), p. 151.

Although humanitarian intervention was considered a timely development for the international community, it was in sheer contrast with the prohibition on the use of force in the first place. Humanitarian intervention breaches the political independence and territorial integrity of the invaded state, for it is the only possible way to halt flagrant human rights violations. Even if one concedes that it introduces only a qualified prohibition, instead of an absolute one, it cannot fit under any proposed interpretation of Art. 2(4). Thus, the legality of humanitarian intervention relies solely on a Chapter VII authorization. Interventions in the name of humanitarian principles exemplify the UNCh's adaptation to the international community's course through teleological interpretation. Nevertheless, the onus is still on "the proposers of new criteria by which to justify exceptions to the Charter's fundamental and stills essentially valid norms" to demonstrate how these criteria would fit the well-established legal framework.[130]

The above propositions leave unilateral / unauthorized recourse to force on humanitarian grounds out of the realm of legality, even though its purpose is tied to morality, natural law or political theory. In an idealistic international plane, any kind of humanitarian intervention would be legal by definition, due to its ultimate goal. In this context, the debate over the legality of unilateral humanitarian intervention is thought

> as one between "positivists" (opposing unilateral humanitarian intervention) and "naturalists" (favoring such intervention by adhering closely – even if not explicitly – to natural law, derived from the rudimentary values held by the "global society"). For the proponents of humanitarian intervention, international law exists only in part to preserve the sanctity of states; the dignity of persons is of equal value and in some situations "trumps" the values protected by strict rules on non-intervention.[131]

Any such "natural" reading of humanitarian intervention would pave the way for the regularization of interventions in states' domestic affairs. In this sense, it would not contravene the prohibition on the use of force only, as states have timelessly secured that "police action" by an established state within its sovereign domains remained lawful".[132] To wit, unilateral / unauthorized recourse to the use of force on humanitarian grounds is not encroaching on the UNCh's regime alone, but it is not embraced by many states either.

Finally, the legality of humanitarian intervention is not confined to the naturalist / positivist argument. The most crucial parameter for the legality of humanitarian intervention is whether the qualitative feature of gross human rights violations is met. This parameter cannot be easily adumbrated, although there is consensus that in the aftermath of the Cold War "international human rights [...] are matters of international concern [and they] are not shielded by domestic jurisdiction".[133] Although the systemic and gross violation of human rights is an easily conceivable

---

[130] Franck (2006), p. 155.

[131] Murphy (2009), p. 349.

[132] Stone (1977), p. 234.

[133] Reisman (1995), p. 795.

concept, its legal perception is a source of confusion. It is asserted, though, that violations of such magnitude imply the political involvement of the perpetrating state.[134] Naturally, the political involvement of the perpetrating sovereign is integral for a motive of systemic and widespread human rights violations. At this point, it should be mentioned by way of digression that shortly after the concept of humanitarian intervention gained ground in the international plane, the concept of "pro-democratic intervention" arose. The conceptual proximity of the two is indisputable: gross human rights violations are perpetuated either by authoritarian regimes, or they take place in collapsed democracies. Discussion over the legitimacy of the use of force to re-establish democratic institutions has occupied theory for quite some time, but it was abandoned, as international law does not favor democracy over other forms of governance. Both on a doctrinal, as well as in practical terms, there has been little association between pro-democratic intervention and the forcible PNA. States which resorted to force to protect their nationals, raised claims over the host states' democratic deficits few times, but this was rarely part of their operational strategy. The US invasion in Panama is probably the clearest example of a state invoking both doctrines simultaneously. The US Department of State invaded Panama on the grounds of self-defense due to its nationals' perilous position. At the same time, it was widely accepted that the US involvement in Panama was opting to overthrow the Noriega regime and allow the democratically elected government take office. The American invasion on pro-democratic terms was strongly condemned by several fora of the international community. The UN, in particular, does not embrace unilateral recourse to force to establish democratic governments, although it promotes democratization through institutions, such as peacekeeping and peacebuilding operations.[135] Yet it is this very aspect of humanitarian intervention which renders the doctrine's legality precarious. For example, the US interventions in Nicaragua and Grenada were judged differently from each other and encountered generally poor response from the international community.[136]

Humanitarian intervention with a view to protecting a state's nationals abroad has been no less problematic. The major line of argumentation has been that if intervention is permitted in the name of gross human rights violations, then such an intervention for the protection of a state's nationals abroad would be *a fortiori* required, bearing in mind the nexus of nationality between the invading state and the victims of the perpetrating state. Humanitarian intervention and forcible PNA are not opposing doctrines as they both share the scope of protecting groups of people from a situation threatening their lives or causing irreparable injury.[137] Apart from this common ground, the two doctrines differ in perspective, promoting the nationality link and human rights protection respectively. In this regard, in the hypothetical

[134] Donnelly (1993), p. 612; Reisman (1995), p. 798.

[135] See, Juan, (2008), pp. 308–310; Wippman (1997), pp. 659–688; UNGA (29 December 1989). Effects of the military intervention by the United States of America in Panama on the situation in Central America. UN Doc A/44/240: Irving (1996), pp. 41–70.

[136] Henkin (1994), p. 387.

[137] Lillich (1969), p. 208: Salako (2016), pp. 152–167.

scenario according to which a state's nationals suffer severe mistreatment by a third state where they reside, it is questioned on what grounds their country of origin can resort to force in order to save them. For a comprehensive response, three considerations are necessary. First, the temporal element is decisive for the legality of both doctrines: in the Cold War era neither humanitarian intervention nor forcible PNA would be legally accepted. As Louis Henkin eloquently points out:

> During the Cold War, the international system did not approve unilateral intervention by a state even on behalf of its own nationals. Only "the Entebbe principle" enjoyed a measure of acceptance: a state may intervene with such force as may be necessary to rescue and extricate hostages - whether or not its own nationals. But that principle did not warrant intervention by a state to conquer territory, or topple a government, or otherwise impose its will, even to end or prevent atrocities.[138]

Ergo, both doctrines' legitimacy was severely doubted before the last decade of the twentieth century. The second and third considerations pertain to the post-Cold War doctrines' invocation. It is questioned whether unilateral and unauthorized recourse to force by a state to protect its nationals suffering in a third state qualifies as humanitarian intervention. In this case, the two doctrines' usefulness becomes identical, as it is limited to the creation of a legitimate narrative to justify the unilateral use of force.[139] It depends on the state's policy to decide whether unauthorized recourse to force would be a matter of protection based on nationality ties or on humanitarian principles.[140] From this point of view, it is immaterial whether a state's discourse will prioritize one over the other doctrine, since they are both driven by the "rescue principle".[141] Humanitarian intervention has attracted criticism by weak states, similarly to forcible PNA. Fear that unilateral use of force by military elites would hide under humanitarian justifications arose, reflecting the legal debate which had taken place regarding forcible PNA at the beginning of the twentieth century.[142]

In turn, this discussion is not affected by the doctrinal correlation between protecting nationals abroad and the inherent right to self-defense, or if it fits the requirements of a qualified use of force prohibition. Finally, one must consider whether forcible PNA and humanitarian intervention could be evoked complementarily in the context of authorized force under Chapter VII. In this scenario, the question is not one of legality *per se*, rather it is evidence of the SC's accepted rationale for authorizing the use of force. So far, practice has shown that humanitarian grounds are more likely to justify the use of force compared to nationality. This does not follow from the superiority or added value of one over the other. In contrast, humanitarian reasons constitute more objective criteria for supporting the recourse to centralized force, while the nationality element justifies a country's strong ties to the

[138] Henkin (1994), p. 386.

[139] Moore (2007), p. 177.

[140] Ayoob (2002), p.85; cf. Bellamy and Wheeler (2008); Bellamy (2015), p. 134.

[141] Wolf (1988), pp. 340–341.

[142] Reisman (2000), p. 6.

population at risk. In this regard, it does not align with the centralized UN regime regarding the use of force.

Although the two share a common justification on use of force, so far theory and state practice avoid connecting them. An interchangeable reference to humanitarian intervention and forcible PNA would allow strong states to resort to force more often, permitting unilateral action on humanitarian grounds.[143]

2.5 Protecting Nationals Abroad and R2P

R2P has come up as the doctrinal evolution of humanitarian intervention. Foreign intervention on humanitarian grounds has gained limited acceptance, as most states have continued to oppose the doctrine's legality and alignment with the UNCh's principles. In this framework, the UN has made gross and systematic violations of human rights a priority of its agenda. In his report "We the peoples: the role of the United Nations in the twenty-first century", former Secretary-General of the UN, Kofi Annan engaged the international community in a serious debate revolving around the clash between gross human rights violations and the principle of state sovereignty. More specifically, Annan, being well aware of the doctrinal problems that "humanitarian intervention" entailed, called on states to reach an agreement on the least problematic response of the international community in such cases. Thus, he stated:

> Although I emphasized that intervention embraced a wide continuum of responses, from diplomacy to armed action, it was the latter option that generated most controversy in the debate that followed. Some critics were concerned that the concept of "humanitarian intervention" could become a cover for gratuitous interference in the international affairs of sovereign states. [...] But to the critics I would pose this question: if humanitarian intervention is, indeed, an unacceptable assault on sovereignty, how should we respond to a Rwanda, to a Srebrenica – to gross and systematic violations of human rights that offend every precept of our common humanity? [...] Humanitarian intervention is a sensitive issue, fraught with political difficulty and not susceptible to easy answers. But surely no legal principle – not even sovereignty – can ever shield crimes against humanity.[144]

This report rebooted the discussion on the interplay between intervention and gross human rights violations. The International Commission on Intervention and State Sovereignty (ICISS) was assigned the challenge to sketch out the relationship between the two. It subsequently came up with the "Responsibility to Protect Report"; while in 2005 the High Level Panel on Threats, Challenges and Change endorsed the R2P concept. The findings of the ICISS have contributed significantly to the understanding of the protection of nationals abroad doctrine. On the one hand,

---

[143] Barrie (1999), p. 794.

[144] UNGA, Report of the Secretary-General (27 March 2000). We the Peoples: The Role of the United Nations in the Twenty-First Century. UN Doc A/54/2000, 34, paras 216–219.

ICISS sets out the core principles regarding the R2P concept. Accordingly, it is described that

> [s]tate sovereignty implies responsibility, and the primary responsibility for the protection of its people lies with the state itself [and] where a population is suffering serious harm [...] and the state in question is unwilling or unable to halt or avert it, the principle of non-intervention yields to the international responsibility to protect.[145]

This report fills an important gap that existed in international law up till that time. It emphasizes states' self-evident obligation to take good care of their citizens and clarifies the legal consequences stemming from it. As Hersch Lauterpacht observes, "the individual in his capacity as an alien enjoys a larger measure of protection by international law than in his character as a citizen of his own State".[146] This absence of protection of a state's own nationals in international law is a result of the dichotomy between the international legal order and the national ones, further denoting that states have until recently considered gross human rights violations to be part of their *domain reservé*.[147] In this regard, systematic and widespread human rights violations of a state's citizens were supposedly covered by the principle of non-intervention, blocking the rest of the international community from taking action accordingly. Thus, the ICISS report takes a clear position by providing that the principle of non-intervention is trumped by international responsibility to protect if specific requisites are met.

On the other hand, the ICISS report takes a firm stance regarding the R2P concept and the protection of nationals abroad doctrine. So, it provides that:

> as to the use of military force by a state to rescue its own nationals on foreign territory, sometimes claimed as another justification for "humanitarian intervention," we regard that as being again a matter appropriately covered under existing international law, and in particular Article 51 of the UN Charter.[148]

Evidently, the ICISS considers the forcible PNA doctrine as legally distinct, falling out of the regulatory ambit of R2P.[149] Additionally, the ICISS does not hesitate to offer its understanding on the theoretical foundation of the doctrine, as a facet of the right to self-defense. The report espouses the proposition that a state's nationals are part of its sovereignty, justifying recourse to force for their sake. At the same time, reference to Art. 51 UNCh shows that no matter the inherent character of the right to self-defense, its exercise is bound by the prerequisites set out in the Article.

The report leaves forcible PNA out of the equation between R2P and the principle of non-intervention; a rational reading in the first place. Nonetheless, there are oversimplifications which question the report's accuracy regarding the protection of nationals abroad. First, if the international community is entitled to employ any kind of intervention to rescue a population from widespread and systematic mistreatment,

---

[145] ICISS (2001), p. xi.

[146] Lauterpacht (1968), p. 150.

[147] Roberts (2001), p. 777.

[148] ICISS (2001), p. 34.

[149] Welsh et al. (2002), p. 499.

then why is this responsibility not recognized for any state whose nationals are in danger? Or, put simply, the nationality nexus enhances a sovereign state's responsibility to protect a population in danger. By categorizing forcible PNA among self-defense clauses, the available protection routes for distinct groups of people residing in a perpetrating state are diminished. In a scenario where a group of nationals are being systematically downgraded by their state of residence, it depends only upon their state of origin to exercise self-defense and does not prompt R2P.

A more concise explanation of R2P would emphasize the concept's protective scope. More specifically, it would be useful to encompass nationals residing abroad within the R2P concept, taking into account the fact that:

> R2P protective intervention against atrocities committed by a government against its own people or another people within its territory can be justified as self-determination assistance or collective self-defense at the request of a victimized people. When a government is unable or unwilling to stop atrocities committed by non-state actors against its own people or another people within its territory, its failure to protect is obvious and self-determination assistance or collective self-defense at the request of a victimized people can be justified.[150]

Therefore, protective intervention includes both the perpetrating state's own people, and another people residing within its territory; the protection of the latter cannot depend on the willingness of their state of nationality to exercise self-defense alone. Conversely, the nationality of the victimized population cannot exclude them from any protective institution, a situation which would thus become discriminatory in terms of international law protection.

All in all, the UN discussion was not occupied with the thematic of nationals abroad; rather, it specified the conditions upon which R2P can be lawfully invoked and exercised. The UN High Level Panel kept pace with the ICISS, and adopted

> the emerging norm that there is a collective international responsibility to protect, exercisable by the Security Council authorizing military intervention as a last resort, in the event of genocide and other large-scale killing, ethnic cleansing or serious violations of international humanitarian law which sovereign Governments have proved powerless or unwilling to prevent.[151]

The UN clarified the substantial and procedural preconditions activating this collective international responsibility. Yet again, it is not clarified if in these four distinct cases (genocide, large-scale killing, ethnic cleansing or serious violations of international humanitarian law) there is a confluence of R2P and the forcible PNA. After all, both concepts start from the same point and recognize "gradually developing legal obligations for the extraterritorial protection of populations".[152] Besides, these four categories of widespread and systematic mistreatment can easily

---

[150] Paust (2017), p. 121.

[151] UNGA (2 December 2004). Follow-up to the Outcome of the Millennium Summit. UN Doc A/59/565, 257, para 203.

[152] Glanville (2012), p. 15.

turn against populations of a different nationality, different national descent or different ethnic origin.

2.5.1 A Duty to Protect Nationals: From R2P to R2Pn

The establishment of R2P by the UN and the concomitant interpretation of the Charter demonstrated a clear shift towards protection from severe human rights violations and a commitment to suppressing international crimes. The concept was meant to "deter states of irresponsible and tyrannical sovereignty"[153] and to shape states' political commitment to taking measures against egregious state practices. Critics concentrated on the diminution of the principle of non-intervention, while ardent supporters emphasized the prospect of a more vertical organization of the international community, further hoping that the association of R2P with international criminal law would enhance its acceptability.[154] The missing part in this discussion is whether acknowledgement of R2P comprises a responsibility to PNA; put simply, if R2P is another source of legitimacy for the forcible PNA, leading towards R2Pn. Although this correlation is rational, given that in "the traditional state-centric international legal system, the responsibility of the wrong-doing state, in general, may be invoked only by the state of nationality of the victim",[155] this view has not been espoused either by states or the UN. States prefer to claim a right over their nationals abroad instead of a duty of protection.

A self-standing right to defend their nationals residing abroad allows states to resort to force if they so choose. Three comments arise from the above. First, states still have the choice whether or not to take measures to protect their nationals abroad from an imminent threat. It remains an executive prerogative depending on a state's financial resources and international policy, or an indication of hard power. A duty to protect and the expectation it entails creates an onerous burden for states unwilling, but most importantly unable, to forcibly protect their nationals. In addition, if one accepts the existence of R2Pn, then states have little room to evaluate which perils justify the use of force and which do not qualify for such actions. Second, the concept of forcible PNA is broader in content than R2P, as it generally refers to imminent threat to life or injury, instead of to systematic human rights violations qualifying as international crimes. Finally, R2P is collective in its conception, referring to violations which create a universal collective interest.[156] This is because it attempts to mobilize the international community when it faces such egregious human rights violations, while states favoring the use of force to protect their

[153] Poposka (2016), p. 69.

[154] Hilpold (2012), p. 72.

[155] Cerone (2012), p. 534.

[156] See, ARSIWA Arts 40, 41 and 48. International Law Commission (November 2001). *Articles on Responsibility of States for Internationally Wrongful Acts*. Supplement No. 10 (A/56/10), chp.IV.E.1.

nationals abroad usually will attempt to avoid the international community's institutional scrutiny.

Overall, states make reference to their right to protect nationals abroad from time to time and only resort to force after careful evaluation. From this viewpoint, the doctrine's formation relies on states' multiple interpretations, which render it susceptible to potential abusive invocation. It remains a question whether the doctrine's legitimacy would be enhanced by its association with R2P, which is bound by strict conceptual limits. However, R2P is subject to fluctuations precisely because it requires centralized agreement for its activation; thus the international community is far from making it a "living reality tool".[157]

In addition, a direct connection between forcible PNA and R2P, or the introduction of R2Pn would contravene states' practice resorting to force in the name of their nationals for less gross violations. In this sense, rescue and evacuation operations, or the use of force for the protection of property rights would be out of discussion, leaving considerable operations without proper justification. Although a duty of protection on such extreme occasions of flagrant violations would build a rational argument, that would put a very high threshold over the concept of protection. There is no legal proximity between forcible PNA and R2P, although they are both founded on an urgent need of protection. It seems that their proximity has more of a discursive character, considering that states invoking forcible PNA usually refer to an inherent duty of theirs to protect their nationals. When speaking of such a duty though, kin-states consider themselves as the only competent to identify and interpret. Nevertheless, the rationale between the two differs significantly and this could explain why the wider legal concept of humanitarian intervention is usually preferred as a legitimate ground for forcible PNA.

2.6 Protecting Nationals Abroad from Terrorist Attacks

The use of force to protect a state's nationals abroad from terrorist attacks forms a distinct aspect of this doctrinal analysis. Most of this discussion arose and revolved around the Tehran Hostages case.[158] This incident attracted international attention.[159] On a legal basis the point of significance became the legitimate response of states whose nationals are taken hostage. More specifically, there is international consensus

[157] Global Centre for the Responsibility to Protect (GCR2P) (August 2009). Retrieved February 22, 2025 from https://www.globalr2p.org/wp-content/uploads/2020/01/2009-UNGA-Debate-Summary.pdf accessed 26 July 2024. See also, UN News, Global Perspective Human Stories (18 January 2012). Responsibility to Protect: Ban Urges Actions to Make UN-backed Tool a 'Living Reality'. Retrieved February 22, 2025 from https://news.un.org/en/story/2012/01/400702

[158] ICJ, *Case Concerning United States Diplomatic and Consular Staff in Tehran (United States of America v. Iran)*, Judgment, ICJ Rep 1980, p. 3.

[159] For a full record of the 1979 US Embassy hostage crisis *see* Eichensehr (2008) 453 et seq; Jeffery (1981), pp. 719–729.

that hostage-taking is outside the legal realm, but no specific response to such incidents has been provided. The two issues which occupied discussion were a) whether states have to first exhaust non-forceful measures before resorting to the use of force and launch a rescue mission, and b) if hostages can raise a rescue claim against their state of nationality, thus demanding the deployment of such a mission.

The first issue pertains to the relationship between the employment of peaceful means and the use of force in international law, and the perpetual question of whether the former is prioritized over the latter. This discussion is fueled by the UNCh's principle that member-states shall settle their international disputes by peaceful means according to Art. 2(3), while they should refrain from the use of force. The UN's commitment to peaceful dispute settlement sets another obstacle before its member-states not to resort unreasonably to force. In the Tehran Hostages case, this issue was of limited value, given that the US employed every available diplomatic tool to release its nationals under Chapter VI UNCh. This would probably have paved the way for the use of force without fear of international condemnation; yet it was not a viable option at the time. This prioritization of peaceful means over force was central to other incidents and determined the success of rescue operations.

A suitable example is that of the Larnaca incident of 1978. It is reported that Cypriot authorities had entered negotiations with gunmen who had seized a plane and taken hostages from Egypt. Egypt launched a rescue operation and obtained authorization from Cypriot authorities to land at Larnaca airport. However, no authorization was granted by Cyprus for the use of force. Egyptian commandos opened fire in an attempt to rescue the hostages, and Cypriots responded. This resulted in the death of fifteen Egyptians and many injured on both sides. The Egyptian mission departed for Egypt, and afterwards the hostages were released and the gunmen were arrested.[160] The same applies, *grosso modo*, and in the Egyptian intervention in Malta in 1985, where the hijacking of a plane has taken place.[161]

The second point of concern relates to the rights of hostages. Taking into account that hostage-taking is a reprehensible act considered a criminal offense by all legal orders, it naturally follows that states ought to deploy a rescue mission abroad to save hostages, just as the police would do if a similar occasion arose within the state's territory. Yet even those states which have enacted legislation on the occasion of international hostage-taking do not embrace this course of thinking. For example, the US Hostage Act provides that:

> Whenever it is made known to the President that any citizen of the United States has been unjustly deprived of his liberty by or under the authority of any foreign government, it shall be the duty of the President forthwith to demand of that government the reasons of such imprisonment; and if it appears to be wrongful and in violation of the rights of American citizenship, the President shall forthwith demand the release of such citizen, and if the release so demanded is unreasonably delayed or refused, the President shall use such

[160] Antonopoulos (2018), p. 234.

[161] Dawson (1987), p. 65.

> means, not amounting to acts of war and not otherwise prohibited by law, as he may think necessary and proper to obtain or effectuate the release.[162]

This piece of legislation is enlightening in three ways. First, it provides national protection from arbitrary deprivation of liberty, incorporating interpretatively hostage-taking abroad. Second, the US introduced the state's responsibility to protect victims of hostage-taking. The national legislation provides for the escalation of national measures for this sake, including the use of force. The legislation does not explicitly refer to the right to self-defense; however, reference to "means, not amounting to acts of war" signifies that smaller-scale use of force is permitted. Third, this legislative piece has been at the epicenter of discussions on a national level, regarding victims' ability to raise claims against their state of origin for not resorting to force to rescue them, in the wake of the Tehran Hostages crisis. Jurisprudence took a firm position that any acts depend on the executive's prerogative, assessing on an *ad hoc* basis the options available to it, further pointing out that its legislative aim was broader than rescuing hostages only. Rather, it was meant to deter terrorist attacks against American citizens. Therefore, even in the event of hostage-taking of nationals whose state provides for the use of force in rescuing them, this is certainly not an obligation for the state of nationality.[163]

Taking a broader look at hostage-taking in conjunction with the forcible PNA doctrine, states condemn this practice and consider that it activates the right to self-defense. This issue, though, remains one of national concern. International documentation on hostage-taking does not touch upon the way in which hostages shall be released, nor does it take a position regarding rescue missions. More specifically, according to Art. 14 of the International Convention against the Taking of Hostages "[n]othing in this Convention shall be construed as justifying the violation of the territorial integrity or political independence of a state in contravention of the Charter of the United Nations".[164] The Convention reiterates the cardinal to the UN system prohibition against the use of force, yet it does not denounce states' right to self-defense in the event of hostage-taking. Otherwise, the release of a state's hostages is cannot be attainable and the relevant documents would be without practical implications. In this sense, it could be argued by way of juxtaposition that hostage-taking is an occasion on which the international community tolerates recourse to force to rescue the victims, perceiving it as a legitimate exercise of self-defense.[165]

The nationality nexus justifies the exercise of self-defense in the event of hostage-taking. Its justification though, resides at the confluence of the arbitrary deprivation of liberty. Hostage-taking has given a push in the doctrinal debate regarding forcible PNA and protection from terrorist groups, or insurgents. This led to a more concrete

---

[162] 22 US para 1732, Release of citizens imprisoned by foreign governments. R.S. para 2001; Pub. L. 101–222, para 9, Dec. 12, 1989, 103 Stat. 1900.

[163] Hughes (1993), p. 565.

[164] International Convention against the Taking of Hostages (17 December 1979). UNTS vol. 1316, p. 205.

[165] Galani (2021), p. 103.

legal framework, which however cannot cover all cases of nationals facing peril due to liberty deprivation, or similar restrictions. Captivity was used above as a more general, descriptive and working term which demonstrates what peril nationals abroad may face, without reducing legal options for their protection. Once more, forcible PNA may well be a response to hostage-taking, yet it is not confined to such occasions. Although the Tehran case and the Entebbe model shaped the doctrine's content in the post-Charter era, they are but a facet of it. Deprivation of liberty applying nationality criteria is a matter not covered by the hostage-taking regime. If a state targets a third state's nationals and systematically deprives them of their liberty, this is a matter which slips away this legal framework. In addition, when such targeting takes place in accordance with legal provisions it is very difficult to invoke any doctrine involving the use of force, even if such practices are massive.

2.7 Nationals Abroad Between Sovereignty and Territorial Integrity

The doctrinal establishment of the forcible PNA doctrine in the post-Charter era is at least challenging. The UN system does not expressly espouse the doctrine, either as an exception to the qualified prohibition of Art. 2(4) or as an aspect of states' right to self-defense. There are many affirmations, though, of the doctrine's acceptance, or at least tolerance, by the UN regime. The proposed inclusion of a right to forcible PNA in the first report of the Special Rapporteur on diplomatic protection is palpable proof of that. According to John Dugart's first report:

> If Article 51 preserves the customary law right of self-defence, it is difficult to contend that the Charter's prohibition on the use of force extends to the protection of nationals abroad. Such contention is made more difficult by the amount of State practice since 1945 in support of military intervention to protect nationals abroad in time of emergency and the failure of courts and political organs of the United Nations to condemn such action. In the words of Jennings and Watts, "there has been little disposition on the part of states to deny that intervention properly restricted to the protection of nationals is, in emergencies, justified".[166]

Thus, there are positive affirmations of the legality of the forcible PNA; by way of extrapolation, it follows that use of force in the name of a state's nationals abroad is not utterly outlawed by the UN regime. Although such an addition was rejected and was not included in the final form of the report, it aptly shows the interconnection between diplomatic protection and forcible PNA both historically and doctrinally. Their starting point is the same. Nationality is a strong cause for protection, no matter what form it takes. This view accepts the exceptional occasion on which protection can only be forcible, despite the unequivocal acceptance of the prohibition to use force.

---

[166] First Report on Diplomatic Protection, by Mr. John R. Dugart, Special Rapporteur (7 March and 20 April 2000). Diplomatic Protection. UN Doc A/CN.4/506 and Add.1, 220, para 58.

Ultimately, the doctrine offers interesting insights into the interplay between state sovereignty, territorial integrity and nationality. First, it emphasizes the importance that nationality still carries in international law. The link between a state and its nationals, whether genuine or not, is strong enough to justify the use of force if needed. Thereby, nationality surpasses the principle of non-intervention on particular occasions. Second, the doctrine separates sovereignty from territorial integrity. More specifically, if forcible protection is an exception to the prohibition on the use of force, which pre-existed and survived the Charter, then it does not violate territorial integrity; otherwise it would be in direct contradiction of Art. 2(4).

Technically, though, such an operation is an intervention in breach of the sovereignty of another state. From a different angle, if use of force for the protection of nationals abroad is part of the right to self-defense, then serious threats against nationals equate to an armed attack. In this course of thinking, forcible PNA is a sovereign act to protect territorial integrity. In both scenarios, territorial integrity is distinct from sovereignty; a general violation of the latter is not by definition a breach of the former, even if this is typically not possible. Territorial integrity is a manifestation of sovereignty in as much as nationals are. Finally, the protection of the nationals abroad theory is a crack in the state-centric orientation of sovereignty, further pointing to the fact that non-intervention is not an absolute correlative to it.[167]

2.8 Conclusions

This chapter has explored the doctrinal underpinnings of the forcible PNA doctrine in the post-Charter era. The debate over the legality of the doctrine's survival after 1945 does not differ much from the general legal contestations regarding the interpretation of the UNCh's provisions. In this regard, this chapter covers quite a broad doctrinal discussion which occupies theory during the last decades. If only one conclusion was to be drawn from the above, then the only one that could be safely made is that forcible PNA cannot be completely excluded from the spectrum of legality. This is not only due to the strength of claims which incorporate the concepts of nationality and protection. It is also related to the continuously changing interpretation of the Charter's provisions. Both Arts 2(4) and 51 have more than one reading and have been the epicenter of states' legal interest. Throughout the years though, both the understanding of the prohibition on the use of force, as well as of the right to self-defense have not remained the same. Their reading has been relativized, and they cannot be considered anymore as an absolute prohibition on one side, and the only exception to it on the other.

The Charter's interpretation developed following the course of history. Therefore, if humanitarian intervention and R2P are compatible with the Charter, then the legality of the forcible PNA doctrine must be reexamined. The doctrine has not

[167] Donnelly (1993), p. 609.

remained static itself. The imperialistic connotation forcible PNA carried from the pre-Charter era was reshaped, following the rise of nation-states and the general principle of the inviolability of borders. In the post-Charter era territoriality was secured from all sides and for this reason it was perceived as a synonym for sovereignty. In this framework, forcible PNA was observed with suspicion, as a means of territorial destabilization. At the same time though, it is suggested that this marginal role it was attributed to the doctrine, is in accordance with its exceptional character and the requirements that shall be fulfilled, for states to invoke it. In other words, forcible PNA has been reshaped after the Charter's entry into force, following the rebranding of sovereignty. Even though territoriality has been elevated as the most important prong of sovereignty, one states cannot oversee how nationality affects their policy. State decision-making regarding the use of force is not always an issue of territorial claims. This is the reason why the doctrine seems to have survived the Charter, under the condition it does not hide territorial claims.

References

Books

Alexandrov SA (1996) Self-defense against the use of force in international law. Kluwer Law International

Biermann W (1999) African crisis response initiative – the new U.S. Africa Policy. LIT Verlag

Brownlie I (1967) International law and the use of force by states. Clarendon Press

Casey CA (2020) Nationals abroad: globalization, individual rights and the making of modern international law. Cambridge University Press

Franck TM (2002) Recourse to force, state action against threats and armed attacks. Cambridge University Press

Galani S (2021) Hostages and human rights, towards a victim-centered approach. Cambridge University Press

Gray C (2018) International law and the use of force, 4th edn. Oxford University Press

Hammerstad A (2014) The rise and decline of a global security actor, UNHCR, refugee protection, & security. Oxford University Press

Higgins R (1994) Problems & process, international law and how we use it. Clarendon Press

ICISS (2001) The responsibility to protect. International Development Research Centre

Johansen SR (2019) The military commander's necessity. The law of armed conflict and its limits. Cambridge University Press

Kralev N (2024) Diplomatic tradecraft. Cambridge University Press

Lauterpacht H (1955) Oppenheim's international law, vol 1, 8th edn. Longmans

Lauterpacht H (1968) International law and human rights. Archon Books

Tzanakopoulos A (2011) Disobeying the security council, countermeasures against wrongful actions. Oxford University Press

Articles

– (1980) State responsibility, state self-help and problems of public international law. Stud Trans Leg Policy 19:19–32
– (2021) Administration of Joseph R. Biden, Jr., 2021 Remarks on United States evacuation efforts in Afghanistan and an exchange with reports. Daily Compilation of Presidential Documents:1–9
Akande D, Liefländer T (2013) Clarifying necessity, imminence and proportionality in the law of self-defense. Am J Int Law 107(3):563–570
Alcala R, Nasu H (2023) The protection of nationals abroad and non-combatant evacuation operations in times of crisis. J Natl Secur Law Policy 14(1):1–28
Antonopoulos C (1999) The unilateral use of force by states after the end of cold war. J Armed Conflict Law 4:117–160
Ayoob M (2002) Humanitarian intervention and state sovereignty. Int J Hum Rights 6(1):81–102
Barrie GN (1999) Forcible intervention and international law: legal theory and realities. S Afr Law J 116(4):791–809
Bellamy AJ, Wheeler NJ (2008) Humanitarian intervention in world politics. Glob World Polit 5:479–496
Boer LJM (2015) Echoes of times past: on the paradoxical nature of Article 2(4). J Conflict Secur Law 20(1):5–26
Bohrer Z (2016) Protecting state soldiers, compatriot civilians or foreign civilians: proportionality's meanings at the tactical operational and strategic levels of war. Isr Yearb Hum Rights 46:171–222
Bohrer Z, Osiel M (2013) Proportionality in war: protecting soldiers from enemy captivity, and Israel's operation cast lead – the soldiers are everyone's children. South Calif Interdiscip Law J 22(3):637–692
Bond D (2016) How should the state manage the contemporary expectation of non-combatant evacuation operations? RUSI J 161(5):28–35
Bowett DW (1957) The use of force in the protection of nationals. Trans Grotius Soc 43:111–126
Brownlie B (1959) Recent appraisals of legal regulation of the use of force. Int Comp Law Q 8(4):707–721
Brownlie I (1961) The use of force in self-defense. Br Yearb Int Law 37:183–268
Brownlie I (2002) International law and the use of force by states revisited. Chinese J Int Law 1(1):1–19
Byman D (2024) A war they are both losing: Israel, Hamas and the Plight of Gaza. Survival 66(3):61–78
Cerone J (2012) Expanding the R2P Tool-Kit: new political possibilities and attendant legal uncertainties. ILSA J Int Comp Law 18(2):531–564
Charters D (1980) Swift and bold: an appraisal of hostage rescue operations. J Conflicts Stud 1(1):26–33
Chilstrom RM (1974) Humanitarian intervention under contemporary international law: a policy-oriented approach. Yale Stud World Public Order 1:93–147
Condon A (2007) Operation *RAMP* – the Lebanon evacuation, overview of a mass NEO and lessons for the future. Aust Army J 4(1):65–75
Corten O (2005) The controversies over the customary prohibition on the use of force: a methodological debate. Eur J Int Law 16(5):803–822
D'Angelo JR (1981) Resort to force by states to protect nationals: the U.S. Rescue Mission to Iran and its legality under international law. Va J Int Law 21(3):485–520
Dannenbaum T, Dill J (2024) International law in Gaza: belligerent intent and provisional measures. Am J Int Law 118(4):659–683
Dawson HG (1987) Civil aviation, hijacking and international terrorism – an historical and legal review. Int Bus Lawyer 15(2):57–66
Day SF (1992) Legal considerations in noncombatant evacuation operations. Naval Law Rev 40:45–64

Dixon GK (2017) The need for a joint support element in noncombatant evacuation operations. Joint Force Q 85(2):50–57
Donnelly J (1993) Human rights, humanitarian crisis, and humanitarian intervention. Int J 48(4):607–640
Dreyfuss M (2012) My fellow americans, we are going to kill you: the legality of targeting and killing U.S. citizens abroad. Vanderbilt Law Rev 65(1):249–292
Duchâtel M, Bräuner O, Hang Z (2014) Protecting China's overseas interests, the slow shift away from non-interference. SIPRI Policy Paper No 41
Dudgeon I (2006) Crisis contingency plans: the Lebanon experience. Defender 23(3):22–25
Eichensehr KE (2008) Defending nationals abroad: assessing the lawfulness of forcible hostage rescues. Va J Int Law 48(2):451–484
Eldred J (2008) The use of force in hostage rescue missions. Naval Law Rev 56:251–274
France – Royaume-Uni (2007) L' Opération Baliste. Sauvegarde Maritime, Enjeux et Perspectives 36:1–121
Franck T (1970) Who killed Article 2(4)? or: changing norms governing the use of force by states. Am J Int Law 64(5):809–837
Franck T (2006) Legality and legitimacy in humanitarian intervention. NOMOS: American Society for Political and Legal Philosophy, pp 143–157
Galani S (2016) Somali piracy and the human rights seafarers. Neth Q Hum Rights 34(1):71–98
Gill TD (2006) The temporal dimension of self-defense: anticipation, pre-emption, prevention and immediacy. J Conflict Secur Law 11(3):361–369
Glanville L (2012) The responsibility to protect beyond borders. Hum Rights Law Rev 12(1):1–32
Gordon DJ (1977) Use of force for the protection of nationals abroad: the Entebbe incident. Case West Res J Int Law 9(1):117–134
Gordon E (1985) Article 2(4) in historical context. Yale J Int Law 10(2):271–278
Græger N, Lindgren WY (2018) The duty of care for citizens abroad: security and responsibility in the in Amenas and Fukushima Crises. Hague J Dipl 13(2):188–210
Green JA (2006) Docking the Caroline: understanding the relevance of the formula in contemporary customary international law concerning self-defense. Cardozo J Int Comp Law 14(2):429–480
Greenwood C (1987) International law and the United States' air operations against Libya. West Va Law Rev 89(4):933–960
Hann MJ (1977) The Pueblo and Mayaguez Incidents: a study of flexible response and decision-making. Asian Surv 17(6):545–555
Henderson C (2020) Self-defense against non-state actors. Am J Int Law 114(4):809–818
Henkin L (1994) Humanitarian intervention. Stud Transnatl Leg Policy 26:383–404
Hilpold P (2012) Intervening in the name of humanity: R2P and the power of ideas. J Conflict Secur Law 17(1):49–80
Hughes KD (1993) Hostages' rights: the unhappy legal predicament of an American held in foreign captivity. Colum J Law Soc Probs 26(4):555–588
Irving KJ (1996) The United Nations and democratic intervention: is sword into ballot boxes enough. Denv J Int Law Policy 25(1):41–70
Jeffery A (1981) The American hostages in Tehran: the ICJ and the legality of rescue missions. Int Comp Law Q 30(3):719–729
Jessup PC (1946) Force under a modern law of nations. Foreign Aff 25(1):90–105
Jiuyong S (2018) Prohibition of use of force in international law. Chin J Int Law 17(1):1–14
Juan MAU (2008) The U.N., the U.S., and the Security Council: regulating the use of force in pro-democratic intervention. Ateneo Law J 53(2):295–322
Kalm S (2013) Diaspora strategies as technologies of citizenship. Glob Soc 27(3):379–397
Kelly MJ (2020) United Nations Security Council permanent membership and the veto problem. Case West Res J Int Law 52(1):101–118
Klein ER (2024) After Afghanistan: the need for a new noncombatant evacuation operation. Joint Force Q 114(2):68–77
Krylov N (1995) Humanitarian intervention: pros and cons. Loy LA Int Comp Law J 17(2):365–408

Levi DF et al (2021) Leaving Afghanistan. Judicature 105(3):30–45
Lillich RB (1968) Forcible self-help by states to protect human rights. Iowa Law Rev 53(2):325–351
Lillich RB (1969) Intervention to protect human rights. McGill Law J 15(2):207–211
Linnan DK (1991) Self-defense, necessity and U.N. collective security: United States and other views. Duke J Comp Int Law 1(1):57–123
Magenis SD (2002) Natural law as the customary international law of self-defense. Boston Univ Int Law J 20(2):413–436
Margo RD (1977) The legality of the Entebbe raid in international law. S Afr Law J 94(3):306–326
McMahan J (2024) Proportionality and necessity in Israel's invasion of Gaza, 2023-2024. Analyse and Kritik 46(2):387–407
Milanovic M (2021) Intelligence sharing in multinational military operations and complicity under international law. Int Law Stud Ser US Naval War Coll 97:1269–1403
Moeckli D, Fasel RN (2017) A duty to give reasons in the security council: making the voting transparent. Int Org Law Rev 14(1):13–86
Moore J (2007) Deciding humanitarian intervention. Soc Res 74(1):169–200
Mrazek J (1989) Prohibition of the use of force and threat of force: self-defense and self-help in international law. Can Yearb Int Law 27:81–112
Murphy SD (1994) The security council, legitimacy, and the concept of collective security after the cold war. Columbia J Trans Law 32(2):201
Murphy SD (2009) Criminalizing humanitarian intervention. Case West Res J Int Law 41(2–3):341–378
Nagler A (2021) Operation allies welcome: the United States' plan to relocate over 65,000 Afghan Asylum Seekers. Geo Immigr Law J 36(1):507 [iii]
O'Connell ME (2002) Lawful self-defense to terrorism. Univ Pitt Law Rev 63:889–908
O'Donoghue A (2005) Humanitarian intervention revisited. Hanse Law Rev 1(2):165–176
Parrish AL (2009) Reclaiming international law from extraterritoriality. Minn Law Rev 93(3):815–874
Parry J (1988) The state of necessity and the use of force to protect nationals. Can Yearb Int Law 26:253–272
Paust JJ (1976) The seizure and recovery of the Mayaguez. Yale Law J 85(6):774–807
Paust JJ (2017) R2P and protective intervention. Temple Int Comp Law J 31(1):109–122
Poposka V (2016) Between David and Goliath: where did we lose R2P between Libya and Syria. J Lib Int Affairs 1(Special Issue):69–70
Raby J (1988) The state of necessity and the use of force to protect nationals. Can Yearb Int Law 26:253–272
Raby J (1989) The right of intervention for the protection of nationals: reassessing the doctrinal debate. Cahiers de Droit 30(2):441–494
Ragazzi F (2014) A comparative analysis of diaspora policies. Polit Geogr 41:74–89
Raina H (2019) The forcible protection of nationals and non-combatant evacuation operations. Maritime Affairs J Natl Maritime Foundation India 14(2):120–137
Reisman WM (1995) Humanitarian intervention and fledging democracies. Fordham Int Law J 18(3):794–805
Reisman WM (2000) Unilateral action and the transformations of the world constitutive process: the special problem of humanitarian intervention. Eur J Int Law 11(1):3–18
Roberts AE (2001) Traditional and modern approaches to customary international law: a reconciliation. Am J Int Law 95(4):757–791
Roele I (2020) Around Arendt's table: bureaucracy and the non-permanent members of the UN Security Council. Leiden J Int Law 33(1):117–138
Ronzitti N (1985) Rescuing nationals abroad through military coercion and intervention on grounds of humanity. Martinus Nijhoff Publishers
Ronzitti N (2006) The expanding law of self-defence. J Conflict Secur Law 11(3):343–360
Sadoff DA (2009) Striking a sensible balance on the legality of defensive first strikes. Vanderbilt J Trans Law 42(2):441–500

Salako SE (2016) Forcible protection of nationals abroad and humanitarian intervention: might or right? Int Law Res 5(1):152–167
Schachter O (1984) The right of states to use armed force. Mich Law Rev 82(5&6):1620–1646
Schachter O (1984–1985) The lawful resort to unilateral use of force. Yale J Int Law 10(2):291–294
Schachter O (1986) In defense of international rules on the use of force. Univ Chic Law Rev 53(1):132–133
Schachter O (1989) Self-defense and the rule of law. Am J Int Law 83(2):259–277
Schweisfurth T (1980) Operations to rescue nationals in third states involving the use of force in relation to the protection of human rights. Germ Yearb Int Law 23:159–180
Shiryaev Y (2007–2008) The right of armed self-defense in international law and self-defense arguments used in the Second Lebanon War. Acta Societatis Martensis 3:80–97
Simmons RR (1978) The Pueblo, EC-121, and Mayaguez Incidents: some continuities and changes. Md Ser Contemp Asian Stud 1978(8):1–58
Stone J (1977) Hopes and loopholes in the 1974 definition of aggression. Am J Int Law 71(2):224–246
Tams CJ (2009) The use of force against terrorists. Eur J Int Law 20(2):359–397
Thomson AWR (2012) Doctrine of the protection of nationals abroad: rise of the non-combatant evacuation operation. Wash Univ Glob Stud Law Rev 11(3):627–668
Turns D (2009) Jus ad Pacem in Bello? Afghanistan, stability operations and the international laws relating to armed conflict. Int Law Stud US Naval War Coll 85:387–410
Wehberg H (1951) L' Interdiction du Recours à la Force. Le Principe et les Problèmes Qui Se Posent. Recueil des Cours 78:62
Welsh J et al (2002) The responsibility to protect: assessing the report of the international commission on intervention and state sovereignty. Int J 57(4):489–512
Whittemore LA (2008) Intervention and post-conflict natural resource governance: lessons from Liberia. Minn J Int Law 17(2):387–434
Williams WL Jr (1980) International law and the American hostages in Iran. Army Law:30–38
Wingfield TC (2000) Forcible protection of nationals abroad. Dickinson Law Rev 104(3):439–469
Wippman D (1997) Defending democracy through foreign intervention. Houston J Int Law 19(3):659–688
Wolf D (1988) Humanitarian intervention. Mich Yearb Int Stud 9:333–366
Yorke GL (2012) Africa and its diaspora: the principal reciprocal benefits to be derived from the amended constitutive act of the African Union. Int J Afr Renaissance Stud 7(2):79–95
Zedalis RJ (1987) Preliminary thoughts on some unresolved questions involving the law of anticipatory self-defense. Case West Res J Int Law 19(2):129–175
Zedalis RJ (1990) Protection of nationals abroad: is consent the basis of legal obligation? Texas Int Law J 25(2):235

Book Chapters

Antonopoulos C (2018) The Larnaca incident – 1978. In: Ruys T, Corten O (eds) The use of force in international law. A case-based approach. Oxford University Press, pp 234–241
Bellamy AJ (2015) Humanitarian intervention. In: Moellendorf D, Widdows H (eds) The Routledge handbook of global ethics. Routledge, pp 127–140
Bowett DW (1986) The use of force for the protection of nationals abroad. In: Cassese A (ed) The current legal regulation of the use of force. Martinus Nijhoff Publishers, pp 39–55
Jureidini R (2011) State and non-state actors in evacuations during the conflict in Lebanon, July-August 2006. In: Koser K, Martin S (eds) The migration-displacement nexus: concepts, cases and responses. Berghahn Books, pp 197–215

Kreß C, Nußberger BK (2018) The Entebbe raid – 1976. In: Ruys T, Corten O (eds) The use of force in international law. A case-based approach. Oxford University Press, pp 220–233
Mignot-Mahdavi R (2021) Drones programs, the individualization of War, and the *Ad Bellum* principle of proportionality. In: Kreß C, Lawless R (eds) Necessity and proportionality in international peace and security law. Oxford University Press, pp 131–168
Piccoli L (2020) Diaspora policies, consular services and social protection for Swiss citizens abroad. In: Lafleur J-M, Vintila D (eds) Migration, social protection in Europe and beyond (Volume 3). A focus on non-EU sending states. Springer, pp 347–362
Randelzhofer A (2002) Article 2(4). In: Simma B et al (eds) The charter of the United Nations: a commentary, vol I. Oxford University Press

UN Documentation

Documents of the United Nations Conference on International Organization (1945) San Francisco, 1945 Vol VI, Commission I, General Provisions. United Nations Information Organizations
First Report on Diplomatic Protection, by Mr. John R. Dugart, Special Rapporteur (7 March and 20 April 2000) Diplomatic Protection. UN Doc A/CN.4/506 and Add.1
HRC (25 March 2024) Report of the Special Rapporteur on the situation of human rights in the Palestinian territories occupied since 1967, Francesca Albanese. UN Doc A/HRC/55/73
International Convention against the Taking of Hostages (17 December 1979) UNTS vol. 1316, p. 205
International Law Commission (November 2001) *Articles on Responsibility of States for Internationally Wrongful Acts*. Supplement No. 10 (A/56/10), chp.IV.E.1
Report of the International Law Commission on its Third Session (16 May to 27 July). *Official Records of the General Assembly, Sixth Session, Supplement No. 9* (A/1858, reproduced in *Yearbook of the International Law Commission 1951*, vol. II, 123–144)
Report of the International Law Commission on its Third Session (1951)
UN, *Vienna Convention on the Law of Treaties*, UNTS Vol. 1155, p. 331 (23 May 1969)
UN News, Global Perspective Human Stories (18 January 2012) Responsibility to Protect: Ban Urges Actions to Make UN-backed Tool a 'Living Reality'. Retrieved February 22, 2025 from https://news.un.org/en/story/2012/01/400702
UNGA (24 October 1970) Declaration on Principles of International Law concerning Friendly Relations and Cooperation among States in accordance with the Charter of the United Nations. A/RES/2625(XXV)
UNGA (25 April–30 May 1973) Report of the Special Committee on the Question of Defining Aggression, 28th Session. UN Doc. Supp. No. 19 (A/9019)
UNGA (14 December 1974) Definition of Aggression. UN Doc. A/Res/3314
UNGA (29 December 1989) Effects of the military intervention by the United States of America in Panama on the situation in Central America. UN Doc A/44/240
UNGA, Report of the Secretary-General (27 March 2000) We The Peoples: The Role of the United Nations in the Twenty-First Century. UN Doc A/54/2000
UNGA (2 December 2004) Follow-up to the outcome of the Millennium Summit. UN Doc A/59/565, 257

Jurisprudence

ICJ

ICJ, *North Sea Continental Shelf*, Judgment, ICJ Reports 1969, p. 3
ICJ, *Case Concerning United States Diplomatic and Consular Staff in Tehran (United States of America v. Iran)*, Judgment, ICJ Rep 1980, p. 3
ICJ, *Case Concerning Military and Paramilitary Activities in and against Nicaragua (Nicaragua v. United States of America)*, Judgment, ICJ Rep 1986, p. 103, para. 194
ICJ, *Case Concerning Armed Activities on the Territory of the Congo (Democratic Republic of Congo v. Uganda)*, Judgment, ICJ Rep 2005, p. 168
ICJ, *The Corfu Channel Case*, Oral Proceedings (Second Part), Reply by Sir Eric Beckett (UK) 19 I 49 555–567
Legal Consequences of the Construction of a Wall in the Occupied Palestinian Territory, Advisory Opinion, ICJ Reports 2004, p. 136
Legal Consequences Arising from the Policies and Practices of Israel in the Occupied Palestinian Territory, Including East Jerusalem, Advisory Opinion, ICJ, 19 July 2024

Online Material

Clark Jr. RL (1995) Noncombatant evacuation operations: major considerations. Naval War Coll Newport Ri Dept of Operations. Retrieved, February 22, 2025 from https://apps.dtic.mil/sti/pdfs/ADA293291.pdf
Department of Homeland Security (11 October 2021) Operation allies welcome fact sheet. Retrieved. February 22, 2025 from https://www.dhs.gov/archive/publication/fact-sheet-operation-allies-welcome
Director Development (2021) Concepts and Doctrine Centre, Joint Doctrine Publication 3–51, non-combatant evacuation operations, 3rd edn. UK Ministry of Defence. Retrieved, February 22, 2025 https://assets.publishing.service.gov.uk/government/uploads/system/uploads/attachment_data/file/979907/20210412-JDP_3_51_NEO_web_V2-O_1_.pdf
Global Centre for the Responsibility to Protect (GCR2P) (August 2009) Implementing the responsibility to protect. The 2009 general assembly debate: an assessment. Retrieved, February 22, 2025 from https://www.globalr2p.org/wp-content/uploads/2020/01/2009-UNGA-Debate-Summary.pdf
Headquarters, Department of the Army (31 July 2019) Stability (Army Doctrine Publications, ADP 3–07). Retrieved, February 22, 2025 https://armypubs.army.mil/epubs/DR_pubs/DR_a/pdf/web/ARN18011_ADP%203-07%20FINAL%20WEB.pdf
Joint Declaration between the Islamic Republic of Afghanistan and the United States of America for Bringing Peace to Afghanistan. Retrieved February 22, 2025 from https://www.state.gov/wp-content/uploads/2020/02/02.29.20-US-Afghanistan-Joint-Declaration.pdf
Kitfield JC (29 August 2022) Remembering the largest non-combatant evacuation operation in US history. Retrieved, February 22, 2025 from https://www.airandspaceforces.com/remembering-the-largest-non-combatant-evacuation-operation-allies-refuge-in-u-s-history%EF%BF%BC/
Massey D (17 October 2007) Operation 'highbrow' debrief report. Retrieved, February 22, 2025 from https://assets.publishing.service.gov.uk/media/5a78f0d840f0b62b22cbe023/lebanon-op-highbrow-debrief.pdf

Milanovic M (14 November 2023) Does Israel have the right to defend itself?. *EJIL:Talk!*. Retrieved, February 22, 2025 https://www.ejiltalk.org/does-israel-have-the-right-to-defend-itself/
The Standing Senate Committee on Foreign Affairs and International Trade (May 2007) The evacuation of Canadians from Lebanon in July 2006: implications for the Government of Canada. Retrieved, February 22, 2025 https://sencanada.ca/content/sen/committee/391/fore/rep/rep12may07-e.pdf
Waldock H (1952) The regulation of the use of force by individual states in international law. Recueil des Cours 81(II):455
Wilmshurst, E. (2008) Definition of aggression. United Nations Audiovisual Library of International Law. Retrieved, February 22, 2025 from https://legal.un.org/avl/pdf/ha/da/da_e.pdf

Miscellaneous

22 US §1732 Release of Citizens Imprisoned by Foreign Governments. R.S. §2001; Pub. L. 101–222, §9, Dec. 12, 1989, 103 Stat. 1900
Federal'nyj zakon ot 24/5/1999 N 99-FZ "O gosudarstvennoj politike Rossijskoj Federacii otnošeenii sootečestvennikov za rebežom" [Federal Law on the State Policy of the Russian Federation in Respect of the Compatriots Abroad of 24 May 1999, No. 99-FZ]

Chapter 3
Protection of Nationals Abroad and State Practice

3.1 Protection of Nationals Abroad: Decolonization and Dependency

The UN's establishment restructured the international legal order in many ways. Apart from the centralization of the use of force, the organization's early years were marked by the departure of colonial powers from their colonial territories and the subsequent independence of these territories. This process was not bloodless, as on many occasions the former colonial powers attempted to display their power and create a state of dependency through coercion. More specifically, there were significant concerns that the end of colonialism was initially a placebo, given that political independence was accomplished only superficially. Former colonial powers developed strong economic ties with their colonies; although they had relinquished sovereignty, their influence remained unchallenged.[1] Control over former colonies took mostly subtle forms, with occasional recourse to force. It was suggested that the end of colonialism only paved the way to neocolonialism.[2]

The UN had a key role in the process of decolonization, as it lent an ear to colonial people and approached political independence as a reality and not a mere formality. The 1960 UNGA Declaration on the Granting of Independence to Colonial Countries and Peoples[3] was a significant moment, as it signified the organization's commitment to the end of colonialism and the attainment of actual political independence. The historical context of decolonization explains why the principle

[1] Zartman (1976), p. 326.

[2] Vengroff (1975), pp. 236–237.

[3] UNGA (24 December 1960). Declaration on the Granting of Independence to Colonial Countries and Peoples. UN Doc A/Res/1514(XV). See also, UNGA (15–17 December 1970). Programme of Action for the Full Implementation of the Declaration on the Granting of Independence to Colonial Countries and Peoples. UN Doc A/Res/2621(XXV).

© The Author(s), under exclusive license to Springer Nature Switzerland AG 2025

I. Pervou, *Protecting Nationals Abroad and the Reconceptualization of Sovereignty*, Studies in the History of Law and Justice 32,
https://doi.org/10.1007/978-3-032-05231-5_3

of non-intervention has been so crucial to the preservation and credibility of the UN regime.[4] The non-intervention of former colonial powers in states which had recently attained their political independence soon became equated with the principle of sovereign equality of the UN member-states, as expressed in Art. 2(1). Sovereign equality among former colonies and colonial powers was a prerequisite for the success of the UN as a trustee of international peace and security: that is, a precondition for the organization's enlargement and establishment of friendly relations between states.

Undoubtedly, these developments have contributed to a sterner view of the forcible protection of nationals abroad doctrine. During the UN's early years, the organization had to strike a fair balance between former colonies' demands for the absence of any kind of intervention and former colonial powers' attempts to exert their influence and authority over these territories. This clash put forward for quite some time the Charter's grammatical reading; at the same time, it decelerated a teleological interpretation which would allow for the doctrines of humanitarian intervention and R2P to be espoused by the international community much sooner. It was thus noted that there was a

> marked increase in conflict in the period from 1945 to 1972 (congruent with decolonization), taking place predominantly in the "Third World", as well as an increase in Western and communist interventions in conflict during these years.[5]

The international and political backdrop of this period better explains why recourse to force to protect a state's nationals abroad was formally repudiated in official policy statements within the UN.

3.1.1 The Case of Congo: A Landmark of Decolonization

The situation in Congo regarding the legality of the Belgian actions in the early 60s caught the international community's attention. Congo may well be characterized as a tormented land. The Belgian-Congolese relationship had been turbulent long before its declaration of independence. It is important to note that Congo was a land of impunity, given that from 1885 till 1908 it was the personal property of King Leopold II. Although the Belgian legal order provided that the king could not act on his own initiative and did not enjoy royal prerogative powers, in Congo the king enjoyed absolute power. It was in 1908 that Congo became a Belgian colony as an outcome of international pressure.[6]

Only two days after the formal declaration of its independence in 1960 the Congolese crisis began, following the mutiny of the Congolese National Army.[7] The

[4] Mushkat (1972), p. 25.

[5] Thompson (2015), p. 52; Azar et al. (1978/1979), pp. 41–60.

[6] Rosoux (2014), p. 19.

[7] Marcum (1961), p. 27.

first crisis lasted for more than three years (from 1960 to 1963) and posed a challenge to the UN, which became actively involved. This crisis exceeded the notion of state turmoil, obliging the UN to launch successive operations. In addition, the crisis was linked to a plane crash which caused the death of the then Secretary-General of the UN.[8]

The situation in Congo was thoroughly discussed both at the SC and GA sessions and became a matter of concern within the organization. The international community focused primarily on the launch of the UN Operation in the Congo (ONUC), because unlike the Emergency Force in the Palestine Dispute (UNEF) and the Korean operation, the ONUC was approved and directly controlled by the UN.[9] An aspect of the first Congolese crisis that formed the basis of confusion was Belgium's forcible intervention ten days after Congo's independence declaration with a view to protecting its nationals. Belgian troops intervened on July 10, 1960 by flying paratroopers into Congo. Only four days later, on July 14, 1960, the UNSC called upon Belgium to withdraw its troops and authorized the deployment of UN troops in Congo. Following its previous decision, the UNSC, on July 22, 1960, called upon Belgium to implement its first decision and withdraw its forces from the Congolese territory. In effect, by July 23 Belgium had withdrawn its forces from the Congolese territory, except for the province of Katanga. There, the Belgian forces remained and delayed their departure as the state continued to refuse to recognize the province's independence. When, finally, they formally withdrew under intense and focused international pressure, Belgium left behind military supplies and personnel to assist Katanga's self-proclaimed president Moise Tshombé.[10]

Thereat, Belgium was actively involved in the Congolese civil war, ensuring its independence. Yet as soon as the military operation to protect their nationals abroad was terminated, Belgium continued intervening in Congo's internal affairs, acting contrary to the UN Charter. In this regard, the Belgian operation to protect its nationals in Congo was broadly seen as a pretext to continue its control over its former colony. Belgium did not even make efforts to better justify its reasons for intervening, and thus its involvement was overt. Viewed through a historical lens,

> Belgium's military intervention elicited varied responses, then and now. Some called it a strictly humanitarian action designed to save lives, while others denounced it as pure neo-colonial aggression.[11]

It is argued that both propositions could stand; on one hand, the Belgian population in Congo was understandably large, given Belgium's long presence in its former colony. On the other hand, Belgium launched a military operation only two days after the Congolese declaration of independence.[12] On top of that, Belgian involvement in Congo lasted till the 80s.

---

[8] James (1996), pp. xviii–xx.

[9] Franck (1961–1962), p. 52.

[10] Marcum (1961), pp. 27–28.

[11] Vanthemsche (2012), p. 210.

[12] Wright (1961), p. 43.

In international law terms, UNSC Res 143(1960) is exemplary, for it demonstrates how the UN perceived the principles of non-intervention and authorization of the use of force. More specifically, according to UNSC Res 143(1960), the SC

> [c]alls upon the Government of Belgium to withdraw its troops from the territory of the Republic of the Congo [and] decides to authorize the Secretary-General to take the necessary steps, in consultation with the Government of the Republic of the Congo, to provide the Government with such military assistance as may be necessary until [...] the national security forces may be able, in the opinion of the Government, to meet fully their tasks.[13]

The Resolution passed with 8 votes in favor and three abstentions, thus it enjoyed formal wide acceptance within the Council. However, it was considered as self-contradicting, because it denounced the unilateral Belgian military operation for the protection of its nationals while in the very next operative clause it authorized the Secretary-General to provide the state's government with military assistance. Notably, the UN realized that the situation in Congo was more than an upheaval, and that use of force was required for the restoration of peace and security. With this in mind, it emerged that the UN did not endorse Belgium's military operation. What remained in question, though, was whether it called upon Belgium to withdraw its forces because it considered forcible PNA to have an unstable legal basis, or if the organization perceived the Belgian operation as a "bold attempt by Belgium to maintain neocolonial control over the nation's economy".[14] Nevertheless, in any event the UN raised a legitimacy issue over Belgium's state practice.

The reintroduction of Belgian troops in Congo two days after its official independence divided the international community. The Soviet Union strongly supported the evacuation of Belgian troops. This was the major reason it did not veto the UNSC Resolution, even though it expressed its concerns about the UN's military assistance for Congo. On the contrary, the US found the launch of a UN military operation necessary, while it did not consider the presence of Belgian troops a problem.[15] This difference of opinion between the two Cold War superpowers reveals that the protection of nationals abroad doctrine did not receive either wide acceptance or disapproval at that time. Thereby, it was a contested concept, dependent on each case's sociopolitical context.[16]

An assessment of Belgium's invocation of the doctrine is anything but simple, for it took place at a critical juncture. Apart from Congo's independence, this marked a significant period for the UN too. Dag Hammarskjöld had assumed a position of leadership within the Organization and he promoted his vision for setting up an "executive administration" for the UN, thus moving towards a more centralized international legal order. This explains to a great extent why the ONUC was established after an agreement was struck between Congo's president and the UN's

[13] UNSC (14 July 1960). The Congo Question. Res 143(1960). UN Doc S/4387.

[14] Gaines (2007), p. 259.

[15] Franck (1961–1962), p. 54.

[16] Kritsiotis (1998), p. 1044.

Secretary-General.[17] This parameter also demonstrates why unilateral and unauthorized use of force could not be tolerated at a time when the UN was willing to act and prevent turmoil.

Eventually, international pressure led Belgium to abandon the forcible protection of nationals abroad rhetoric during the second phase of the Congolese crisis, which began in 1964. More specifically, in September 1964 the insurgent Popular Liberation Army took control of Stanleyville and announced that foreigners would not be permitted to leave the city. Foreigners trapped in Stanleyville were treated as hostages and the insurgents were willing to use them for political bargaining. According to records, there were 63 Americans and 525 Belgians in the territories controlled by the rebels. Besides, Greeks, Italians and Canadians were also held captive. Surprisingly, the US and Belgium did not opt for the forcible protection of their nationals at once; rather they referred to the UN and the Organization of African Unity, while the International Red Cross was also informed. Finally, this situation was resolved after the Congolese authorities gave permission to the Belgian and American governments to proceed with a rescue operation and evacuate the hostages. Nevertheless, this operation was authorized by the official government of Congo and not the insurgents. Thus, the American and Belgian forces would operate in a hostile environment. The rescue operation was not a success, given that very few hostages were released.[18]

The situation in Congo in 1964 proved extremely perilous for foreigners. Yet states did not resort to forcible protection of their nationals abroad and abided by the principle of non-intervention.[19] They secured permission from the host state and notified the UN accordingly, taking as a given that "there is no agreed norm forbidding active military support for the recognized government of a country, at least before the rebellion has made great headway".[20] Of course, this shift in Belgium's policy was not only a matter of respect for the UN regime and Congo's territorial integrity and political independence. It resulted from the environment of extreme violence which dominated the Congolese provinces at the time.

Overall, Belgium's rhetoric during the first phase of the Congolese crisis echoed the pre-Charter perception of the doctrine. Although many Belgian nationals were found in Congo when mutiny erupted, the means employed by Belgium were consistent with the behavior of a colonial power. Belgium actively intervened in Congo's political life in many ways, taking advantage of the suddenness of the violence and disarray that followed its independence.[21] The Charter's entry into force may have shifted the doctrinal debate over forcible PNA, but on a practical level it remained a tool in the hands of stronger states to exert power over weaker

[17] Özsu (2020), p. 611.

[18] Weisberg (1972), pp. 262–263.

[19] UNSC (9 December 1964). Questions Concerning the Democratic Republic of Congo. Res 199(1964), UN Doc S/6129, op. clause 1.

[20] Henkin (1979), pp. 156–157.

[21] Grant (2009), p. 22.

and secure their political interests. The hegemonical perception over sovereignty continued at least during UN's first years of operation. The most significant change was that the UN, as a pillar of stability, had an active role and involvement in the events. As such, it restrained and prevented further escalation.

The case of Congo demonstrates how decolonization changed the foundations of sovereignty. Although colonial powers abandoned their territorial claims over their former colonies, they did not grant them political autonomy. Territorial claims were replaced by increased presence and continuous interventions in the domestic affairs of the former colonies. Sovereignty was not a matter of territorial gains anymore, rather a matter of political influence. This was achieved through several paths, like permanent sovereignty over their natural resources, while it is also suggested that it gave birth to the concept of humanitarian intervention.[22] However, the UN regime and the progress of decolonization marginalized forcible interventions and required justification by the intervening states, which were under the scrutiny of the international community. Sovereignty became a synonym for power and control, while its territorial aspect became less significant, since it was legally secured. The two exceptions to this rule were doctrines allowing the use of force, like humanitarian intervention and forcible PNA, or control over resources. That is limited, or veiled territorial power over former colonies.[23] The transformation of the perception of sovereignty was evident soon after the UNCh's entry into force. The example of the Belgian intervention of Congo demonstrates how forcible PNA became an *ultimum refungium* for those states willing to impose their interest on others. As nationality is an indispensable aspect of sovereignty, it became the most suitable shield to forcible intervention. Afterall, the instrumentalization of nationality ties was not something new to the international community.

3.2 Forcible PNA and American Foreign Policy

The doctrine has time and again been invoked by the US and has to an extent shaped its foreign policy. From 1945 onwards the US has resorted to force on many occasions to protect American nationals residing abroad. The forcible PNA without any prior authorization by the UN, or without third state consent, has been a central tenet of debate as far as American foreign policy is concerned. However, the US policy is consistent in at least two points: the US interprets Art. 2(4) as a provision introducing a qualified prohibition, and at the same time it adheres to the inherent character of the right to self-defense. The combined reading of these two elements suffices to reveal the American perspective towards the use of force in general. The right to self-defense is central in the pursuit of the state's national interests.[24] In

[22] Stilz (2019), p. 262; Geyer (2016), p. 50.

[23] Rezvani (2014), p. 248 et seq.

[24] Corn (2016), pp. 229–233.

addition, self-defense is not circumscribed by the concept of territoriality; on the contrary, it is also attached to nationality ties. American policy has repeatedly underlined the extraterritorial facet of its sovereignty, and its jurisdiction in turn.[25] Thus, self-defense is not exercised when an armed attack occurs against the territory of a state alone, but when a state's nationals are in a perilous condition. This fact explains why the US, in most of its military operations, projects protection of nationals abroad as one of its key claims.

Only in 1958 did the US send forces abroad: to Lebanon, to protect the lives of approximately 2500 American citizens.[26] The American President Dwight Eisenhower in his special message to the Congress on July 15, 1958, following the landing of US marines in Lebanon, mentioned, among others, that

> United States forces are being sent to Lebanon to protect American lives and by their presence to assist the Government of Lebanon in the preservation of Lebanon's territorial integrity and independence, which have been deemed vital to United States national interests and world peace.[27]

The American policy put the safety of American nationals to the foreground and acted to protect them. The message demonstrated the American president's attempt to clarify that the US intervention was not only driven by national interests but served the purpose of international peace and security too. In support of this line of argument, he added that the US wished to withdraw its forces "as soon as the United Nations has taken further effective steps designed to safeguard Lebanese independence".[28] The 1958 American intervention in Lebanon verified the hypothesis that American policy endeavored to satisfy international requirements without relinquishing its own interests. The American stance, though, received severe criticism very early. The US had been accused of feigning respect for the UN standards, as it only formally informed the organization after it had intervened in another state. Thereat, it had been suggested that on many occasions, American claims that it supported foreign governments were nothing but the instrumentalization of domestic disorder, and ultimately a way of disguising imperial interventions.[29] However, the Eisenhower doctrine which was introduced in the 1958 intervention of Lebanon was carefully construed. The use of force would be limited and employed only on the condition that the third state would provide its consent. In this regard, the US kept in alignment with the Charter's standards, further making the argument that criticism stemmed from US opponents in the Cold War framework.[30] After all, the American actions had been discussed both in the SC and the GA, but both fora did

---

[25] Chehtman (2010), p. 71.

[26] Wright (1959), pp. 123–124.

[27] The American Presidency Project (15 July 1958). Retrieved February 22, 2025, from https://www.presidency.ucsb.edu/documents/special-message-the-congress-the-sending-united-states-forces-lebanon.

[28] idem.

[29] Weede (1978), p. 498.

[30] Graber (1958), p. 322.

not reach conclusions on its legitimacy. The American troops remained onsite for so long as they were considered able to secure US national interests and withdrew only when the situation eased, having secured that the state's political system will not pose dangers against its nationals in the near future. In the Cold War times, the demand for political stability and security of citizens abroad was synonymous with anti-communism.[31] However, this is the political foundation of the US interventions and skipped the legal debate.

This pattern was repeated many times, and in some cases, it drew international attention. Use of force against the Dominican Republic (a), Grenada (b), and Panama (c), have been thoroughly researched in this regard.

3.2.1 The 1965 Dominican Crisis: Aspects of American Foreign Policy

During the 60s, the Dominican Republic suffered a severe crisis due to political instability. After President Trujillo's assassination in 1961, the state was divided between pro-Soviet and pro-American supporters, making no exception to the rule of the time. On April 24, 1965, a revolutionary movement emerged in the country, resulting in heavy fighting in the Dominican capital of Santo Domingo for at least three days. The revolutionaries demanded the return of the state's former President Juan Bosch and met strong opposition from the country's authorities.

Overall, this upheaval resulted in the death of many and injuries to thousands of people, creating a state of chaos. Four days after the occurrence of these incidents, the US Embassy in the Dominican Republic announced that the US would proceed with a military operation to evacuate American citizens and nationals of other states residing therein. To safeguard the evacuation of American nationals from Santo Domingo, 400 marines were deployed in the field, while more than 1000 marines were on standby in case of further escalation of violence. Eventually, as the evacuation process unfolded, American marines and airborne troops were deployed in an effort to "restore order and deter" the rebels, who were considered "Communist elements".[32]

This revolution resulted in the establishment of "two entirely antagonistic governments [...] in the Dominican territory: one called Constitutionalist Government and the other, Government of National Reconstruction".[33] Both governments requested the Organization of American States (OAS) to assign a representative of the Inter-American Commission on Human Rights and authorize an onsite visit to investigate alleged human rights violations. The Inter-American Commission

---

[31] Hahn (2006), p. 44; Little (1996), p. 42.

[32] Naughton (1965), p. 547.

[33] OAS (June 1 to August 31, 1965). Report on the Activities of the Inter-American Commission on Human Rights in the Dominican Republic. OEA/Ser.L/V/II.13 doc 14 Rev., Chapter I.

approved the approval of the competing Dominican authorities, formed a special committee in the Dominican Republic and appointed its chairman to represent it. At the same time, the OAS Council was formally informed and convened on the initiative of the US to make a decision regarding the situation in the Dominican Republic. Accordingly, the OAS demanded an immediate ceasefire and launched the Inter-American Peace Force (IAPF) with a mandate to end the state's turmoil and guarantee that safe and free elections would take place. More specifically, the OAS Resolution provided that the IAPF should operate in a spirit of democratic impartiality to

> 1. Cooperate in the restoration of peace in the Dominican Republic, 2. Maintain the security of its inhabitants and the inviolability of human rights, 3. Establish an atmosphere of peace and conciliation which would permit the functioning of democratic institutions.[34]

The IAPF consisted of six OAS member-states, namely the US, Brazil, Nicaragua, Costa Rica, Paraguay and Honduras.[35] The IAPF was composed of 1700 troops from six Latin American Countries and 12,400 from the United States.[36] Thus, US troops were the core of the IAPF.[37] Apart from regional responses, the UN also took action concerning the situation in the Dominican Republic. It sided with the OAS and asked for an immediate and strict cease-fire, and in addition it invited the UN Secretary-General to send a representative to the Dominican Republic to report to the Security Council on the situation.[38] The Dominican crisis ended in July 1966 after general elections took place. These elections were the turning point that marked the withdrawal of foreign troops from the Dominican state and guaranteed a gradual return to normalcy.[39]

The use of force in the Dominican crisis was unique in many aspects. The most significant aspect was the OAS decision to launch the IAPF and take military action to enforce peace and guarantee political representation. Recourse to force by regional organizations was definitely not usual practice, and OAS was strongly condemned for such and for its involvement in the Dominican crisis.[40] Taking for granted that the Dominican crisis had strong Cold War implications, in conjunction with the immediate intervention by the US, raised multiple questions for the decision by the OAS council. Although the OAS had abolished unilateral intervention and recourse to force over time, being in full alignment with the UN Charter, in the Dominican case it deviated from its standard policy and upheld the American

---

[34] Bogen (1966), p. 297.

[35] For the composition, mission and accomplishments of the Inter-American Peace Force (IAPF) see US Army Center of Military History. Retrieved February 22, 2025, from https://history.army.mil/html/bookshelves/resmat/dom_republic/IAPF_Stability_Ops_Rpt.pdf.

[36] See Dominic Republic – DomRep, Background. Retrieved February 22, 2025, from https://peacekeeping.un.org/mission/past/domrepbackgr.html.

[37] Nanda (1966), p. 440.

[38] UNSC (14 May 1965). Res 203(1965).

[39] Palmer, Jr. (1989).

[40] Dreier (1968), pp. 477–493.

position. The OAS launch of the IAPF retrospectively legitimized the American actions right after the outbreak of the crisis.[41] Although the US initially sent marines and airborne troops to the Dominican Republic for a large-scale evacuation mission, it turned out soon enough that the US involvement in the crisis exceeded the protection of its nationals. In this sense, the disputed legitimacy of the American intervention rendered the OAS Council decision controversial, given that Art. 19 of the OAS Charter provides that no member-state shall intervene

> directly, or indirectly, for any reason whatever, in the internal or external affairs of any other state [and that] the foregoing principle prohibits not only armed force but also any other form of interference or attempted threat against the personality of the State or against its political, economic, and cultural elements.[42]

The US made several claims to substantiate the legitimacy of its acts in the Dominican Republic. Even though the protection of its own nationals was the first claim made by the US, it soon became clear both from the rapidly increasing number of its forces onsite and from the statements by President Johnson that its main objective was to prevent a communist government takeover. In his speech on the Dominican Republic intervention, President Johnson stated that:

> We believe that change comes and we are glad it does, and it should come through peaceful process. But revolution in any country is a matter for that country to deal with. It becomes a matter calling for hemispheric action only – repeat – only when the object is the establishment of a communistic dictatorship. Let me also make clear tonight that we support no single man or any single group of men in the Dominican Republic. Our goal is a simple one. We are there to save the lives of our citizens and to save the lives of all people. Our goal, in keeping with the great principles of the inter-American system, is to help prevent another Communist state in this hemisphere. And we would like to do this without bloodshed or without large-scale fighting.[43]

This address received intense scrutiny as it introduced the so-called "Johnson Doctrine", according to which the prevention of the spread of communism in the Western hemisphere was of utmost importance for the American continent; as a result, such a threat justified hemispheric collective intervention.[44] The Johnson Doctrine was manifest proof that US involvement in the Dominican crisis did not aim at the protection of nationals alone, while it explained why the US did not turn to the UN in the first place and activated the OAS instead. The US reasonably expected a Soviet veto if intervention was to be discussed in the UNSC and for this it addressed the Dominican crisis as a regional issue.[45]

No matter the effectiveness and degree of international acceptance of the Johnson Doctrine, as far as PNA was concerned its invocation undermined the credibility of

---

[41] McLaren (1966), pp. 184–185.

[42] OAS (30 April 1948). Charter of the Organization of American States. Bogota OAS T.S. Nos 1-C and 61.

[43] Johnson (May 2, 1965). Retrieved February 22, 2025, from https://loveman.sdsu.edu/docs/1965JohnsonDoctrine.pdf.

[44] Papermaster (1989), p. 496.

[45] Rabe (2006), p. 55.

American reference to rescue operations. Put simply, it clarified that the US reference to forcible PNA veiled its national interests: to intervene so as to control other states' political course. Additionally, rescue operations are tiny part of the forcible PNA doctrine, whose legality is rarely doubted. However, there are cases when the lines between military rescue operations and military operations to secure political interests in foreign soil, while protecting nationals, are blurred. The same legal concerns, more or less, came to light in the US intervention in Grenada too.

3.2.2 The 1983 American Invasion of Grenada

On October 25, 1983, President Reagan authorized an invasion of Grenada by American forces to protect approximately 1000 American nationals, mostly university medical students. More specifically, violence escalated on the island when Bernard Coard took control of the government, after he ordered the assassination of the state's former president, Maurice Bishop. Coard encountered strong opposition from civilians due to the violent government takeover—and not due to his Marxist views, as is sometimes implied. Therefore, national turmoil was not provoked by Coard's political position, given that the late Maurice Bishop had been a communist and during his four-year office had moved Grenada gradually closer to the Soviet-bloc states. As soon as American troops landed in Grenada to rescue American nationals, they met strong opposition from the joint Grenadan and Cuban armed forces. The latter were found on the island assisting in the repair of the island's airport. The American forces lacked intelligence about the operational environment, and they soon asked for reinforcements.[46]

The intervention in Grenada fit into the wider context of US attempts to decelerate Soviet infiltration in the American continent and build strong ties with the established governments. As far as Caribbean states are concerned though, it was reported that the US had on many occasions considered themselves as their protector. In the aftermath of European colonialism in the Caribbean, combined with the rising Latin American nationalism and Cuba's attempts to become the leading power of the region, the US had been seen by many as a credible partner, able to establish and guarantee stability.[47] Thereby, it is no surprise that the Organization of Eastern Caribbean States (OECS) required assistance from the US.[48]

The key elements of the US invasion of Grenada are the American claim to protect its nationals abroad (a), the request by the OECS to the US for military assistance and to stabilize the situation in Grenada (b), and the invitation by many actors in Grenada to the US to intervene (c). It is suggested that taken together they

[46] See United States invades Grenada. This Day in History. Retrieved, February 22, 2025, from https://www.history.com/this-day-in-history/united-states-invades-grenada.

[47] Thomson (1985), p. 384.

[48] Quigley (1986–1987), p. 274.

confirmed the legality of American actions, considering that the intervention in Grenada was yet another example of US involvement in the politics of another state under the pretext of protecting nationals abroad. In this case, too, American forces multiplied in the field and were not limited to protecting and evacuating their nationals. An evacuation mission would not require 8000 American troops to be deployed. Although the US proclaimed that this was an evacuation mission and spread this message worldwide, it was not one technically speaking. The US invaded alongside security units from six member-states of the OECS, which formed the Caribbean Peace-Keeping Force. Just like the Dominican incident, American troops formed the core of the allied forces, given that the Caribbean Peace-Keeping Force counted only 300 members.[49] In this sense, it was not a unilateral intervention—at least, not a typical one. Rather, it was a joint US-Caribbean action, formulated at the request of the OECS to the US for military assistance. Finally, allied forces had also received a request for action by Grenada's Governor-General, Sir Paul Scoon, as soon as Maurice Bishop was assassinated. State consent tallied with regional request suffices on principle to legitimize a state's military assistance. At the same time, the intervening state did not need to invoke protection of nationals abroad as an alternative legal basis. Yet the incident in Grenada demonstrated that both a regional organization's request as well as state consent might lack reliability. First, several national actors, including Grenada's Governor-General, asked the US for its immediate intervention. But their requests did not come from official state bodies. Even though Coard took over the government by force and imposed his authority, he was still considered head of Grenada. If this proposition is not true, and one accepts that Grenada was an ungoverned country at the time, then again pleas for military help from state actors were not equivalent to a request from the official government.

Turning to the OECS plea for military support from the US, this request was based on their collective defense treaty. The OECS evaluated the situation in Grenada as a threat to peace in the region, requiring further action. The OECS mentioned in its letter to the US that:

> The current anarchic conditions, the serious violations of human rights and bloodshed that have occurred and the consequent unprecedented threat to the peace and security of the region created by the vacuum of authority in Grenada.[50]

This created perilous conditions for everyone on the island. Apart from Grenada's political instability, the OECS drew international attention to the state's rapid militarization. In particular, the letter stated that:

> Military forces and supplies are likely to be shortly introduced to consolidate the position of the regime and that the country can be used as a staging post for acts of aggression against its members [...] the capability of the Grenada armed forces is already at a level of sophistication and size far beyond the internal needs of that country.[51]

[49] Gordon (1984), pp. 334–335.

[50] The New York Times (26 October 1983). Retrieved February 22, 2025, from https://www.nytimes.com/1983/10/26/world/letter-asking-us-to-act.html.

[51] idem.

The OECS directly implied that Grenada could proceed with military action against its neighboring states. Thus, this reference was also used as a justification for anticipatory self-defense. Taking also into consideration the historical context, it may well be suggested that the OECS was worried about Grenada's close political ties with Cuba and its role in the region. These fears were substantiated by the "Grenada-Cuba Association", which was created much earlier in 1978 at the initiative of the Bishop Presidency.[52] Indeed, both the OECS and the US raised claims of anticipatory self-defense alongside collective self-defense and protection of nationals abroad. More specifically,

> the United States set forth as a reason for its participation in the Grenada intervention the "unprecedented threat to the peace and security of the region" created by the Grenadian military buildup, the Soviet-Cuban influence, and the subsequent breakdown of order on the island.[53]

It follows that the statements made by the OECS and the US were in full alignment. Both the regional organization and the US considered Grenada as a potential threat to regional peace and security and speculated that any upheaval in the country could prove detrimental for the Western hemisphere.

The final point of concern regarding the legitimacy of the military intervention in Grenada relates to the legal weight and importance of the OECS letter to the US. To offer a complete analysis on this point, one needs to delve into the scope and purposes of the OECS, and further explain how regional collective self-defense functions alongside the UN regime. From this viewpoint, a short digression on the historical aspects and role of the OECS is necessary.

This regional organization was established on June 4, 1981, and its Treaty of Establishment (the Treaty of Basseterre) entered into force a few days later. In essence, the OECS was the successor of the West Indies (Associated States) Council of Ministers, which dated back to 1966.[54] According to Art. 8 para 4 of the 1981 Establishing Treaty,

> [t]he Defence and Security Committee shall have responsibility for co-ordinating the efforts of Member States for collective defence and the preservation of peace and security against external aggression and for the development of close ties among the Member States of the Organisation in matters of external defence and security, including measures to combat the activities of mercenaries, operating with or without the support of internal or national elements, in the exercise of the inherent right of individual or collective self-defence recognized by Article 51 of the Charter of the United Nations.[55]

Two conclusions can safely be drawn from the above. First, the OECS was a newly established state when the intervention in Grenada took place. The situation

[52] Hardt (1987), p. 291.

[53] Maizel (1986), p. 70.

[54] ibid, pp. 48–49.

[55] Treaty establishing the Organisation of Eastern Caribbean States (Treaty of Basseterre) (18 June 1981). Retrieved February 22, 2025, from http://ctrc.sice.oas.org/CARICOM/OECS/Treaty_basseterre.pdf, 8.

in Grenada was unprecedented for this regional organization, and it had to interpret Art. 8 for the first time. Second, the reading of Art. 8 promoted by the OECS members was arbitrary, or extraordinary at least. The legislative provision in question refers explicitly to external aggression which might trigger defense against external actors. If external aggression occurs, then regional self-defense follows the requirements of Art. 51 UNCh. Therefore, the conditions of necessity, imminence and proportionality remain.

The novelty of this provision is the term "external aggression", which signifies that the attack must emanate from a state or actor (mercenaries without the support of internal elements) outside the organization, while the use of the term "aggression" instead of the term "armed attack" demonstrates that the OECD drafters were referring to acts against the sovereignty, territorial integrity or political independence of a state, adhering to the language of the 3314/74 UNGA Resolution. In this framework, it readily emerges that the OECS Establishing Treaty provided for collective self-defense from external actors alone. Conversely, its wording does not leave space for humanitarian or pro-democratic intervention. Any attempt at interpretation according to Art. 31 VCLT would not fit the Grenada intervention.[56] The internal turmoil had lasted only a short time when the third states invaded Grenada, and therefore no risk of the region's destabilization could have been foreseen.

Even if one accepts that this action served the scope and purposes of the OECS, the question whether it was in accordance with the centralized collective security system set by the UNCh remains. It is aptly pointed out that the OECS adopted

> the thesis that neighboring states may be entitled to use military force – and to legitimize military force by others – in order to meet a threat to their security by a country perceived as potentially aggressive and dangerous to the peace goes far beyond the right of collective self-defense or international "peacekeeping" as generally understood. Such action would have been legally valid if undertaken pursuant to a Security Council decision under chapter VII.[57]

This view is consistent with the subsequent decisions made by the OAS and the UNCh, which did not support the OECS plea for third states' intervention. More specifically, the OAS treated the intervention in Grenada differently to the action taken in the Dominican Republic. Many voices had raised concerns that the OAS authorization in the Dominican crisis was in sheer violation of the sacrosanct prohibition against intervention that the OAS Charter provided. Following this course of thinking, it was made clear that the OAS was attempting to right the wrongs of the past by maintaining this stance in Grenada. It was reported that the intervention in Grenada was "overwhelmingly condemned initially and acquiesced in accepting the action was neither swift nor unanimous",[58] which further denotes that the OAS

[56] Acevedo (1984), p. 73.

[57] Schachter (1984b), pp. 1620–1646, 1640–1641; cf Maizel (1986), p. 82.

[58] Karas and Goodman (1984), p. 83.

could not rotate 180 degrees, and thus took a more moderate position in the end.[59] From a more realistic viewpoint, the discrepancy in the OAS approach between the incident in the Dominican Republic and the one in Grenada demonstrates the decrease of American influence in the organization. In the same way, the UNSC could not reach a decision on the situation in Grenada, while the UNGA Resolution concluded that it

> deeply deplores the armed intervention in Grenada, which constitutes a flagrant violation of international law and of the independence, sovereignty and territorial integrity of that State.[60]

Thereat, the UN took a more stringent position regarding the intervention in Grenada. Although factual resemblance between the two incidents is striking, nevertheless the international community did not enact the same legal treatment. As a result, the proposition that the intervention in Grenada was nothing but the resurrection of the Johnson Doctrine by the Reagan administration is not entirely accurate.[61]

Overall, the legitimacy of the 1983 intervention in Grenada has been heavily contested, even though the military operation lasted only a few days. By October 28, 1983, the major military and operational objectives had been accomplished. Most Americans were evacuated in the first couple of days. Finally, the US troops withdrew and only support personnel and security units remained on the island.[62] This controversy over the intervention's conformity with international law was primarily due to the fact that

> there was little evidence that the Americans on the island were actually in any danger and that there is some doubt, as well as to whether or not the OECS followed correct treaty procedures or had the right to invade a member state. The United States relied upon an amalgam of its various justifications, appearing to understand how shaky each was on its own and hoping that together, they would stand stronger and be accepted.[63]

In other words, the US was considered to have used the forcible PNA doctrine as a cover to obscure the real grounds for its engagement in the conflict. This accumulation of legal claims continues to be considered a safe pathway for a state's policy; yet it is detrimental to the credibility of the doctrine. The example of Grenada differs from the ones previously referred, in two aspects. First, due to the doubt of the existence of imminent threat for the rescued nationals. An evacuation operation in face of unprecedented peril is a cause not easy to overcome. However, when this element is missing then forcible PNA is at least precarious. The second peculiarity regarding the intervention of Grenada, is that the US had secured institutional support by international organizations. So far, the involvement of any international organization or even the institutional cooperation of states in military operations is

[59] Diuguid (30 October 1983). Retrieved February 22, 2025, from https://www.washingtonpost.com/archive/politics/1983/10/30/oas-fails-to-draft-grenada-resolution/2ddb1376-3a9d-4345-84d6-246802550f1a/.

[60] UNGA (2 November 1983). The Situation in Grenada. UN Doc A/Res/38/7, op. clause 1.

[61] Dore (1984), pp. 173–190.

[62] Riggs (1985), pp. 10–11.

[63] Meyer (1993), pp. 402–403.

deemed to have a positive impact, offering the necessary balancing of interests and restraint to the use of force. However, Grenada demonstrates the manipulative role that politics may develop over small regional international organizations.[64] The demand for peace and security was both global and regional too. Smaller organizations developed parallel, or even competitive action against the UN, challenging its monopoly on authorizing the use of force. The example of Grenada demonstrates how decentralized collective security systems flourished at the Americas at that time.[65]

Apart from issues of legitimacy regarding the American intervention of Grenada, the authorization of the use of force by regional organizations such as the OAS, or the OECS, raises questions as to states' perception as far as the collective security system and the UN Charter's prerogative on this domain are concerned. The Grenada incident is interesting not only in terms of state policy but is also revealing regarding the institutional guarantees on peace and security. First, it is suggested that forcible PNA is not only espoused by certain states in the post-Charter era, but by regional organizations too. In effect, this could raise the argument that there is a regional precedent on forcible PNA, or even that the involvement of OAS and the OECS indicate the existence of a regional customary norm permitting the use of force to protect one's nationals abroad.

Second, the Grenada incident has further implications regarding the Charter's interpretation. The previous chapter went through the doctrinal interpretative paths on the use of force. A restrictive view according to which there shall be no violence and therefore forcible PNA is outlawed, cannot stand the Grenada incident. This is not only because states invoked the doctrine considering it consistent with their obligations emanating from the Charter, but mostly due to regional security systems which developed a role counter to that of the UN regime.[66] However, it shall also be noted that the regional organizations under question were unable to explain how and why Grenada was a state capable of moving to aggressive acts.[67]

3.2.3 The American Invasion of Panama

The American policy regarding forcible PNA unfolded fully in the case of Panama. Unlike interventions in the Dominican Republic and Grenada, the Panama incident differed in its core aspects. The presidential address to the nation on the Panama invasion is revealing. On December 20, 1989, President George H.W. Bush declared that:

[64] Hakimi (2007), p. 665.

[65] Hickey (2004), p. 80.

[66] Wood and Sthoeger (2022), p. 219.

[67] Harrell (2008), pp. 437–438.

> The goals of the United States have been to safeguard the lives of Americans, to defend democracy in Panama, to combat drug trafficking, [...] to protect the integrity of the Panama Canal Treaty [and] to bring General Noriega to justice in the United States.[68]

American foreign policy was based on the accumulation of numerous reasons to substantiate the legitimacy of its actions. The major differences from the other interventions relied primarily on two points. First, although the claim for democratic restoration existed in all three incidents, in the case of Panama pro-democratic intervention did not stem from Cold War politics. Panama's president, Manuel Noriega, had been for years a close ally of the American authorities, developing a key role in the deployment of the Contras in Nicaragua and providing information to the US intelligence agencies. Therefore, the US efforts to overthrow Noriega's government and bring him before the national courts to be charged was not due to any pro-Soviet policies, rather it resulted from a gradual deterioration in the two states' relations.[69]

In addition, it was not common before that time to officially declare that the ultimate goal of a military operation was to arrest the head of a state, and it accordingly received heavy criticism.[70] Second, unlike the Dominican and Grenadian precedents, the American operation in Panama had been carefully designed and planned for a long time. Although Panama suffered from internal turbulence from time to time, the overthrow of the Noriega regime was not a response to an imminent threat.[71] On the contrary, it was predetermined. Nevertheless, the US discourse relied on defensive terms, and many considered the American actions as an exercise of the right to self-defense, and a cool-headed and careful, well-designed project.[72]

On the basis that Operation Just Cause did not result from the occurrence of an imminent threat, the prerequisites of Art. 51 UNCh could not be met easily. Accordingly, the US discourse was based mostly on the grounds of pro-democratic intervention and a roughly worded early form of R2P.[73] In this context, the question that arose was whether the protection of nationals abroad claim, which was made the primary focus of American reasoning, was invoked as an exception to the qualified prohibition of Art. 2(4) UNCh, like the other claims,[74] or if the confluence of American claims did not alter its legal basis and was a manifestation of Art. 51 UNCh. The second hypothesis is closer to American established state practice, according to which forcible PNA was tied to the state's inherent right to self-defense.[75]

---

[68] Bush (20 December 1989). Retrieved February 22, 2025, from https://www.americanrhetoric.com/speeches/ghwbushpanamainvasion.htm.

[69] Quigley (1990), p. 278; Clayton et al. (2017), p. 606.

[70] Berman (1990), p. 784.

[71] Rumage (1993), p. 2.

[72] Terry (1990), p. 9.

[73] Murphy (2009), p. 373.

[74] Akehurst (1977), pp. 3–23.

[75] Lillich (1992), p. 218.

Finally, the point which differentiated Operation Just Cause from other incidents was that the US brought forward a moral claim. More specifically, the intervening state foregrounded the argument that it ought to save all Panama citizens from an established tyranny which was ruining all aspects of their lives. The US emphasized Panama's corrupt juridical system, the state of criminal impunity which permeated the country, and the fact that the Noriega presidency was openly assisting and cooperating with the drug cartels. Altogether, these parameters were considered to necessitate a response from the international community, and even more from states which had strong legitimate interests in Panama. That is, the US should intervene not only in the name of 35,000 American nationals residing in Panama, but also to guarantee the enforcement of the Panama Canal Treaty.[76] From this viewpoint, the US intervention in Panama was both legitimate and awaited by the international community.[77] It was suggested that if the US did not opt to proceed with this military operation, then the lives of thousands would be in extreme peril. This theory directly linked the use of force to human rights. As Anthony D'Amato pointed out:

> Tyrannical leaders are being replaced in nation after nation by governing bodies that are more responsive to the citizenry. Contributing to the momentum of popular sovereignty are the Grenada and Panama interventions. Not only did the United States remove tyrannical leaders from those two countries, but more importantly it set an example that has undoubtedly shaken other ruling elites that enjoy tyrannical control in their own countries. For even if some of those entrenched elites regard themselves as secure against popular uprising in their own countries (usually by the application of torture and brutality against political dissidents), they cannot now feel totally insulated against foreign humanitarian intervention. Thus, Grenada and Panama may very well act as catalysts in the current global revolution of popular sovereignty. In this respect, as well as on their own merits, the two interventions underscore the unraveling of statist conceptions of international law.[78]

This view demonstrates the progressive character of international law, which shall be responsive to citizenry and prioritize human rights clauses in above state interests. The use of force prohibition and the prerequisites for the legitimate invocation of the right to self-defense are clearly articulated by the international community to regulate international law and must not be obstacles to the protection of values that are of cardinal importance to the international community. In this sense, the use of force to halt systematic human rights violations, or to put an end to state corruption, is legitimate due to the moral claims it serves. Yet this course of thinking, although correct in principle, does not correspond to the realities of the international stage. Further, it prioritizes morality over legality, thus depriving the rules on the use of force of any sense of objectivity.

---

[76] United States of America and Panama (7 September 1977). Panama Canal Treaty. UNTS Vol. 1280, I. Nos 21086–21107, p. 3.

[77] Furlong (1993), p. 21.

[78] D'Amato (1990), p. 524; see also Nanda (1990), p. 498; cf Millett (1990), p. 3.

These concerns over the 1989 invasion of Panama were expressed by many scholars, as well as by states,[79] which considered it a flagrant violation of well-established international law norms. Yet, there was no consensus over the operation's legality and international fora were inconclusive, as they could not come up with a solid resolution. There was general difficulty in determining the attitude of many states regarding the American invasion of Panama. The UNSC could not reach a decision, while in the UNGA Resolution, which strongly deplored the American intervention in Panama, many states abstained. Therefore, no uniform position regarding the legality of the 1989 incident can be tracked.[80] In the words of Louis Henkin,

> If the Panama invasion and the attempts to justify it sought to change the law whether to permit the use of force where there has been no armed attack but to defend *soi disant* "vital interests," to permit the use of force to impose more legitimate governments or to capture thugs – we can only hope that the attempt to effect such changes in the law will not succeed. The United States, I am deeply persuaded, will regret it if such a change in the "common law" occurs, and will itself seek to prevent that change. Indeed, the history of the common law rejects its use as an analogy to justify the U.S. invasion of Panama. When the common law proved inadequate, when society could not tolerate the law's ambiguities and uncertainties and its dependence on imperfect institutions, the law was codified, made more clear, more firm, leaving less room for violators and for reliance on an imperfect judiciary. So too, some fifty years ago, the common (customary) international law may have allowed every state to decide for itself whether it was justified in using force to defend its "vital interests," or in what it considered a "just cause."[81]

Henkin's critique touches upon the ambiguity of Operation Just Cause, which attempted to substitute legitimacy gaps for moral propositions. This general view over the American invasion of Panama, although moving in the right direction, missed the point regarding the protection of American nationals.

In the case of the Panamanian intervention, the US indeed received information that its nationals were the subject of hostile behaviors by the state; what is more, the American population in Panama counted around 35,000 people.[82] These parameters would suffice to substantiate the claims to legitimacy of an evacuation mission protecting American nationals onsite. However, the US operation exceeded by far the purpose of protecting American citizens. The American discourse put forcible PNA first, but this purpose was diminished in importance by the other claims made. That

---

[79] See Items Relating to the Situation in Panama. Decision of 23 December 1989 (2902nd meeting): Rejection of a Draft Resolution on the Situation in Panama. Retrieved February 22, 2025, from https://www.un.org/securitycouncil/sites/www.un.org.securitycouncil/files/en/sc/repertoire/89-92/Chapter%208/AMERICA/item%2013_Panama%20-%203%20items%20-%20consolidated.pdf, 395; UNGA (29 December 1989). Effects of the Military Intervention by the United States of America in Panama on the Situation in Central America. UN Doc A/44/PV.88, op. clause 1.

[80] Ronzitti (2019), p. 439.

[81] Henkin (1991), p. 312.

[82] Sofaer (1991), pp. 285–286.

is, protection of nationals abroad was an important but not the central tenet in Operation Just Cause.

The above analysis of the American state practice relating to the protection of nationals abroad is not exhaustive: only selected incidents in which the claim was brought up are examined.[83] Yet, it is indicative of a potentially emerging pattern regarding its use and validity. Overall, the US has accumulated various legal claims in support of its military operations. The forcible PNA doctrine aims at a wider audience; as such, it was put to the forefront of America's foreign policy. To delineate the major constituents of US state practice regarding PNA, three points stand out. First, the US did not hesitate to invoke jointly the protection of American nationals residing abroad with pro-democratic or humanitarian interventions. Although these doctrines differed in their legal foundation, this was not considered a handicap to the American strategic argumentation. Second, there was an apparent shift in the American discourse. The interventions in the Dominican Republic and Grenada were strongly characterized by Cold War rhetoric, while the invasion of Panama served "vital American interests".[84] The US turned to a broader concept to justify recourse to force. Third, the US sought international institutional support in all such occasions as proof of its actions' legitimacy. The course of history demonstrates the decreasing support for this approach by the wider international community.

The importance of this analysis pertains also to the interpretation of the PNA doctrine, in terms of the evaluation of peril and the necessity to recourse to force. Apart from policy issues and national interests, a specific pattern over the interpretation of what constitutes a peril for US nationals can be traced in the above analysis. Necessity for recourse to force relates to the danger faced by US nationals irrespective of the number of the group in jeopardy. This approach regarding which conditions are deemed perilous for American citizens is in line with the state's practice before the UN Charter and is apt proof of how the US perceives sovereignty as a concept not restrained by territoriality. America's strong conviction that sovereignty is also extraterritorial has been part of its legal justifications throughout time.

As far as the American policy is concerned, the doctrine's invocation manifests its entanglement with other doctrines regarding recourse to force. The American policy is exemplary regarding the interchangeable use of justifications for its forcible interventions. Forcible PNA is invoked irrespective of the importance attributed to the peril envisaged by American nationals each time. It is a strong cause for intervention and develops a supportive and complementary role when the rest of the justifications are precarious. On an operation level, the American paradigm has two implications. First, the state's decision to forcibly protect its citizens abroad is not based on quantitative criteria. It is a complex decision which prioritizes the kind and magnitude of peril faced by them. In this sense, significant deviations from the

[83] For a full account of American operations in the Charter era see Wingfield (2000), p. 467.

[84] Gilboa (1995–1996), p. 540.

American standards on democratic governance are a cause for the use of force.[85] Second, the above incidents showcase the operation challenges of forcible PNA. Even if it is designed to be an evacuation operation, it involves the military, if there are hostile environments.

Sovereignty is extraterritorial according to the American rationale. Forcible PNA is not only fueled by nationality clauses; in addition, it extends to guarantees of governance that will not bring American citizens into a perilous condition. However, apart from these observations, it is evident that the American understanding of sovereignty is not exhausted in territoriality and nationality. It is also a matter of power to implement national jurisdictional standards.

Although these incidents were not clearly in accordance with the Charter's obligations, they were tolerated by the UN, leading to the question whether the international community consented to their doctrinal rightness, or if there is a new hegemonic trend which evolved within the international organization.

3.3 The Entebbe Raid: A Decisive Point in the Doctrine's Perception

The third part of the analysis regarding state practice and forcible PNA in the post-Charter era emphasizes on the Entebbe rescue operation. This incident is one of a time and for this reason it is analyzed separately. The incident changed the doctrinal and operation discussion regarding forcible PNA and introduced a new paradigm for such operations. The Entebbe raid was a catalyst for the evolution of the doctrine and subsequent state practice. From Entebbe onwards, two things were made clear: first that forcible PNA was widely considered a breach of the principle of non-intervention, and second that even such small-scale rescue operations were under the scrutiny of UN organs. Nevertheless, the Entebbe incident paved the way for NEOs.

The raid concerned a series of airplane hijackings that took place during the 70s and 80s, all following the same pattern. On June 27, 1976, an Air France airplane with more than two hundred passengers, en route from Tel Aviv to Paris via Athens, was hijacked after it took off from Athens. The hijackers declared they were members of the Popular Front for the Liberation of Palestine and ordered the plane to land at the airport of Entebbe, Uganda. A few hours after landing, the hijackers allowed a few passengers to disembark, and they were transferred to another terminal. The hijackers then demanded the release of 53 "freedom fighters" in exchange for the return of the passengers and crew members of the plane. If their demands were not satisfied, they threatened to kill all hostages. Israel decided to negotiate with them, and as a sign of goodwill the hijackers released 101 hostages, keeping only those with Israeli nationality and those who were believed to be Jews. Almost

[85] Schachter (1984a), pp. 646–647.

a week after the plane was hijacked Israel proceeded with a military raid to rescue the remaining captives. This counter-terrorist hostage-taking mission was code-named Operation Thunderbolt.[86] During the battle between the Israeli defense forces and the hijackers there were casualties. It was reported that three captives, all of the hijackers, around twenty Ugandan soldiers and an Israeli member of the armed forces lost their lives.[87] The operation was fairly deemed a success, as previous rescue raids had not ended well.

3.3.1 Bewilderment Regarding the Legal Classification of the Raid

The raid was not well received by the international community, even though it was a success. The key aspects regarding this 90-minute raid were fourfold. First, the hostages were kept due to their nationality. That is, the hijackers intended to keep them to exert pressure on Israel and secure the release of their comrades. From this perspective, Israeli action was expected and anticipated. The taking of Israeli hostages (and simultaneous release of passengers who were not Israeli nationals) reaffirms that nationality ties are a strong reason to trigger a state's actions. Although Entebbe demonstrated a discrepancy between states' perceptions on the use of force to protect nationals abroad facing imminent peril, it cemented the view that states are expected to act in assistance of their nationals. Otherwise, hostage-taking would not have been a popular means of pressure at the time. As was eloquently put, to show the spread of this non-state practice:

> Throughout the world, the number of kidnapping and hostage/barricade situations long ago surpassed the crisis level. The latter years of the 70's saw scores of such attacks [...] It continues to grow. The victims are as varied in their backgrounds as are their captors. Diplomats, international business personalities, members of the judiciary, airline employees and passengers, and people generally who are in the proverbial "wrong place at the wrong time" are abducted by countless terrorist groups.[88]

Second, unlike other hostage-rescue operations, the Ugandan government did not give permission to the Israeli forces either to land or use force. On the contrary, Uganda condemned Israel for having violated its sovereignty and territorial integrity, characterizing the raid an act of aggression. According to the Ugandan Minister of Foreign Affairs in his address to the UNSC:

> three Zionist Israeli transport planes landed by surprise and without any authority from the Ugandan Government at Entebbe International Airport. Soon after landing, they proceeded straight to the old airport building where the hostages and the crew of the French airbus, which was hijacked in flight between Tel Aviv and Paris, were being held by Palestinian

[86] See Dunstan (2012).

[87] Boyle (1980–1981), pp. 771–772.

[88] Wilder (1981), p. 374.

> commandos. Out of the aircraft, two military jeeps drove and the invaders, using hand grenades, machine-guns, bazookas and other explosives, indiscriminately attacked the airport building and the Ugandan soldiers who were guarding the building at a distance of 200 metres and who were armed only with lights arms in accordance with the conditions laid down by the hijackers. As a result of this attack on the building, the invaders killed seven hijackers and some hostages and a number of Ugandan soldiers, injuring many others as well. The Israeli invaders also blasted the old airport terminal building, damaged the runway and destroyed a number of Ugandan aircraft and extensive installations.[89]

The Idi Amin government vehemently opposed the Israeli actions; they were not considered a rescue mission, nor were they welcome. On the contrary, the language used by the country's representative at the UN demonstrated that Uganda perceived the operation as a breach of the principle of non-intervention and a violation of its sovereignty, in full alignment with the language of UNGA Res 3314. Of course, this view was not espoused by all states. The US position was diametrically opposed to that of the Ugandans, as the address by the US Representative to the UNSC proved. According to the US,

> Israel's action in rescuing the hostages necessarily involved a temporary breach of the territorial integrity of Uganda. Normally such a breach would be impermissible under the Charter of the United Nations. However, there is a well-established right to use limited force for the protection of one's own nationals from an imminent threat of injury or death in a situation where the state in whose territory they are located either is unwilling or unable to protect them. The right, flowing from the right of self-defense, is limited to such use of force as is necessary and appropriate to protect threatened nationals from injury.[90]

This sort of divergence of opinion was not new and showed to the fullest why UN member-states could not reach a decision on the incident. A wide range of views were expressed, unveiling the international community's confusion over how to characterize the incident. Although hostage-taking was unanimously condemned, as an act contrary to the principles of international law, the Israeli action received mixed responses: from being considered a flagrant violation of international law—and the UNCh in particular—to a lawful act of self-defense or self-help against a terrorist attack. The then UN Secretary-General Kurt Waldheim characterized the raid as a "serious violation of the sovereignty of a member state of the United States".[91] UNSC debates were inconclusive, affirming the fact that the incident had led to a morass of confusion.[92]

Third, this operation re-established the foundations for the proportionate use of force. The Israeli operation was deemed proportionate, as its measures of protection

[89] UNSC Official Records (9 July 1976). Complaint by the Prime Minister of Mauritius, current Chairman of the Organization of African Unity, of the "act of aggression" by Israel against the Republic of Uganda, para 31.

[90] Schachter (1984b), p. 1630.

[91] UNSC Official Records (14 July 1976). UN Doc S/PV.1943, 4.

[92] Shaw (2021), p. 1004; McDowell (1976), pp. 1224–1234.

were "strictly confined to the removal of the danger"[93] that hung over the nationals.[94] Overall, the Israeli response became ever-more necessary as the window of time decreased. In this regard, it was suggested by many that a proportionate evacuation mission should have been permissible, given that it would only involve "temporary and proportionate use of military force in order to withdraw the victims".[95] The question of how states are expected to legally respond to a terrorist attack or an international offense in general has always troubled legal scholarship. If the view was taken that the use of force was permitted, since it was necessary and proportionate, then the forcible PNA was in accordance with Art. 51 UNCh. Likewise, if it was considered a legitimate act of self-help, it would not contradict the prohibition of Art. 2(4) since it would not target a state's sovereignty, territorial integrity or political independence. If none of these options were adopted, then it must be considered that states have no means of responding to such incidents, which would consequently require the existence of a more centralized international system.[96]

Finally, the Entebbe crisis prompted international negotiations about the 1979 Convention against the Taking of Hostages. The ensuing debate revealed a gap between developed and developing states. On one hand, developed states were concerned about the possibility that their nationals might be held captives, and thus required a strict cooperation scheme between state-parties. On the other hand, developing states were mainly worried about potential interventions in their territories to combat hostage-taking incidents.[97] In the aftermath of Entebbe, the major question whether the use of force for the protection of nationals abroad was in accordance with international law remained unanswered. For this reason, negotiations regarding the adoption of the Hostages Convention carefully avoided touching upon this point.[98]

Although the raid qualifies as legitimate use of force under all legal bases, this did not prevent the intense political debate which ensued. The raid was a necessary, imminent and proportionate response by the Israeli military forces. This assessment is mostly factual and thus it cannot be easily overturned.[99] Yet, it heated the political dialogue and prompted legal responses. The disagreement between states over the raid's legality and consistency with the Charter is indicative of the inconclusive results of the forcible PNA discussion up till that time. Afterall, this raid was nothing but the ideotype of how forcible PNA should look like to be compatible with the Charter's most restrictive interpretations on the use of force.

[93] Knisbacher (1977), p. 73.

[94] Gordon (1977), p. 133.

[95] Paust (1978), p. 89.

[96] Franck (2001), p. 63.

[97] Byers (2004), p. 168.

[98] International Convention against the Taking of Hostages (17 December 1979). UNTS vol. 1316, p. 205.

[99] Fairley (1980), p. 54.

3.3.2 *The Raid's Contribution to the Protection of Nationals Abroad Doctrine*

The Entebbe raid took place at a time when there was no international legal context either on hostage-taking or on terrorism. Political debate followed the legal framework of the time, and it is not surprising that the same facts would have been treated in a completely different manner nowadays. Operation Thunderbolt conceptualized how small-scale military operations for the protection of nationals facing imminent threat should be organized. In retrospect, the raid was in alignment with the UNCh prerequisites in terms of necessity, imminence and proportionality.

Apart from the exact legal characterization of airplane hijacking, the crucial aspect concerned whether the legitimacy of such an operation relies on the consent of the state where the nationals are. Technically, a raid violates a state's territorial integrity even if it meets the prerequisites of Art. 51 UNCh. For this reason, willingness to cooperate or give consent by the host state are preconditions. In the Entebbe raid, Uganda's position was considered precarious at the very least. The Idi Amin government had been officially negotiating with the hijackers to release hostages, yet it had a poor history of cooperation with the Israeli authorities. This position was the source of the splitting of UN member-states. The cardinal question of the debate was posed by the UK delegation, namely, what a state could do to protect its nationals facing such a peril without trespassing on the territorial integrity of another state. Yet the query whether the means employed by Israel were justified by its ultimate goal was left unanswered. Current practice acknowledges that no rescue operation can take place without trespassing on a state's territory. Therefore, PNA is by default a difficult task for states to carry.

The Entebbe raid is deemed a necessary and proportionate rescue operation *ex post facto*. Despite the debate it raised at that time, it would nowadays make a rational choice for a state's whose nationals are taken hostages. Also, it poses inevitably a matter of comparison between the Entebbe hostages and the Israeli hostages of 2023. Although the peril is of the same type as victims are in both cases taken in captivity, making the necessity of a rescue operation a given in both cases, there is clear differentiation regarding proportionality. The Entebbe raid was deemed a success, judging by its result. Yet, it is not guaranteed that a rescue mission will succeed in protecting nationals.

What is not answered by these ascertainments is what are the limits of forcible PNA. Apart from the criteria of necessity, imminence and proportionality, there is no answer as to when a military operation aiming at releasing hostages must end. If protection is seen in sheer terms, then military operations must persist for as long as all nationals are released. However, this is a theoretical scenario far from the reality of most operations. In this regard, although the Entebbe incident is exemplary from an operational perspective, and led to the concept of NEOs, it does not provide solid responses to current problems regarding forcible PNA.

All in all, the doctrine's legitimacy walks a delicate line between the principle of non-intervention and the protection of a state's nationals and sovereign rights in turn. The technical aspect of territorial breaches is relegated to the need to rescue and release hostages.[100] Although Thunderbolt is exemplary, one cannot oversee that the captives' location was known, thus rendering the operation sharp and successful. However, if this condition is met, then again, an operation's success is not guaranteed.[101] This is the difference between Thunderbolt and Operation Eagle Claw for the release of the Tehran hostages.[102] If this condition was not met, then such an operation would not be a viable option. The same is not applicable on most occasions, turning rescue missions into large-scale military operations.

3.4 Protecting Nationals and Property Abroad: The British State Practice as the New Normal

The UK's practice regarding forcible PNA has been in the spotlight over the last years, emphasizing certain aspects of the doctrine. The UK has been among those states which embraced the doctrine from its naissance. It supports the view that a customary rule allowing states to have recourse to force to protect their nationals in jeopardy abroad existed before the UN, and insists that the norm survived the UNCh. The unique feature of the UK's policy is that it opts for a broadened version of the doctrine and considers recourse to force legitimate and permissible not only when nationals' lives are at risk, but also when nationals' vital interests are at stake.[103] In other words, the doctrine encompasses both life threats and property risks.[104]

The UK's state practice has been consistent over recent decades and earlier. The Pacifico incident and the development of gunboat diplomacy evolved during time. Apart from such pre-Charter incidents, as well as through the affirmation of the doctrine's existence in the *Corfu Channel* case,[105] the UK put forward the need to use force to protect their nationals' interests during the Suez Canal Crisis. The crisis was officially triggered by Egypt's decision to nationalize the Suez Canal Company, which administered the canal, and simultaneously its move to seize the canal on July 26, 1956. These acts led to military response by three states, namely Israel, France and the UK, in late October of the same year. France and the UK sent paratroopers to Egypt aiming at reversing the canal's nationalization and thus safeguarding the interests of the Suez Canal Company's shareholders. In this context, the UK invoked its right to self-defense under Art. 51 UNCh. Records of the debate in the

[100] Ruys (2014), p. 200.

[101] Kaztár and Balász (2021), p. 875.

[102] Gazit (1981), p. 115.

[103] Warbrick (1988), p. 1010.

[104] Güven and Ribbelink (2016), p. 60.

[105] See Chap. 2.

House of Commons on September 13, 1956, shed light on the major argumentative line adopted by the UK.

The then Secretary of State, Selwyn Lloyd, emphasized the interests of British nationals in Egypt and raised specific questions:

> How many expatriate soldiers are under martial law of our country? They are our own nationals. I am dealing with people who are not nationals of Egypt, but who are expatriates. I find it extraordinary that anyone should deny the right of these British citizens to withhold their labour, or complain because their employers propose to give them compensation for loss of employment.[106]

In addition, other members of the British Parliament referred to threats against British nationals that they would end up imprisoned if they refused to work on the nationalized canal. These statements are indicative of how the doctrine was perceived by British representatives. The invasion of Egypt lasted only a few days, and it ended without any tangible gains for the UK. Both the UK and France withdrew their military personnel, primarily due to intense diplomatic pressure exerted by the US and the USSR,[107] without securing military or strategic advantage.[108] Their attempts to reassert their prominent role in the canal zone failed at the first hurdle.[109]

There have been doubts over the invocation of Art. 51 UNCh, regarding the imminence and necessity of the intervention in particular. Although Secretary of State Lloyd made explicit reference to the Waldock criteria, most commentators have underlined that they were not met.[110] The lives of British nationals were not in immediate danger, although the deterioration of relations between Egypt and the UK was inevitable. In addition, it came to the surface that the three states that invaded Egypt had been planning the operation jointly, and for this some have called the crisis the "Tripartite Aggression".[111] Although this was not contrary to any international law norm, the careful planning of this intervention by three states reduced the strength of the self-defense argumentation.

As far as British discourse was concerned, PNA played an important role. In this framework, two elements stood out. First, the UK placed a protective shield over their citizens abroad. It was not only their lives that mattered, but also their economic interests, labor rights and fear of mistreatment. In this sense, the UK adopted the widest version of the doctrine; recourse to force was a means to guarantee their nationals' well-being and not just their existence. Second, the UK broadly

---

[106] UK Parliament, House of Commons (13 September 1956). Retrieved February 22, 2025, from https://hansard.parliament.uk/Commons/1956-09-13/debates/f95cd24b-6a90-4dfe-a1ef-c8119bdf2a8a/SuezCanal.

[107] Foreign Relations of the United States (1955–1957). Suez Crisis (July 26–December 31, 1956). Volume XVI, Document 35. Retrieved February 22, 2025, from https://history.state.gov/historicaldocuments/frus1955-57v16/d35.

[108] Bassiouni (1975), pp. 1070–1074; Smolansky (1965), pp. 581–605; Withana (2008), pp. 156–160.

[109] Lahav (2015), pp. 1309–1310.

[110] Fordoński (2022), pp. 197–198.

[111] Shlaim (1997), pp. 509–530.

interpreted the term "nationals". There were not only citizens who happened to be abroad during this dangerous outbreak of violence, but also people with dual citizenship, or British nationals who worked permanently in other states. The term "expatriates" was used interchangeably with that of "nationals" and denoted the ties between people abroad with the UK, either officially—meaning citizenship—or unofficially. The notion referred specifically to "citizens with long-term residence abroad" or else to "long-term external citizens".[112] The British foreign policy at the time regarding the right to use force is summarized in three reasons:

> (a) if an armed attack occurs, or is immediately threatened, against it; (b) if one of its rights is illegally and forcibly denied or threatened and no other remedy is available; or (c) if the lives of its nationals abroad are threatened.[113]

The above elements constituted British foreign policy regarding forcible PNA and of their interests in general. What differentiated this operation from the Congo example, referred to earlier, was predominantly the fact that the military intervention was brief. Attempting to draw a line between Belgium's invasion of Congo and the Suez Canal crisis, proportionality is the element which makes the difference. Although it is evident that both states acted as former colonial powers and attempted to prolong their influence in Congo and Egypt respectively, the UK was not criticized in such a harsh manner as Belgium, given that its use of force was not excessive and was focused only on the canal area. Overall, the UK's decision to resort to force was criticized only as humiliating.

The UK's state practice is actually best conceptualized through recent examples, *id est* operations in Sierra Leone.[114]

3.4.1 The UK Operation in Sierra Leone: NEOs and UN Authorization

The British military intervention in Sierra Leone took place in 2000. However, Sierra Leone was a state devastated and torn by civil war. Sierra Leone's capital, Freetown, had originally been created by the UK as a colony for free slaves, and eventually the rest of Sierra Leone's territory had fallen under British rule as a protectorate.[115] It had experienced trouble since it gained independence from the UK in 1961. During its short course of independence, Sierra Leone had not managed to reach internal peace, and political instability had been a reality. In 1991 a civil war between dominant tribes in Sierra Leone intensified. By 1999, when fighting erupted in the capital, Sierra Leone's infrastructure and public institutions were destroyed

---

[112] Bauböck (2009), p. 478.

[113] Marston (1988), p. 794.

[114] For a more comprehensive record of British military interventions see Gegout (2018), pp. 209–242.

[115] See Hargreaves (1956).

almost completely. Violence, alongside corruption and human rights abuses, were witnessed as everyday phenomena in Sierra Leone.[116]

The state faced an ongoing humanitarian crisis that resulted from ongoing battles.[117] The UN and the Economic Community of West African States (ECOWAS) took efforts to rescue people from extreme poverty and to guarantee minimum order in the state through aid packages and peacekeeping operations.[118] However, even international and regional initiatives were ineffective. Due to these circumstances, many states as well as international organizations considered Sierra Leone a failed state.[119] The turning point which prompted UK's military involvement in the situation in Sierra Leone was when the Revolutionary United Front (RUF) initiated "No Living Thing" in Freetown in May 2000. This insurgent movement resulted in more than 6000 deaths in Freetown and indiscriminate violence against civilian populations. The RUF's actions overturned the Lomé Peace Agreement which had been signed between the government of Sierra Leone and the RUF in 1997, providing for the cessation of hostilities and power sharing arrangements between them.[120]

The UK responded to this situation by launching Operation Palliser. UK's Prime Minister at the time, Tony Blair, mentioned shortly before the invasion of Sierra Leone that "the most pressing foreign policy problem we face is to identify the circumstances in which we should get actively involved in other people's conflicts" and further posed five distinct questions:

> First, are we sure of our case? War is an imperfect instrument for righting humanitarian distress; but armed force is sometimes the only means of dealing with dictators. Second, have we exhausted all diplomatic options? [...] Third, on the basis of a practical assessment of the situation, are there military operations we can sensibly and prudently undertake? Fourth, are we prepared for the long term? [...] And finally, do we have national interests involved?[121]

These were the pillars of British foreign policy from then on. Blair's establishment of the Doctrine of the International Community paved the way for the UK's intervention in Sierra Leone, and later in Iraq. As far as Sierra Leone was concerned, all of the above questions readily fulfilled the criteria for an affirmative answer. The safety of British citizens in Sierra Leone topped the list of national interests. At the same time, Sierra Leone was on the verge of chaos. Peace accords

[116] See Mitton (2015), pp. 14–20.

[117] Williams (2001), p. 146.

[118] Olonisakin (2017), pp. 629–641.

[119] Rotberg (2003), p. 6.

[120] UNSC (12 July 1999). Letter Dated 12 July 1999 from the Chargé d' Affairs ad interim of the Permanent Mission of Togo to the United Nations Addressed to the President of the Security Council. UN Doc S/1999/777, Annex; National Legislative Bodies / National Authorities, Sierra Leone: The Lomé Agreement between the Government of Sierra Lone and the Revolutionary United Front of Sierra Leone (7 July 1999). Retrieved February 22, 2025, from https://www.sierra-leone.org/Laws/1999-3.pdf.

[121] Blair (22 April 1999). Retrieved February 22, 2025, from http://www.britishpoliticalspeech.org/speech-archive.htm?speech=279.

had been breached, and diplomatic routes had been cut. In this framework, the British military intervention in 2000 received widespread acceptance from the international community.

More specifically, on May 6, 2000, the UK government ordered the deployment of a Joint Rapid Reaction Force to conduct a NEO and evacuate British, European, Commonwealth and American citizens from Sierra Leone. The rescue mission did not exclude other states' nationals, on the precondition that there was a previous agreement between their state of nationality and the UK. Within three days from the beginning of the NEO, UK forces evacuated the majority of approximately 1000 British nationals and transferred them safely to Senegal. According to reports, some people decided to remain in Sierra Leone as they felt that UK forces created a sense of stability, while some could not be evacuated as they resided in remote rural areas.

The UK had long been prepared for this NEO, and when the crisis began it was strategically and operationally ready. More specifically, British military personnel were trained for a potential operation in Sierra Leone. The British government had authorized similar smaller missions in Sierra Leone in the years preceding the NEO. According to military terminology, "two fact-finding and reconnaissance missions" to Sierra Leone had already taken place, with a view to familiarize military personnel with the environment and to get in touch with government and UN authorities onsite.[122]

Right after the evacuation had been accomplished, Operation Palliser transitioned and focused on counterinsurgency actions, aiming to stabilize the country and achieve an immediate end to hostilities. Initially, Operation Palliser was a NEO and was not meant to deploy counterinsurgency operations.[123] The operation was officially terminated on June 15, 2000, and it is considered a success to this day. Nevertheless, the UK continued to maintain enhanced military presence in the area and its personnel have aided regional and international peacekeeping missions in Sierra Leone.[124]

Unlike other similar operations, Operation Palliser was warmly welcomed by the international community, as well as by civilians in Sierra Leone.[125] The UK was not perceived as a violator of the principle of non-intervention, rather it was seen as a state willing to take on the burden of rescuing foreign citizens and guaranteeing stability in Sierra Leone. In operational terms, Palliser was mainly characterized by two features: it involved approximately 4500 British soldiers, sailors and marines and it was a low-intensity operation: that is, involving the deployment and use of soldiers in occasions other than war, such as non-state actors or counter insurgents. Clearly, the military personnel operating in Sierra Leone exceeded the needs of a rescue mission and targeted the defeat of the rebels.

---

[122] Berman and Labonte (2006), p. 181.

[123] Krieg (2013), p. 98.

[124] Gowan(2018), p. 859.

[125] Wheeler (2001), pp. 20–21.

On the international plane, Operation Palliser set a precedent. The UNSC issued eight resolutions regarding Sierra Leone in 2000. It kept a close eye on the conflict. Its resolutions regulated a wide range of issues, varying from the mandate, size and duration of the UN peacekeeping operation in Sierra Leone, the rules governing the trade of diamonds, as well as the establishment of a special court.[126] The British operation was a typically unilateral one, since there was no prior authorization by the UNSC. In turn, the use of force by the UK in Sierra Leone was in grammatical terms against the provisions of the UNCh and constituted a breach of Art. 2(4) and the principle of non-intervention. What is more, it soon became obvious that British involvement exceeded the limits of self-defense, assuming that Operation Palliser was established on such a legal basis. Not only were British actions not condemned by the UNSC, but on the contrary, UNSC Res 1299(2000), which was adopted amidst the British operation, among others, declared that it:

> Expresses its appreciation to all States who, in order to expedite the rapid reinforcement of UNAMSIL, have accelerated the deployment of their troops to UNAMSIL, made available additional personnel, and offered logistical, technical and other forms of military assistance, and calls upon all those in a position to do so to provide further support.[127]

The above wording left room for unilateral rescue missions and counter-insurgency operations, given that it refers to "other forms of military assistance". Indeed, after the evacuation of British nationals, military personnel assisted the UN peacekeeping forces in Sierra Leone and cooperated with them for as long as they remained onsite. In addition, the UN Secretary-General in his statement on May 11, 2000, mentioned that

> the United Kingdom has made an invaluable contribution by securing the airport. The presence of British troops, even for a limited time and with a limited mandate, is a very important stabilizing factor.[128]

Many SC members were drafted in the Secretary-General's opinion, emphasizing mostly the UK's contribution to securing the airport, which allowed additional peacekeeping forces to reach Freetown. Yet the language used by them varied. The US recognized that the UK's military deployment "helped stabilize the situation",[129] France welcomed "the speedy intervention of the United Kingdom",[130] Portugal stressed the fact that an EU member-state had made "an important military contribution" to the conflict,[131] while Namibia expressed its "high appreciation to the United Kingdom Government".[132] These statements affirmed the UN's positive

---

[126] UNSC (7 February 2000). Res 1289(2000); UNSC (5 July 2000). Res 1306(2000); UNSC (4 August 2000). Res 1313(2000); UNSC (14 August 2000). Res 1315(2000); UNSC (5 September 2000). Res 1317(2000); UNSC (22 December 2000). Res 1334(2000).

[127] UNSC (19 May 2000). Res 1299(2000), op. clause 2.

[128] UNSC S/PV.4139 (11 May 2000), p. 3.

[129] ibid, 8.

[130] ibid, 18.

[131] ibid, 22.

[132] ibid, 14.

reaction to this unilateral military operation. Stepping back from the UN Secretary-General's position, the references to a "limited time" and "a limited mandate" revealed the confines of unilateral military operations within the UN system in the first place. Reading this part in conjunction with the UK's position, though, clarifies why the UK's actions in Sierra Leone were significant in relation to the forcible PNA doctrine. The representative of the UK in the UNSC stated that:

> The United Kingdom has taken a number of important steps to support UNAMSIL. Last weekend we deployed the British Spearhead Battalion to Freetown. That deployment is primarily for the evacuation of United Kingdom nationals. But we also believe that the deployment of our troops, who have secured Lungi airport, made a real contribution to the efforts of UNAMSIL. We have kept that vital link open and thus freed up UNAMSIL troops to concentrate on their wider task. I am grateful to the Secretary-General for his kind words about the effect the presence of our forces has had, and I will ensure that they are passed on to those concerned.[133]

That is, the UK's foreign policy relied primarily on the necessity to protect its nationals abroad, and on occasion to offer military support to UN peacekeepers. This is why the timeframe and content of its military operation was limited in the first place. According to official policy statements made before the UNSC, and Kofi Annan's speech, it seems that the forcible protection of nationals abroad was not outlawed by the UN regime. References to limited time and mandate pointed directly to the requirements set by Art. 51 UNCh, and in particular to NEOs.[134]

In this regard, the British evacuation operation in Sierra Leone set the foundations for the doctrine's re-interpretation. The Sierra Leone incident provided a solid answer to the question whether the doctrine had survived the UNCh and in what form it was permitted by the international legal system. NEOs seem to have been a substitute for the archetypical understanding of the protection of nationals abroad doctrine and to provide an alternative way which does not put states in a position to choose between their obligation to protect their nationals abroad and that of respecting the principle of non-intervention. According to the UK's Ministry of Defence

> [n]on-combatant evacuation operations involve the relocation of designated non-combatants, threatened in a foreign country, to a place of safety. In the event of a crisis that requires the evacuation of eligible persons, it will be the Foreign, Commonwealth and Development Office that coordinates the evacuation and they may request support from the Ministry of Defence. Land forces can be committed to provide security to the evacuation operation. Examples include Operation Pitting in Kabul (2021), Operation Highbrow in Beirut (2006) and Operation Palliser in Sierra Leone (2000).[135]

This description reveals which operations form the new normal regarding forcible PNA. Protection of a state's nationals facing peril abroad is a good cause for the design and execution of a rescue operation. Although such operations are not meant to breach international norms, their non-combatant character can only be secured through the support of defense forces. This depends on the military risks, the level

---

[133] ibid, 7.

[134] Thomson (2012), pp. 665–668.

[135] Ministry of Defence (2023), p. 53.

of hostility at the operation's location etc. From this perspective, NEOs are not meant to involve the use of force, but are designed to do so if needed, for the safety of both rescuers and civilians in peril. This admission puts forcible PNA and NEOs in a realistic perspective, where operational guarantees are pivotal for all those involved in such operations. Apart from the doctrinal part, evacuation and / or rescue operations involve by definition a certain degree of risk which shall be avoided or at least mitigated. Operation Palliser and the ones to follow demonstrated how doctrinal remarks differ from operational concerns. This discrepancy is no novelty in this legal field. According to the British take on forcible PNA, if the protection of nationals requires an evacuation or rescue operation, then the kin-state shall be prepared to use force if needed. In simple terms, if PNA takes the form of a NEO then it is designed to be forcible. This scheme resembles a lot that of peacekeeping operations where force is permitted at a tactical level, as a means of self-defense, or defense of the mandate.[136] This is the reason why according to the British manual it is the Ministry of Defence holding a role in support of NEOs.

3.5 The Embracement of NEOs by the UNSC

Acceptance of the British evacuation operation in Sierra Leone changed the international landscape regarding NEOS. The case which best describes this development is the UNSC's response to the situation in Libya in 2011. On February 15, 2011, rebellion against Muammar Al-Qaddafi's forty-year rule broke out in the context of the so-called Arab Spring, which had affected several states' political structure up to this time. However, in Libya this revolt met harsh repression by Al-Qaddafi's forces and civil war began.[137] Violence quickly escalated, attracting the attention of the international community and further necessitating action. The UNSC showed quick reflexes and added the situation in Libya to its agenda on February 22, 2011.[138] The major issue of concern, following numerous debates and briefings, was the cessation of violence and more specifically the protection of the civilian population which had suffered excessive casualties from the very beginning. The UN Secretary-General Ban Ki-moon described the situation as extremely critical and pointed out that

> the first obligation of the international community is to do everything possible to ensure the immediate protection of civilians at demonstrable risk. Indeed, if further proof is required it should be sought simultaneously with measures to afford protection.[139]

---

[136] Tsagourias (2015), pp. 399–402.

[137] Anderson (2011), p. 6.

[138] UNSC (22 February 2011). Official communiqué of the 648th (closed) meeting of the Security Council. UN Doc S/PV.6486.

[139] UN Doc S/PV.6490 (25 February 2011), p. 3.

These circumstances prompted UNSC Resolutions under Chapter VII, mainly with the scope of bringing stability to Libya, which was spiraling deeper into civil war. In this framework, a side issue which concerned the UNSC a few days later was the rescue of foreign citizens trapped in Libya at the time. Many states communicated their concerns at consecutive meetings. India was the first to mention that it was alarmed for "the safety of Indian nationals and their assets in Libya" and further urged "the authorities there to ensure their safety and welfare and facilitate the departure of those desirous of leaving the country".[140] This course of thinking was adopted by numerous members of the UNSC, namely the UK, Portugal[141] and Mauritania, which highlighted the need to secure a free evacuation route for migrant workers who desperately sought to escape from Libya.[142]

As a result, the two UNSC Resolutions adopted under Chapter VII addressed the issue of the protection of foreigners in Libya and provision for their safe evacuation. In UNSC Res 1970(2011), states expressed their concern "for the safety of foreign nationals and their rights in the Libyan Arab Jamahiriya" and further requested "all Member States, to the extent possible, to cooperate in the evacuation of those foreign nationals wishing to leave the country".[143] The fact that this resolution was unanimously adopted by the UNSC member-states demonstrates that their views coincided on the issue. States upheld the need to evacuate foreign nationals from a land where they faced imminent threat to life. In this sense, the UNSC endorsed states' obligation to facilitate their nationals' evacuation from troubled regions.

Building on this decision, UNSC Res 1973(2011) repeated the Council's resolute concern for the safety of foreign nationals and their rights and further authorized the use of force in Libya according to the international community's R2P.[144] The UNSC authorization gave the green light for numerous NEOs led either by the US or the EU under the condition that the UN Secretary-General was duly and timely notified.[145] The US launched Operation Odyssey Dawn, assisting in a multinational safe evacuation from Libya and Tunisia, while the UK proceeded with Operation Deference. At the same time, Germany launched Operation Pegasus and Canada ran Operation Mobile.[146] Finally, it is worth mentioning that China was the state with the largest population in Libya; approximately 16,000 Chinese citizens were evacuated from Libya via Greek passenger ships.[147] The above is indicative of the extensive cooperation between states for citizens' protection, and also of China's

[140] UN Doc S/PV.6491 (26 February 2011), p. 2.

[141] UN Doc S/PV.6498 (17 March 2011), p. 8.

[142] UN Doc S/PV.6555 (15 June 2011), p. 2.

[143] UN Doc (26 February 2011). S/Res/1970(2011), preambulatory clause, op. clause 3.

[144] UN Doc (17 Match 2011). S/Res/1973(2011), preambulatory clause, op. clause 4.

[145] UN Doc S/PV.6505 (24 March 2011), pp. 3–4.

[146] Dixon (2017), p. 55.

[147] Reuters Staff (27 February 2011). Retrieved February 22, 2025, from https://www.reuters.com/article/uk-libya-protests-evacuation-idUSLNE71M02220110227.

180 degree turn on this issue.[148] The fact that these NEOs were endorsed by the UN was a guarantee for states to approve their participation in kinetic operations.[149]

In the end, NATO began assuming responsibilities and coordinated the operations of twelve states deployed in the territory of Libya. Operation Odyssey Dawn was renamed Unified Protector.[150] However, as soon as NATO took on the whole military operation in Libya, after UNSC authorization, there has been a distinct shift in the operational character of the intervention. Operation Unified Protector was not related to evacuation of foreign nationals in Libya; rather, its scope was to protect civilians and civilian-populated areas under threat of attack.[151]

The case of Libya simplified the legal debate revolving around forcible PNA. Given that the UNSC authorized the use of force in Libya on humanitarian grounds, these evacuation operations had a clear, distinct aim. In this sense, there could be no confusion about their scope or extent, and invocation of the forcible PNA doctrine was uncontroversial.[152] The UNSC endorsed state cooperation on the evacuation of foreign nationals from Libya, thus accepting the concept of multinational rescue operations. These resolutions were considered to mark a shift in the UNSC's approach towards R2P and by extension to the forcible PNA doctrine.[153] Nevertheless, legal scholarship remained divided as to whether PNA was still tolerated by the UNCh, or if these UNSC decisions bore proof of its legitimacy in the UN regime.[154] In addition, given the involvement of NATO in Libya and the duration of these operations, it became evident that PNA was not the epicenter of attention. Both the UN and NATO aimed at securing civilians from the war that had started tearing apart Libya. In this sense, it is suggested that the use of force, even for the protection of nationals in peril, was finally a pretext for intervention, taking advantage of the UNSC authorization. Several states upheld that NATO's interpretation of the UNSC Resolution was a result of misinterpretation and manipulation,[155] further pointing at the dangers hidden in invoking, or accepting forcible PNA.

3.6 The Proliferation of NEOs

State cooperation for the protection of nationals residing abroad, or for the shield of financial interests, is by now intensified. Multinational NEOs are institutionalized and incorporated in most states' military manuals. Multinational NEOs have become

148 Baum (2020), pp. 259–273.

149 Quartararo et al. (2012), p. 144.

150 Alton and Struble (2014), p. 9; Phinney (2014), p. 89.

151 Wester (2020), p. 223.

152 Grimal and Melling (2011), p. 166.

153 Bellamy and Williams (2011), pp. 825–850.

154 Shesterinina (2016), p. 820.

155 Ulfstein and Christiansen (2013), p. 170; Payandeh (2012), p. 383.

a useful tool in the hands of states for two reasons. First, their multinational character is thought to offer them legal justification. States do not resort to force unilaterally, but they share with others the policy that a NEO is necessary for the promotion of their interests. Second, the multinational character of NEOs implies a more prudent management of human and financial resources. States allocate military operational tasks and there is a preferential use of the sectors they are more specialized in.

During the last years, multinational military operations have multiplied. This new trend is the result of the entangled globalized world, meaning that certain actions affect simultaneously more than one state. The question that has occupied legal discussion recently is whether PNA is not exhausted to nationals residing in a third state abroad, but it includes all perils nationals may face outside their country's borders and jurisdiction. The example of the "new multinational security initiative", codenamed "Operation Prosperity Guardian",[156] for the protection of international shipping in the Red Sea by the Houthis attacks is revealing. This occasion is unique in many aspects. To begin with, Operation Prosperity Guardian is oriented towards freedom and security of navigation. The states involved attempt to limit and eventually stop attacks by the Houthis against private and public ships. In this sense, this multinational operation is not a NEO. However, the scope of securing free navigation is not only an issue of financial interest. It also aims at protecting people onboard. Therefore, PNA is an indispensable part of the operation. So far, theory has approached the current situation through the lens of the law of the sea. Thus, Operation Prosperity Guardian qualifies as a response to acts of piracy, according to the UN Convention on the Law of the Sea (UNCLOS),[157] and as such its legality is not doubted.

This view is prevalent, and rightly so, given that the operation takes place at sea, and it shall be governed by the relevant legal regime. Yet, examining only the law of the sea aspects of it, is oversimplifying. The states involved openly proclaimed that protection of their nationals, or ships with their flag, is one of the prominent scopes of this operation. More specifically, American commanders are instructed to defend designated non-U.S. military forces, and foreign nationals against hostile acts, or hostile intent, when they receive such an authorization. This view demonstrates how the states participating in this multinational operation perceive their acts as acts of self-defense and adopt the doctrine of "collective self-defense".[158]

The second unique feature relates to the operational parameters of this coalition. One would normally expect that protection from hostile acts would cover only those vessels flagged with a flag of the participating states, or their allies, and normally any intervention would take place after the consent of the flag state. Yet, this doctrinal prerequisite cannot be achieved, taking into account how hostile the

[156] U.S. Department of Defense (18 December 2023). Retrieved, February 22, 2025, from https://www.defense.gov/News/Releases/Release/Article/3621110/statement-from-secretary-of-defense-lloyd-j-austin-iii-on-ensuring-freedom-of-n/.

[157] Papastavridis (2024). Retrieved February 22, 2025, from https://www.eliamep.gr/wp-content/uploads/2024/01/Insights-2-Red-Sea-EN.pdf, p. 8.

[158] Pedrozo (2024), pp. 65–66.

environment is. If prior consent was an unbreakable term for intervention, then the effectiveness of such an operation would be minimized.[159] This deviation from use of force standards is considered minor, as it is imposed by the imminence of the threats confronted onboard and thus is tolerated. At the same time though, a paradoxical scheme is created. Multinational forces guarantee the safety of foreign civilians, and foreign vessels without having necessarily attained their prior consent. If these acts are seen through the forcible PNA perspective, then the doctrine is highly relativized, given that a state uses force to protect its nationals, or any nationals, as well as its property, or any property. From this perspective it resembles multinational NEOs, except there is no prior arrangement on the nationality of the ones to be saved.

If Operation Prosperity Guardian is to be related to forcible PNA then the new trend relativizes the concepts both of territoriality, and nationality. Territoriality is legal fiction, given that the operation takes place in international waters and breach of territoriality comes only as a matter of the flags of the vessels. Respectively, there is no certainty that nationality ties exist, given that in private vessels the crews are by definition multinational. This is an operational novelty and shows how state practice reshapes the forcible PNA doctrine, and use of force theory in general.

3.7 Conclusions

The preceding analysis is definitely not exhaustive, yet some patterns on the doctrine's use have come up, also revealing how state practice copes with the obligations stemming from the UN Charter. Forcible PNA has been used occasionally, as a pretext for a state's intervention in the domestic affairs of another. The doctrine's invocation on such occasions is discrediting its legal value. However, this was not anew; forcible PNA is inextricably linked with states' strategic national interests and the line between them is obscure. Taking into consideration that it lies upon states absolute discretion whether they will recourse to force to protect their nationals, in conjunction with the fact that nowadays people can reside anywhere, it comes that forcible PNA is not only a matter of factual necessity, but also a political choice. In this sense, the fact that a state's nationals can today be spread all over the globe, renders the doctrine a suitable justification for intervening in a state's national affairs.

This conclusion also implies that the doctrine is employed by states with the political power and financial resources to deploy operations for the protection of their citizens abroad. It is a realistic feature which partly reaffirms why the doctrine is invoked by states with some degree of international power and/or influence. Finally, recent post-Cold War practice points at the operational value of NEOs. The value of these operations rest on their dissociation from the principle of

[159] See, U.S. Navy, U.S. Marine Corps and U.S. Coast Guard (March 2022).

non-intervention. Technically, non-combatant evacuation operations breach a state's territorial integrity and sovereignty, yet they do not equate to an invasion. In addition, NEOs are recognized as necessary under certain circumstances. That is, when the international community confronts situations where states are on the verge of chaos, jeopardizing the lives of both national and foreign civilian populations, it tolerates recourse to force for PNA.[160]

The above make up a mosaic which renders it difficult to conclude in objective legal criteria regarding the doctrine's invocation. NEOs enjoy a certain level of acceptance among states as they are considered the least intrusive tool, when the lives of nationals are at stake. This level of acceptance relies both on their necessity and most importantly on the fact that NEOs offer a standardized pattern of force, which minimizes the threat of rampant use of force. However, it is already mentioned that NEOs do not cover the doctrine's ambit. Although there seems to be general consensus as to their use and necessity, nevertheless NEOs are not the answer regarding the doctrine's legal basis. The preceding analysis emphasizes on states' invocation of the doctrine in a wide range of cases: some invoke the doctrine echoing pre-Charter hegemonical policies, other occasions are based on a more realistic need for protection, while there are cases where forcible PNA is the only viable solution.

Forcible PNA's legality is not only a matter of doctrinal interpretation, rather the appraisal of a series of criteria, like the type of peril faced by nationals, the number of people in jeopardy, the existence of hostile environment and so on. In this sense, it is more than expected to have many different readings of the doctrine. If one was to determine which is the common denominator in state practice regarding forcible PNA, then the only safe reference point would be the detachment of sovereignty from territoriality. This proposition goes both ways: first, states consider their prerogative, or duty to protect their nationals abroad, thus affirming the extraterritorial aspect of sovereignty. A state consists of its people, ergo sovereignty is where a state's peoples are. Reversely, a military operation to protect people facing imminent peril is technically a violation of a state's soil, but not necessarily a violation of its sovereignty, as long as these operations do not have a permanent impact on its territorial integrity.

This reading of forcible PNA serves states' national interests to protect their citizens abroad and fend them from ravaged areas. However, any proposition for a slight detachment of territoriality from sovereignty is a point of friction and carries risks, as will be seen below. Overall, when emphasis is put on the practical and operational aspects of forcible PNA, the multifaceted character of sovereignty is highlighted. There cannot be an absolute perception of sovereignty, given that both its limbs, territoriality and nationality have changed over the course of time. This fluidity has reshaped state practice creating a new reality, where rescue or evacuation operations are founded on coalitions and have a multinational character. Simultaneously, these shifts affect the doctrinal value of forcible PNA and cast

[160] Alcala and Nasu (2023), p. 16.

away any doubts regarding its legality in the post-Charter era. Afterall, the absolute prohibition of the use of force is out of question, given the doctrines which have developed during the last decades, coupled with state practice. Forcible PNA is no exception to this. The doctrine has long been invoked by states; its transformations follow those of sovereignty and the understanding of territoriality and nationality.

UN Documentation

International Convention against the Taking of Hostages (17 December 1979). UNTS vol. 1316, p. 205.

UNSC

UN Doc S/PV.6555 (15 June 2011).
UN Doc S/PV.6505 (24 March 2011).
UN Doc S/Res/1973(2011) (17 March 2011).
UN Doc S/PV.6498 (17 March 2011).
UN Doc S/Res/1970(2011) (26 February 2011).
UN Doc S/PV.6491 (26 February 2011).
UN Doc S/PV.6490 (25 February 2011).
UNSC (22 February 2011). Official communiqué of the 648th (closed) meeting of the Security Council. UN Doc S/PV.6486.
UNSC (22 December 2000). Res 1334(2000).
UNSC (5 September 2000). Res 1317(2000).
UNSC (14 August 2000). Res 1315(2000).
UNSC (4 August 2000). Res 1313(2000).
UNSC (5 July 2000). Res 1306(2000).
UNSC (19 May 2000). Res 1299(2000).
UNSC (11 May 2000). S/PV.4139.
UNSC (7 February 2000). Res 1289(2000).
UNSC (12 July 1999). Letter Dated 12 July 1999 from the Chargé d' Affairs ad interim of the Permanent Mission of Togo to the United Nations Addressed to the President of the Security Council. UN Doc S/1999/777.
UNSC Official Records (14 July 1976). UN Doc S/PV.1943.
UNSC Official Records (9 July 1976). Complaint by the Prime Minister of Mauritius, current Chairman of the Organization of African Unity, of the "act of aggression" by Israel against the Republic of Uganda.
UNSC (14 May 1965). Res 203(1965).
UNSC (9 December 1964). Questions Concerning the Democratic Republic of Congo. Res 199(1964). UN Doc S/6129.
UNSC (14 July 1960). The Congo Question. Res 143(1960). UN Doc S/4387.

UNGA

UNGA (29 December 1989). Effects of the military intervention by the United States of America in Panama on the Situation in Central America. UN Doc A/44/PV.88.

UNGA (2 November 1983). The situation in Grenada. UN Doc A/Res/38/7.

UNGA (15–17 December 1970). Programme of action for the full implementation of the Declaration on the Granting of Independence to Colonial Countries and Peoples. UN Doc A/Res/2621(XXV).

UNGA (14 December 1960). Declaration on the Granting of Independence to Colonial Countries and Peoples. UN Doc A/Res/1514(XV).

OAS

OAS (June 1 to August 31, 1965). Report on the Activities of the Inter-American Commission on Human Rights in the Dominican Republic. OEA/Ser.L/V/II.13 doc 14 Rev.

OAS (30 April 1948). Charter of the Organization of American States. Bogota OAS T.S. Nos 1-C and 61.

Miscellaneous

Ministry of Defence, Joint Doctrine Publication 0-20, UK Land Power (6th edn.). Retrieved February 22, 2025, from https://assets.publishing.service.gov.uk/media/6523da4aaea2d000132199d4/20231008-JDP_0_20_UK_Land_Power.pdf.

National Legislative Bodies / National Authorities, Sierra Leone: The Lomé Agreement between the Government of Sierra Lone and the Revolutionary United Front of Sierra Leone (7 July 1999). Retrieved February 22, 2025, from https://www.sierra-leone.org/Laws/1999-3.pdf.

Treaty establishing the Organisation of Eastern Caribbean States (Treaty of Basseterre) (18 June 1981). Retrieved February 22, 2025, from http://ctrc.sice.oas.org/CARICOM/OECS/Treaty_basseterre.pdf.

United States of America and Panama (7 September 1977). Panama Canal Treaty. UNTS Vol. 1280, I. Nos 21086–21107, p. 3.

U.S. Navy, U.S. Marine Corps and U.S. Coast Guard (March 2022). The Commander's Handbook on the Law of Naval Operations. NWP 1-14M, MCTP 11-10B, COMDTPUB P5800.7A.

References

Books

Chehtman A (2010) The philosophical foundations of extraterritorial punishment. Oxford University Press

Clayton LA, Conniff ML, Gauss SM (2017) A new history of modern Latin America, 3rd edn. University of California Press

Dunstan S (2012) Israel's lightning strike: the Raid on Entebbe 1976. Bloomsbury Publishing

Gegout C (2018) Why Europe intervenes in Africa: security prestige and the legacy of colonialism. Oxford University Press

Henkin L (1979) How nations behave, law and foreign policy, 2nd edn. Columbia University Press

James A (1996) Britain and the Congo Crisis, 1960–63. Macmillan Press Ltd.

Krieg A (2013) Motivations for humanitarian intervention, theoretical and empirical considerations. Springer

Mitton K (2015) Rebels in a rotten state: understanding atrocity in the Sierra Leone Civil War. Oxford University Press

Palmer B Jr (1989) Intervention in the Caribbean: the Dominican crisis of 1965. The University Press of Kentucky

Rezvani DA (2014) Surpassing the sovereign state, the wealth, self-rule, and security advantages of partially independent territories. Oxford University Press

Shaw MN (2021) International law, 9th edn. Cambridge University Press

Stilz A (2019) Territorial sovereignty, a philosophical exploration. Oxford University Press

Vanthemsche G (2012) Belgium and the Congo 1885-1980 (trans: Cameron A, Windross S). Cambridge University Press

Wester K (2020) Intervention in Libya, the responsibility to protect in North Africa. Cambridge University Press

Withana R (2008) Power, politics, law: international law and state behaviour during international crises. Martinus Nijhoff Publishers

Wood M, Sthoeger E (2022) The UN Security Council and International Law. Cambridge University Press

Articles

Acevedo DE (1984) Collective self-defense and the use of regional or subregional authority as justification for the use of force. Am Soc Int Law Proc 78:69–73

Akehurst M (1977) The use of force to protect nationals abroad. Int Relat 5(5):3–23

Alcala R, Nasu H (2023) The protection of nationals abroad and combatant evacuation operations in times of crisis. J Natl Secur Law Policy 14(1):1–28

Alton RAC, Struble JR (2014) The constitutionality and advancement of international humanitarian ideals in Libya by NATO and United States' Operations Odyssey Dawn and Unified Protector. Tulane J Int Comp Law 23(1):1–36

Anderson L (2011) Demystifying the Arab Spring, parsing the differences between Tunisia, Egypt, and Libya. Foreign Aff 90(1):2–7

Azar EE, Jureidini P, McLaurin R (1978/1979) Protracted social conflict: theory and practice in the Middle East. J Palest Stud 8(1):41–60

Bassiouni MS (1975) Suez 1956: international crisis and the role of law. DePaul Law Rev 24(4):1070–1074

Bauböck R (2009) The rights and duties of external citizenship. Citizenship Stud 13(5):475–499

Baum TJ (2020) The responsibility of power: shifts in Chinese conceptualization of the legitimacy of overseas intervention to protect nationals abroad. Global Change Peace Secur 32(3):259–273
Bellamy AJ, Williams PD (2011) The new politics of protection? Côte d'Ivoire, Libya and the responsibility to protect. Int Aff 87(4):825–850
Berman A (1990) In mitigation of illegality: the U.S. Invasion of Panama. Kentucky Law J 79(4):735–800
Bogen DS (1966) The Law of Humanitarian Intervention: United States Policy in Cuba (1898) and in the Dominican Republic (1965). Harv Int Law Club J 7(2):296–315
Boyle FA (1980–1981) International law in time of crisis: from the Entebbe Raid to the Hostages Intervention. Northwest Univ Law Rev 75:769–856
Byers M (2004) Agreeing to disagree: Security Council Resolution 1441 and international ambiguity. Global Gov 10(2):165–186
D'Amato A (1990) The invasion of Panama was a lawful response to tyranny. Am J Int Law 84(2):516–524
Dixon GK (2017) The need for a joint support element in noncombatant evacuation operations. Joint Force Q 85(2):50–57
Dore II (1984) The U.S. Invasion of Grenada: Resurrection of the Johnson Doctrine. Stanford J Int Law 20(1):173–190
Dreier JC (1968) New wine and old bottles: the changing Inter-American System. Int Organ 22(2):477–493
Fairley HS (1980) State actors, humanitarian intervention and international law: reopening Pandora's Box. Georgia J Int Comp Law 10(1):29–64
Fordoński R (2022) Regime change on the pretext of forcible protection of nationals abroad: selected case studies including Ukraine, Dominicana and Egypt. Studia Prawnoustrojowe 57:191–203
Franck T (1961–1962) Political problems incident to United Nations Intervention in the Congo. Proc Am Branch Int Law Assoc 1961:52–55
Franck TM (2001) When, if ever, may states deploy military force without prior security council authorization? Wash Univ J Law Policy 5:51–71
Furlong WL (1993) Panama: the difficult transition towards democracy. J Interam Stud World Aff 35(3):19–64
Gazit S (1981) Risk, glory, and the rescue operation. Int Secur 6(1):111–135
Gilboa, E. (1995–1996). The Panama Invasion Revisited: lessons for the use of force in the post cold era. Polit Sci Q, 110(4), 539–562.
Gordon DJ (1977) Use of force for the protection of nationals abroad: The Entebbe Incident. Case West Reserve J Int Law 9(1):117–134
Gordon E (1984) International law and the United States action in Grenada. Int Lawyer 18(2):331–380
Graber DA (1958) The Truman and Eisenhower doctrines in the light of the doctrine of non-intervention. Polit Sci Q 73(3):321–334
Grant TD (2009) Regulating the creation of states from decolonization to secession. J Int Law Int Relat 5(2):11–58
Grimal F, Melling G (2011) British action in Libya 2011: the lawful protection of nationals abroad? Denning Law J 23(1):165–177
Hahn PL (2006) Securing the Middle East: The Eisenhower Doctrine of 1957. Pres Stud Q 36(1):38–47
Hakimi M (2007) To condone or condemn? Regional enforcement actions in the absence of security council authorization. Vanderbilt J Transnatl Law 40:643–685
Hardt DB (1987) Grenada reconsidered. Fletcher Forum 11(2):277–308
Hargreaves JD (1956) The establishment of the Sierra Leone Protectorate and the Insurrection of the 1898. Camb Hist J 12(1):56–80
Harrell PE (2008) Modern-day guarantee clauses and the legal authority of multinational organizations to authorize the use of military force. Yale J Int Law 33:417–446

Henkin L (1991) The Invasion of Panama under international law: a gross violation. Columbia J Transnatl Law 29(2):293–318

Hickey JE (2004) Challenges to Security Council monopoly power over the use of force in enforcement actions: the case of regional organizations. Ius Gentium 10:75–129

Karas JM, Goodman JM (1984) The United States Action in Grenada: an exercise in realpolitik. Univ Miami Inter-Am Law Rev 16(1):53–108

Kaztár G, Balász GB (2021) Beyond Tehran and Nairobi: can attacks against embassies serve as a basis for the invocation of self-defence? Eur J Int Law 32(3):863–888

Knisbacher M (1977) The Entebbe Operation: a legal analysis of Israel's Rescue Action. J Int Law Econ 12(1):57–84

Kritsiotis D (1998) Reappraising policy objections to humanitarian intervention. Mich J Int Law 19(4):1005–1050

Lahav P (2015) The Suez Crisis of 1956 and its Aftermath: a comparative study of constitutions, use of force, diplomacy and international relations. Boston Univ Law Rev 95(4):1297–1354

Lillich RB (1992) Forcible protection of nationals abroad: the Liberian Incident of 1990. German Yearb Int Law 35:205–223

Little D (1996) His finest hour? Eisenhower, Lebanon, and the 1958 Middle East Crisis. Diplomatic Hist 20(1):27–54

Maizel SR (1986) Intervention in Grenada. Naval Law Rev 35:47–86

Marcum JA (1961) Unilateral intervention in the Congo and its political consequences. Am Soc Int Law Proc 55(First Session):27–29

Marston G (1988) Armed intervention in the 1956 Suez Canal Crisis: the legal advice tendered to the British Government. Int Comp Law Q 37(4):773–817

McDowell EC (1976) United Nations: Security Council Debate and Draft Resolutions concerning the operation to rescue hijacked hostages at the Entebbe Airport. Int Leg Mater 15(5):1224–1234

McLaren JPS (1966) The Dominican Crisis: an Inter-American Dilemma. Can Yearb Int Law 4:178–193

Meyer JA (1993) Collective self-defense and regional security: necessary exceptions to a globalist doctrine. Boston Univ Int Law J 11(2):391–434

Millett RL (1990) The Aftermath of Intervention: Panama 1990. J Interam Stud World Aff 32(1):1–15

Murphy SD (2009) Criminalizing humanitarian intervention. Case West Res J Int Law 41(2–3):341–378

Mushkat M (1972) The process of decolonization international legal aspects. Univ Baltimore Law Rev 2(1):16–34

Nanda VP (1966) The United States' Action in the 1965 Dominican Crisis: Impact on World Order – Part I. Denver Law J 43(4):439–479

Nanda VP (1990) The validity of United States Intervention in Panama under international law. Am J Int Law 84(2):494–503

Naughton JF (1965) The Dominican Crisis: an examination of traditional and contemporary concepts of international law. Duquesne Univ Law Rev 4(4):547–566

Özsu U (2020) Organizing internationally: Georges Abi-Saab, the Congo Crisis and the Decolonization of the United States. Eur J Int Law 31(2):601–619

Papermaster DI (1989) A case study of the effect of international law on foreign policy decisionmaking: the United States Intervention in the Dominican Republic in 1965. Tex Int Law J 24(3):463–498

Paust JJ (1978) Entebbe and self-help: the Israeli response to terrorism. Fletcher Forum 2(1):86–91

Payandeh M (2012) The United Nations, military intervention, and regime change in Libya. Va J Int Law 52(2):355–403

Pedrozo P (2024) Protecting the free flow of commerce from Houthi Attacks off the Arabian Peninsula. Int Law Stud 103:49–73

Phinney TR (2014) Reflections on operation unified protector. Joint Force Q 73(1):86–92

Quartararo J, Rovenolt M, White R (2012) Libya's Operation Odyssey Dawn, Command and Control. PRISM 3(2):141–156
Quigley, J. (1986–1987). The United States Invasion of Grenada: stranger than fiction. Univ Miami Inter-Am Law Rev, 18(2), 271–352.
Quigley J (1990) The legality of the United States Invasion in Panama. Yale J Int Law 15(2):276–315
Rabe SG (2006) The Johnson Doctrine. Pres Stud Q 36(1):48–58
Riggs RM (1985) The Grenada Intervention: a legal analysis. Mil Law Rev 109:1–82
Ronzitti N (2019) Rescuing nationals abroad revisited. J Conflict Secur Law 24(3):431–448
Rosoux V (2014) The two faces of Belgium in the Congo: perpetrator and rescuer. Eur Rev Int Stud 1(3):16–38
Rumage SA (1993) Panama and the myth of humanitarian intervention in U.S. foreign policy: neither legal nor moral, neither just nor right. Ariz J Int Comp Law 10(1):1–76
Ruys T (2014) The meaning of "force" and the boundaries of the Jus Ad Bellum: are "minimal" uses of force excluded from UN Charter Article 2(4)? Am J Int Law 108(2):159–210
Schachter O (1984a) The legality of pro-democratic invasion. Am J Int Law 78(3):645–650
Schachter O (1984b) The right of states to use armed force. Mich Law Rev 82(5&6):1620–1646
Shesterinina A (2016) Evolving norms of protection: China, Libya and the problem of intervention in armed conflict. Camb Rev Int Aff 29(3):812–830
Shlaim A (1997) The Protocol of Sèvres, 1956: anatomy of a war plot. Int Aff 73(3):509–530
Smolansky OM (1965) Moscow and the Suez Crisis, 1956: a reappraisal. Polit Sci Q 80(4):581–605
Sofaer AD (1991) The legality of the United States Action in Panama. Columbia J Transnatl Law 29(2):281–292
Terry JP (1990) The Panama Intervention: law in support of policy. Naval Law Rev 39:5–14
Thompson A (2015) Humanitarian principles put to the test: challenges to humanitarian action during decolonization. Int Rev Red Cross 97(897/898):45–76
Thomson AWR (2012) Doctrine of the protection of nationals abroad: rise of the non-combatant evacuation operation. Wash Univ Glob Stud Law Rev 11(3):627–668
Thomson R (1985) The Caribbean after Grenada. Int J 40(2):377–386
Ulfstein G, Christiansen HF (2013) The legality of the NATO Bombing in Libya. Int Comp Law Q 62(1):159–171
Vengroff R (1975) Neo-colonialism and policy outputs in Africa. Comp Polit Stud 8(2):234–250
Warbrick C (1988) Protection of nationals abroad. Int Comp Law Q 37(4):1002–1012
Weede E (1978) U.S. support for foreign governments: or domestic disorder and imperial intervention, 1958-1965. Comp Polit Stud 10(4):497–528
Weisberg HL (1972) The Congo Crisis 1964: a case study in humanitarian intervention. Va J Int Law 12(2):261–276
Wheeler N (2001) Introduction: the political and moral limits of western military intervention to protect civilians in danger. Contemp Secur Policy 22(3):1–27
Wilder SH (1981) International terrorism and hostage-taking: an overview. Manitoba Law J 11(3):367–387
Williams P (2001) Fighting for freetown: British Military Intervention in Sierra Leone. Contemp Secur Policy 22(3):140–168
Wingfield TC (2000) Forcible protection of nationals abroad. Dickinson Law Rev 104(3):439–469
Wright Q (1959) United States Intervention in the Lebanon. Am J Int Law 53(1):112–125
Wright Q (1961) The United Nations and the Congo Crisis. J Bassett Moore Soc Int Law 2(2):41–55
Zartman IW (1976) Europe and Africa: decolonization or dependency. Foreign Aff 54(2):325–343

Book Chapters

Berman EG, Labonte MT (2006) Sierra Leone. In: Durch WJ (ed) Twenty-first-century peace operations. US Institute of Peace and The Henry L. Stimson Center, pp 141–228

Corn GP (2016) Developing rules of engagement: operationalizing law, policy, and military imperatives at the strategic level. In: Corn GS et al (eds) U.S. military operations, law, policy, and practice. Oxford University Press, pp 209–248
Gaines KK (2007) Pauli Murray in Ghana: The Congo Crisis and African American Woman's Dilemma. In: Campbell JT et al (eds) Race, Nation, & Empire in American History. University of North Carolina Press, pp 250–276
Geyer M (2016) Humanitarianism and human rights: a troubled rapport. In: Klose F (ed) The emergence of humanitarian intervention, ideas and practice from the nineteenth century to the present. Cambridge University Press, pp 31–55
Gowan R (2018) European involvement in United Nations Peacekeeping. In: Meijer H, Wyss M (eds) The handbook of European defence policies & armed forces. Oxford University Press, pp 854–869
Güven O, Ribbelink O (2016) The protection of nationals abroad: a return to old practice? In: Paulussen C et al (eds) Fundamental rights in international and European law, public and private law perspectives. TMC Asser Press, pp 45–72
Olonisakin F (2017) United Nations Mission in Sierra Leone. In: Koops JA et al (eds) The Oxford handbook of United Nations Peacekeeping Operations. Oxford University Press, pp 629–641
Rotberg RI (2003) Failed states, collapsed states, weak states: causes and indicators. In: Rotberg RI (ed) When states fail, causes and consequences. Princeton University Press, pp 1–25
Tsagourias N (2015) Self-defence, protection of humanitarian values, and the doctrine of impartiality and neutrality in enforcement mandates. In: Weller M (ed) The Oxford handbook of the use of force in international law. Oxford University Press, pp 398–415

Online Material

Blair T (22 April 1999) Doctrine of the International Community. Retrieved February 22, 2025, from http://www.britishpoliticalspeech.org/speech-archive.htm?speech=279
Bush GHW (20 December 1989) Address to Nation on Panama Invasion. American Rhetoric Online Speech Bank. Retrieved February 22, 2025, from https://www.americanrhetoric.com/speeches/ghwbushpanamainvasion.htm
Diuguid LH (30 October 1983) OAS Fails to Draft Grenada Resolution. The Washington Post. Retrieved February 22, 2025, from https://www.washingtonpost.com/archive/politics/1983/10/30/oas-fails-to-draft-grenada-resolution/2ddb1376-3a9d-4345-84d6-246802550f1a/
Dominic Republic – DomRep, Background. Retrieved February 22, 2025., from https://peacekeeping.un.org/mission/past/domrepbackgr.html
Foreign Relations of the United States (1955–1957). Suez Crisis (July 26–December 31, 1956). Volume XVI, Document 35. Letter from President Eisenhower to Prime Minister Eden. Retrieved February 22, 2025, from https://history.state.gov/historicaldocuments/frus1955-57v16/d35
Items Relating to the Situation in Panama. Decision of 23 December 1989 (2902nd meeting): Rejection of a Draft Resolution on the Situation in Panama. Retrieved February 22, 2025., from https://www.un.org/securitycouncil/sites/www.un.org.securitycouncil/files/en/sc/repertoire/89-92/Chapter%208/AMERICA/item%2013_Panama%20-%203%20items%20-%20consolidated.pdf
Johnson L (May 2, 1965) Published Text of Speech on the Dominican Republic Intervention (The Johnson Doctrine Speech). Retrieved February 22, 2025, from https://loveman.sdsu.edu/docs/1965JohnsonDoctrine.pdf
Papastavridis E (2024) Red Sea Attacks and the International Response: An International Law Insight. Hellenic Foundation for European and Foreign Policy. Retrieved February 22, 2025, from https://www.eliamep.gr/wp-content/uploads/2024/01/Insights-2-Red-Sea-EN.pdf

Reuters Staff (27 February 2011) Libya Evacuations by Country. Retrieved February 22, 2025, from https://www.reuters.com/article/uk-libya-protests-evacuation-idUSLNE71M02220110227
The American Presidency Project (15 July 1958) Special Message to the Congress on the Sending of United States Forces to Lebanon. Retrieved February 22, 2025, from https://www.presidency.ucsb.edu/documents/special-message-the-congress-the-sending-united-states-forces-lebanon
The New York Times (26 October 1983) Letter Asking U.S. to Ask. Retrieved February 22, 2025, from https://www.nytimes.com/1983/10/26/world/letter-asking-us-to-act.html
U.S. Department of Defense (18 December 2023) Statement from Secretary of Defense Lloyd J. Austin III on Ensuring Freedom of Navigation in the Red Sea. Retrieved, February 22, 2025, from https://www.defense.gov/News/Releases/Release/Article/3621110/statement-from-secretary-of-defense-lloyd-j-austin-iii-on-ensuring-freedom-of-n/
UK Parliament, House of Commons (13 September 1956). Suez Canal (Volume 558). Retrieved February 22, 2025, from https://hansard.parliament.uk/Commons/1956-09-13/debates/f95cd24b-6a90-4dfe-a1ef-c8119bdf2a8a/SuezCanal
United States invades Grenada. This Day in History. Retrieved, February 22, 2025., from https://www.history.com/this-day-in-history/united-states-invades-grenada
US Army Center of Military History. Retrieved February 22, 2025., from https://history.army.mil/html/bookshelves/resmat/dom_republic/IAPF_Stability_Ops_Rpt.pdf

Chapter 4
Forcible PNA and the Recent Russian Discourse

4.1 Introduction

The invasions of Georgia in 2008 and of Ukraine in 2014—further resulting in Crimea's illegal annexation—and the 2022 ongoing war against it, have all been justified more or less by the alleged threat to Russian nationals in the invaded areas. Russia's policy from 2008 onwards was the outcome of a gradual shift that was introduced with the Federal Legislation on State Policy of the Russian Federation in Respect of the Compatriots Abroad. This legislation is in alignment with the Russian Constitution, which provides in Art. 61 para 2 that the Russian Federation "shall guarantee its citizens defense and patronage beyond its boundaries".[1] For many commentators, this legislation is indicative of Russia's attempts to establish its influence in former Soviet Union republics; as such, it has brought Russia's discourse and policy parallel with the neo-colonial rhetoric of the early 60s.[2]

It is astonishing that during the Cold War era the Soviet Union did not invoke the doctrine, although it developed a rhetoric on the use of force against third countries in the light of self-help and self-defense. Even within this framework, it is reported that the former Soviet Union did not bother to offer legal justifications for the times it used force. The Soviet Union's legal argumentation regarding the use of force during this period was based equally on two pillars: first, that it was a state with augmented "national interests to protect and national rights to assert" and second, that it considered itself as "the vanguard of a world socialist revolution".[3] In this context, the Brezhnev doctrine emerged. According to it:

---

[1] Russian Federation 1993 (rev. 2014) (Constitution of the Russian Federation). Retrieved February 22, 2025, from https://www.constituteproject.org/constitution/Russia_2014, Art. 61 para 2; Blitt (2024), pp. 1–90.

[2] Kushnir (2018), pp. 75–79.

[3] Rostow (1981), p. 214.

© The Author(s), under exclusive license to Springer Nature Switzerland AG 2025

I. Pervou, *Protecting Nationals Abroad and the Reconceptualization of Sovereignty*, Studies in the History of Law and Justice 32,
https://doi.org/10.1007/978-3-032-05231-5_4

> The socialist countries have their own vital interests, their own obligations, including the obligation to protect their mutual security, and their own socialist principles of mutual relations based on brotherly assistance, solidarity and internationalism. This commonwealth is an indissoluble whole, cemented together by indissoluble ties such as history has never known. [...] The Soviet Union and the other socialist countries have often warned those who are tempted to try to embarrass the socialist commonwealth that we will neither tolerate nor allow even one of its links to be torn off.[4]

The Soviet rhetoric at the time introduced the term "socialist commonwealth", echoing the already existing discourse of the US and the UK, a counterpart of the Johnson doctrine.[5] The Brezhnev doctrine reflected the Soviet understanding of superpowers' supremacy vis-à-vis weaker countries.[6] The doctrine was invoked to justify the Soviet invasion of Czechoslovakia in 1968 and for this reason it was built on the rhetoric the US developed in the Dominican crisis.[7] Yet, unlike the Johnson argumentation, the Soviets did not make any reference to the protection of nationals abroad.

During the Cold War, the Soviet Union did not count on PNA as a causal factor for breaching the principle of non-intervention. This was not due to ideological factors, rather it resulted from the Soviet Union's state structure as a federation. In effect, this could also explain why Russia only belatedly added the doctrine to its argumentation regarding the use of force.

4.2 The 2008 Intervention in Georgia: A Turning Point in Russia's Foreign Policy

The chronicle of Russia's invasion of Georgia dates back to 8 August 2008, when Georgian forces bombarded Tskhinvali, the capital city of South Ossetia. The days that followed were characterized by increased tensions and violence which soon engulfed the autonomous districts of South Ossetia and Abkhazia in the northern part of Georgia, a federal republic. Within a few hours, Russian forces were engaging in hostilities with the Georgian army. The conflict lasted only a few days, and for this reason it is known as the "Five-Day War". On August 12, 2008, the two states agreed to a ceasefire, which was signed by both sides on August 15 and 16 respectively. Afterwards there were a few minor incidents. The situation in the regions of South Ossetia and Abkhazia returned to normalcy soon after Russia and Georgia had concluded the Six-Point Peace Plan on the initiative of French President Sarkozy, who acted as a mediator on behalf of the European Union. Within a month's time, Russian troops had withdrawn from Abkhazia and South Ossetia, and

[4] UNGA, Thirty-Third Session, 1679th Plenary Meeting (3 October 1968). UN Doc A/PV.1679, paras 68–73.

[5] Franck and Weisband (1970), p. 1013; Reisman (1988), pp. 171–198.

[6] Hilpold (2015), p. 269.

[7] Goodman (1969), p. 76.

on September 8, 2008, the two states signed the Agreement on Implementing Measures.[8]

The five-day armed confrontation resulted in approximately 850 casualties in total from both parties. Immediately after the ceasefire, the autonomous districts of South Ossetia and Abkhazia declared their independence from Georgia on August 26, 2008. The Russian President Dmitry Medvedev immediately issued Decrees on the Recognition of the Republic of Abkhazia and the Republic of South Ossetia by the Russian Federation and subsequently presented them before the UNSC, as the result of the "freely expressed will of the population to live in an independent State".[9] These declarations of independence did not have a strong impact in the international plane. The former Georgian districts have still only been recognized as states by five UN member-states so far, namely Russia, Nicaragua, Venezuela, Nauru and Syria. The rest consider them as entities. Recognition of the two states is Russian-led, and it comes as no surprise that the Nagorno-Karabakh and Transnistria entities also recognize the two Caucasus republics.[10]

To better understand how the Five-Day War broke out, one needs to look further into the historical dimension of the two Caucasian regions. The historical dimension is of significance to the conflict's particularities, as is how the protection of nationals abroad doctrine played a central role in Russia's claims.

4.2.1 The Special Status of the Two Caucasian Districts: A Historical Overview

A brief account of the relationship between Russia and Georgia explains the special legal status of Abkhazia and South Ossetia. For many centuries the two states have peacefully co-existed, taking into consideration that the two nations share a common cultural background. Georgia was a republic of the Soviet Union from 1992 till 1991: the Georgian Soviet Socialist Republic or SSR.[11] Throughout the centuries, Georgia has been a bone of contention between powerful states due to its strategic geopolitical position. This partly explains why South Ossetia and Abkhazia were given special status within the Soviet Union, when Georgia was one of its republics. The two districts had received the status of oblast; that is, they were second-level administrative units of the Soviet Union. In turn, both districts had the right to make decisions without any interference about their legal status. Shortly before the dissolution of the Soviet Union, both Abkhazia and South Ossetia declared their

[8] Amnesty International (2008), p. 10.

[9] UNSC (28 August 2008). The Situation in Georgia. UN Doc S/PV.5969, p. 4.

[10] Tokarev et al. (2021), pp. 93–119.

[11] Suny (1994).

independence, in 1990 and 1991 respectively. Their attempts to gain their freedom were unsuccessful, however, and tensions soon arose between Russia and Georgia.[12]

The war in South Ossetia was between Georgian troops and Ossetian separatist forces. Units of the Soviet Army sided with the separatists, with the result that the region's stability was at risk. And when Abkhazia refused to become a constituency of independent Georgia the conflict began. From 1992 till 1993 Georgia and Abkhazia engaged in hostilities. It was alleged that Russia interfered and conducted air-strikes in support of the Abkhazians, an accusation that was formally denied. On both occasions, the conflict periods ended with agreements initiated by Russia. Although there were serious indications that Russia was directly taking part in the hostilities, this was not formally recognized. Therefore, Russia took on the role of the main mediator.

As far as South Ossetia is concerned the 1992 Sochi Agreement[13] provided that Russian peacekeepers would be present in the region, with a view to preventing the two parties from engaging in hostilities. Low-scale tensions were to be monitored by a tripartite peacekeeping mission, consisting of Russian, Georgian and Ossetian forces, collaborating under the instructions of the OSCE. The establishment of Russian peacekeeping forces in the region was considered a stabilizing factor.[14]

With regards to Abkhazia, its independence claim did not receive international support. Hostilities in Abkhazia amounted to civil war. Thus, they were considered a threat to international peace and security by the UNSC. The UNSC decided on the deployment of observers[15] and subsequently of an advance team of observers.[16] Afterwards, it established the UN Observer Mission in Georgia (UNOMIC) with a mandate to report on cease-fire compliance. At the same time, the UNSC welcomed the deployment of

> mixed interim monitoring groups of Georgian/Abkhaz/Russian units designed to consolidate the cease-fire, and request[ed] the Secretary-General to facilitate cooperation between the United Nations observers and these units within their respective mandates.[17]

All of the above were put forward by the UNSC as guarantees of non-violation of the ceasefire agreement. Eventually, the situation in Abkhazia eased with the 1994 Moscow agreement which affirmed the establishment of a ceasefire. This agreement was endorsed by the UNSC in effect.[18]

---

[12] Crawford (2006), p. 403.

[13] Agreement of Principles of Settlement of the Georgian—Ossetian Conflict (Sochi Agreement) (24 June 1992). Retrieved, February 22, 2025, from https://peacemaker.un.org/sites/default/files/document/files/2024/05/ge20ru920624agreemenonprinciplesofsettlementgeorgianossetianconflict.pdf.

[14] Kostelyanets (2019), p. 541.

[15] UN Doc S/Res/849(1993) (9 July 1993), op. clause 2.

[16] UN Doc S/Res/854(1993) (6 August 1993), op. clause 1.

[17] UN Doc S/Res/858(1993) (24 August 1993), op. clause 6.

[18] UN Doc S/1994/583 (17 May 1994), Annex 1.

Despite the unsuccessful attempts made by Abkhazia and South Ossetia to become independent states, their previous federal status as oblasts, coupled with their 1990–1993 fight for independence predetermined their subsequent recognition as autonomous districts with the Georgian state. All in all, several opinions have been expressed on the reasons why the two regions received autonomous status. According to some, it was due to their national affinity with Russia, while others have suggested that it resulted from the two regions' support for the Bolsheviks.[19]

The ceasefire agreements brought forth a new era in the historical course of Abkhazia and South Ossetia. The agreements were successful up till the 2008 Five-Day War, as they brought stability and peace to the region. From 2004 the relations between the two countries deteriorated. It is revealing that in 2007 Georgia instituted proceedings against Russia before the European Court of Human Rights (ECtHR). Georgia claimed that in 2006 and 2007 Russia had issued more than 4600 expulsion orders against Georgian nationals. Georgians residing in Russia were targeted; before their expulsion they had been arbitrarily arrested and detained. Over a six-month period more than 4600 Georgian nationals had allegedly been expelled from Russia. Over the same period, the Russian embassy in Georgia had suspended issuing Russian visas to Georgians.[20] In addition, the situation in the two districts worsened day by day: small-scale hostilities broke out and the ceasefire agreements were broken. Incidences of violence were an everyday reality in both regions. There are, again, many contentions as to the reasons which led to the resurgence of violence. Although this is part of political analysis, most tend to attribute tensions to the policy of the Georgian President Saakashvili. By 2008 the Caucasus region had become a place of insecurity. Repeated violent outbursts had eventually rendered the peacekeeping forces ineffective.[21] Although the two conflicting sides provided completely different accounts of events, it is undeniable that the conditions for armed conflict were met. In the aftermath of the Five-Day War the two regions were at point zero regarding their international legal status.

4.2.2 The Six-Point Peace Plan and International and Regional Attempts to Establish Peace

The ceasefire agreement between Georgia and Russia was the source of heated legal debate. The six principles agreed upon were: no recourse to violence by Georgians, Russians, Abkhazians and Ossetians (a), the cessation of hostilities (b), access granted to humanitarian aid (c), the return of Georgian armed forces to the Georgian mainland (d), withdrawal of Russian armed forces from the regions, and Russian peacekeepers to remain onsite and implement additional security measures until

---

[19] Hewitt (2008), pp. 187–188.

[20] *Georgia v. Russia (I)*, App. No 13255/07 (ECtHR, 3 July 2014); Bloed (2006), p. 194.

[21] Shanahan Cutts (2007), p. 304.

international monitoring mechanisms could resume their role in the area (e) and, finally, continued dialogue in good faith for the establishment of peace and stability in the two regions (f). The plan was the result of a compromise between the two parties. For Western and European states, though, the agreement was not balanced but favored the Russian interests. By vesting Russian peacekeepers with the power to guarantee peace and stability in the regions it further legitimized the presence of Russian forces onsite. It was considered that the Six-Point Peace Plan reduced Georgia's sovereignty and territorial integrity.[22]

Apart from discussion of the conflict in the internationally competent forum for international peace and security—the UNSC—the European Union acted and created an Independent International Fact-Finding Mission on the Conflict in Georgia (IIFFMCG).[23] This decision was expected, hence unprecedented for Europe. The IIFFMCG was the first fact-finding mission established by the European Union. Its mandate was to

> investigate the origins and the course of the conflict in Georgia, including with regard to international law, humanitarian law and human rights, and the accusations made in that context. The geographical scope and time span of the investigation will be sufficiently broad to determine all the possible causes of the conflict. The results of the investigation will be presented to the parties to the conflict, and to the Council, the Organisation for Security and Cooperation in Europe (OSCE) and the United Nations (UN), in the form of a report.[24]

The IIFFMCG's 2009 report offers significant insights into the 2008 Five-Day War, as it explored in depth the argumentation of both sides in the conflict. Read in conjunction with the UNSC records of the debate meetings, the IIDFFMCG's report aimed to demonstrate how the Five-Day War broke out. This was a difficult task, taking into account that both parties claimed that they acted in self-defense.

Georgia, on one hand, argued that recourse to force was necessary to protect its sovereignty and territorial integrity. It also claimed that turbulence was caused by Russia's interference in the two districts. Nevertheless, Georgia did not openly refer to self-defense in international fora, as this would constitute accepting that it had not exercised effective control over the two districts. In turn, this would have reduced its argumentation that recourse to force was necessary to safeguard its territorial integrity. In addition, if it conceded that its control over the two districts had been diminished, this would enhance South Ossetia's and Abkhazia's claims for independence. Georgia's limited control over the disputed territories during hostilities was affirmed by the ECtHR, according to which neither Georgia nor Russia exercised

[22] United Nations Office for the Coordination of Humanitarian Affairs (OCHA) (15 August 2008). Background: Six-point Peace Plan for the Georgia-Russia Conflict. Retrieved February 22, 2025, from https://reliefweb.int/report/georgia/background-six-point-peace-plan-georgia-russia-conflict.

[23] Council of the European Union (2 December 2008). Concerning an Independent International Fact-Finding Mission on the Conflict in Georgia. Council Decision 2008/901CFSP.

[24] Ibid., Art. 1(2).

effective control over South Ossetia during the Five-Day War.[25] According to the Georgian representative at the UNSC,

> the illegal separatist authorities and armed formations are under the control and direction of the security and defence agencies of the Russian Federation. Numerous high ranking Russian officers from among the ranks of the peacekeepers, as well as other officials from the Russian military, intelligence, and law-enforcement services, are serving in senior roles in Tskhinvali. [...] The Government's military action was taken in self-defence after repeated armed provocations and with the sole goal of protecting the civilian population and preventing further loss of life among residents of various ethnic backgrounds. We believe that every democratic State would have reacted in a similar fashion to protect its own citizens. The Government acted because the separatists not only defied the ceasefire but sharply escalated the violence, killing several peacekeepers and civilians within hours of the ceasefire.[26]

Therefore, the state's discourse revolved around defense of its sovereignty in the two districts and the preclusion of separatist movements. It is striking, though, that reference to self-defense came without reference to Art. 51 UNCh.

On the other hand, Russia also claimed self-defense, based on two distinct legal grounds. First, that it was vested by the 1992 peace accords with the power to protect the peace and stability in Abkhazia and South Ossetia. Second, that it rushed to protect its peacekeepers, as well as Georgians of Russian origin residing there. It proclaimed that the situation stemmed from the inability of the Georgian government to maintain the delicate political balance required for the regions' prosperity. Russia accused Georgia of failing to keep a fine line between the populations of different ethnic origin residing in South Ossetia.[27]

4.2.3 *Forcible PNA and the Five-Day War*

The Russian discourse regarding the use of force against Georgia was nothing but clear. Even though self-defense in the name of its nationals residing in the two regions was at the forefront of its rhetoric, Russia also called upon humanitarian intervention due to the ongoing humanitarian crisis which threatened the lives of innocent civilians.[28] Russia's accusations about the brutality of Georgia were elevated to the point of accusing it of genocide against ethnic Ossetians.[29]

Astonishingly, the Permanent Representative of Russia to the UNSC used the terms "genocide" and "ethnic cleansing" interchangeably, resulting in other UNSC

---

[25] *Georgia v. Russia (II)*, App. No 38263/08 (ECtHR, 21 January 2021), para 111; Sicilianos (2017), p. 4; Longobardo and Wallace (2022), pp. 145–177.

[26] UN Doc S/PV.5951 (8 August 2008), pp. 4–5.

[27] Ibid., 3.

[28] Hafkin (2010), p. 226; UN Doc S/PV.5952 (8 August 2008), p. 4.

[29] Petro (2009), p. 1538.

member-states calling for softer and more cautious language.[30] These claims undermined the Russian rhetoric and provoked reactions both by Georgia and by third states.[31] This is verified considering that on August 12, 2008, the two states agreed upon a ceasefire; the very same day Georgia instituted proceedings before the ICJ against Russia relating to "its actions on and around the territory of Georgia in breach of the 1965 International Convention on the Elimination of All Forms of Racial Discrimination". Georgia claimed that

> the Russian Federation, through its State organs, State agents, and other persons and entities exercising governmental authority, and through the South Ossetian and Abkhaz separatist forces and other agents acting on the instructions of, and under the direction and control of the Russian Federation, is responsible for serious violations of its fundamental obligations under CERD, including Articles 2, 3, 4, 5 and 6.[32]

Russia gradually dropped the inflammatory rhetoric, following international pressure on manipulative language. In its official correspondence with the IIFFMCG, Russia conceded that references made by it for

> acts of genocide perpetrated against the Ossetian people by the Georgian side in August 2008 should be viewed in the context of the preliminary information that was received during the first hours of the conflict and prior to it.[33]

Claims about ethnic cleansing or genocide were soon abandoned and discredited by the international community.[34] In this context, Russia's main argumentation relied on the forcible PNA doctrine.

Russian President Medvedev invoked forcible PNA in the clearest possible terms. More specifically, he claimed that Russia was and would remain a security guarantor for the Caucasus people. From this viewpoint, protection of Russian compatriots was detrimental to Russia's existence.[35] In his words, Russia promised to "protect the life and dignity of Russian citizens wherever they are. We will not allow their deaths to go unpunished. Those responsible will receive a deserved punishment".[36] Three significant conclusions can be directly inferred from this statement. First, Russia upheld the forcible PNA doctrine. Second, it went a step

[30] UN Doc S/PV.5953 (10 August 2008), pp. 8, 14.

[31] See OSCE, Group of Friends of Georgia (2 September 2022). Russia's 2008 Military Invasion of Georgia. Retrieved February 22, 2025, from https://www.gov.uk/government/speeches/russias-2008-military-invasion-of-georgia-joint-statement-to-the-osce.

[32] See *Application of the International Convention on the Elimination of All Forms of Racial Discrimination (Georgia v. Russian Federation)*, Preliminary Objections, Judgment, I.C.J. Reports 2011, p. 70.

[33] IIFFMCG, Report Vol. II, (September 2009). Retrieved February 22, 2025, from http://www.ceiig.ch/pdf/IIFFMCG_Volume_II.pdf, p. 426.

[34] Human Rights Watch (13 January 2009). Retrieved February 22, 2025, from https://www.hrw.org/report/2009/01/23/flames/humanitarian-law-violations-and-civilian-victims-conflict-over-south.

[35] Chatham (2011), pp. 88–89.

[36] Reuters (8 August 2008). Retrieved, February 22, 2025, from https://www.reuters.com/article/idUSL8661071.

further in recognizing its duty to protect its nationals abroad (R2Pn). Finally, it considered that recourse to force was necessary not only to protect populations in peril, but also to function as a form of punishment for the perpetrators. The first contention was common to all states which referred to the doctrine from time to time. The second and third, though, are quite interesting and reveal much about Russian discourse at that time. Russia reiterated its pre-Charter discourse and declared that it had a responsibility to protect its citizens wherever they were. It assumed responsibility to protect them, echoing the policy followed by superpowers till the early twentieth century.[37] It elevated all such claims of protection of compatriots beyond its boundaries. It was no longer a matter of discretion based on political will and the availability of resources, but a duty owed to its nation. This shift, although slight in doctrinal terms, is considerable in terms of state practice and explains Russia's choice to engage in certain areas it considered conflicting and of significant national interest.

Finally, it deemed recourse to force as a means of protection, as well as a permissible countermeasure against those who put its nationals in jeopardy.[38] The Russian justification of the use of force was nebulous. Russia put forward the forcible PNA as a matter of self-defense under Art. 51 UNCh. Recourse to force was triggered after Russian peacekeepers and civilians were attacked by Georgian troops in South Ossetia. Simultaneously, to some extent it introduced a responsibility to protect nationals abroad (R2Pn), which is *prima facie* a contradiction of the traditional self-defense argument. Furthermore, self-defense requires the proportionate use of force, while reprisals or countermeasures do not follow the same strict criteria.[39]

The UNSC debate records reveal that most states denounced the deployment of Russian military forces in South Ossetia, and in Georgia in general. The debate was developed on three levels. First, it was not contested that Russian peacekeepers had confronted a hostile environment and found themselves in great danger. Neither the UNSC nor the EU Council of Ministers doubted that Russian peacekeepers had died during hostilities.[40] Self-defense for their protection would be totally understandable and legitimate and would probably justify a rescue or evacuation mission, even though this proposition was not openly suggested by third countries. However, it is uncertain whether a potential deployment of a NEO for the evacuation of Russian peacekeepers and citizens would be welcomed by the international community. The role of Russian peacekeepers in the Five-Day War was the crux of the matter; it was their involvement in hostilities that was disputed.

On one hand, Georgia alleged that their presence was shielding separatist movements in South Ossetia and that, furthermore, their numbers had been extraordinarily high in the region during the conflict. On the other hand, Russia claimed that

---

[37] Allison (2009), p. 175.

[38] Criddle (2015), p. 296.

[39] Cannizzaro (2001), p. 901; Franck (2008), pp. 715–767.

[40] UNSC (8 August 2008). Security Council Hears Conflicting Russian, Georgian Views on Worsening Crisis. UN Doc SC/9418; UN Doc S/PV.5952 (8 August 2008), p. 7; UN Doc S/PV.5961 (19 August 2008) p. 2; IIFFMCG, Report Vol. II (September 2009), pp. 221–222, 265.

Russian peacekeepers had been targeted by the Georgian troops, and it referred to previous smaller-scale incidents of aggression against them. Second, states perceived Russia's actions as a form of aggression and attacks against the territorial integrity of Georgia. More specifically, even if Russia were entitled to act in self-defense, the force it had used exceeded legal boundaries, and was disproportionate. Russian troops had advanced into the Georgian mainland, tearing the country into two pieces. In this regard, CoE's Parliamentary Assembly (PACE) noticed that the Russian operation included

> large military actions in central and western Georgia and in Abkhazia [and] failed to respect the principle of proportionality and international humanitarian law and constituted a violation of Council of Europe principles.[41]

This proportionality breach was deemed evident due to the Russian operation's magnitude, compared to the level of hostilities preceding it. In this sense, PACE considered that Russia's scope was to occupy part of Georgia's territory. Third, states avoided making direct mention of the doctrine, even though forcible PNA subtly ran through the debate.

Both the US and the UK tackled the legitimacy of Russia's invocation of the doctrine, which went against the well-established nature of the policy. The Five-Day War was the first time Russia had founded its rhetoric on the forcible protection of nationals abroad. Many considered it a resurrection and full realization of the Brezhnev doctrine; protection of compatriots abroad was integral to the Russian Federation, and formed part of its "near abroad policy".[42] Following the same rationale, the doctrine's legitimacy was also questioned by the IIFFMCG, which mentioned in its report that

> since 1945, numerous states have led military actions by pointing to the need to protect their own nationals abroad. In many cases the legality of these actions was disputed. There is no customary law allowing such actions. If at all, such actions should be limited in scope and duration and exclusively focused on rescuing and evacuating nationals. In the case at hand, the action was not solely and exclusively focused on rescuing and evacuating Russian citizens, but largely surpassed this threshold by embarking upon extended military operations over large parts of Georgia. Consequently, it must be concluded that the Russian military action outside South Ossetia was essentially conducted in violation of international law.[43]

The IIFFMCG's doctrinal position though was rudimentary. It recognized the legitimacy of rescue and evacuation missions, but cast doubts on the doctrine itself. Furthermore, it completely refused to acknowledge the existence of a customary rule on the forcible protection of nationals abroad, ignoring the historical course of the doctrine. Nonetheless, it pinpointed that the Russian military operations were disproportionate. The IIFFMCG linked proportionality to territoriality. The

---

[41] PACE (30 September – 2 October 2008). The Consequences of the War between Georgia and Russia. Res 1633(2008), op. clause 6.

[42] Götz (2022), p. 1536.

[43] IIFFMCG, Report Vol I (September 2009). Retrieved, February 22, 2025, from https://www.echr.coe.int/Documents/HUDOC_38263_08_Annexes_ENG.pdf, pp. 24–25.

magnitude of Russia's actions went unnoticed, as the report emphasized the fact that operations covered large parts of Georgia. In this context, it considered that operations outside South Ossetia breached international law rules. By way of contrast, one could argue that the IIFFMCG did not argue for the legitimacy of Russian military operations in South Ossetia, and nor uphold their necessity, even though this was part of its mandate.[44] Thereat, the IIFFMCG's position on the matter raised concerns in every respect, particularly due to doctrinal inconsistencies and in effect legal characterization of the acts attributed to the two conflicting states.

4.2.4 The Five-Day War and Russia's Passportization Policy

In the conflict between Russia and Georgia the major issue of concern revolved around the notion of nationals. Unlike all previous cases, where legal interest focused on the prerequisites of necessity, imminence and proportionality—in this case the Russian line of argumentation—were scrutinized for the excessive issuance of Russian passports to South Ossetians before the war's outbreak. Russia proceeded with the mass-scale issuance of passports to nationals of South Ossetia, and by the time the conflict had begun the largest percentage of the district's nationals had acquired Russian nationality. Russia was accused of weaponizing nationality; that is, offering South Ossetians Russian nationality so as to be able to intervene in their name.[45] In this regard, passportization was a means to achieve collective naturalization, and as such it functioned as a manipulative state practice which "annexes populations" with the view to founding territorial claims.

However, one cannot avoid the opposite view, based on the argument that South Ossetians and Abkhazian constituted minorities within the Georgian state since day one of its creation. Their strong communal links, as well as the autonomous status of their regions in the Soviet Union system, explains why these groups felt threatened by the creation of the Georgian state. This line of argumentation attempts to justify the Russian policy and the necessity of its operations.[46]

The issue of passportization was brought up by Georgia in international debates and attracted the attention of the international community. States disapproved of the Russian policy to intervene in the name of "new-born citizens". Passportization was at the epicenter of legal research and many authors pointed out that the Russian policy disrupted the necessary bond that ought to exist between a state and its nationals, echoing Nottebohm's "genuine link" concept. According to it, the validity of an individual's nationality is dependent on a "genuine connection" between

---

[44] cf. Tagliavini (2011), p. 90.

[45] Natoli (2010), pp. 389–417.

[46] Maco (2016). Retrieved, February 22, 2025, from https://www.securityoutlines.cz/nationalism-soviet-legacies-and-majority-minorities-dynamic-amid-the-establishment-of-the-independent-state-of-georgia/.

the person and the state which extends its nationality to them. The ICJ had in this matter held that

> nationality is a legal bond having as its basis a social fact of attachment, a genuine connection of existence, interests and sentiments, together with the existence of reciprocal rights and duties. It may be said to constitute the juridical expression of the fact that the individual upon whom it is conferred, either directly by the law or as the result of an act of the authorities, is in fact more closely connected with the population of the State conferring nationality than with that of any other State.[47]

Restoration of the Nottebohm dictum was *prima facie* rational. Russia's passportization policy was not included in the ordinary means of nationality acquisition. All the same, it did not violate any international law principle. The Nottebohm dictum does not reflect the current views on nationality law. In the 1955 case, the "genuine connection" was a necessary concession to the international community, aiming at tackling impunity for the crimes of the Third Reich. Thus, the historical context in which this dictum occurred differed significantly from today's international legal regime. States' decision whether or not to confer their nationality to individuals is at their absolute discretion, one of the major manifestations of sovereignty. Yet, even if the Nottebohm dictum is considered valid, then again Russia's actions fulfill its prerequisites. The strong ties between the state and residents of Abkhazia and South Ossetia are indisputable. Therefore, inability to establish the illegality of mass-passportization in international law, is a matter of how state sovereignty is perceived, and it does not relate to the understanding of nationality. Therefore, alternative bases for the outlawing of mass-passportization were sought.

In this context, it has also been suggested that mass-passportization breaches the principle of good neighborliness, as established by the 2625(1970) Declaration on Friendly Relations.[48] Collective naturalization is potentially proof of the lack of good neighborly relations between states. Indeed, when a state proceeds with the mass issuance of passports and naturalizes citizens of a neighboring state, this cannot go unnoticed. The Russian policy was the epitome of controversy, considering that it conferred Russian citizenship on the citizens of a region whose historical course was troubled. South Ossetia's claims for independence after the Soviet Union's dissolution remained strong in the following years. In this respect, Georgia's complaints about Russia's deceitful role in the region were not unfounded.[49] These complaints better demonstrated the legal gap regarding collective naturalization practices in international law. Although some collective naturalization practices have been deemed inadmissible by judicial authorities in the past, the mass issuance of passports has passed under the radars of international law.[50] This omission had escaped international attention, given that the interest in creating a body of

---

[47] *Nottebohm Case (second phase)*, Judgment of April 6th, 1955: ICJ Reports 1955, p. 4, p. 23.

[48] UNGA (25 October 1970). Declaration on Principles of International Law Concerning Friendly Relations and Co-operation Among States in Accordance with the Charter of the United Nations. UN Doc. A/RES/2625 (XXV), preamble.

[49] Natoli (2010), p. 417.

[50] International Law Commission (1952). UN Doc A/CN.4/50, p. 8.

nationality rules focused on its loss, that is statelessness and denationalization, while collective naturalization through peaceful practices was not deemed a problem. It was not until Russia employed the practice in these regions that it returned in the spotlight.

Passportization remains an unresolved question as far as the Five-Day War is concerned; a recorded event about which the international community did not arrive at a clear resolution. There is no evidence that either South Ossetians or Abkhazians were coerced by Russia into accepting its nationality. Thus, it may well be considered a deliberate choice of theirs. If this proposition is true, not only did collective naturalization of the two districts' citizens not contravene international law, but it demonstrates these people's alienation from the state of Georgia. This view has long been expressed in international legal discourse. It has been asserted that collective naturalization, "provided that it reflects a sufficient connection with the naturalising state [...] may not be contrary to international law – and certainly not if the person concerned has in some way consented".[51]

It follows that it is immaterial to international law whether there is state practice of the mass issuing of passports that results in collective naturalization. International law only cares for the individual's clear consent, or, conversely, that the individual is not exploited by the state which confers nationality on them. Yet even though large-scale conferrals of nationality are not problematic in the first place, the element of extraterritoriality is indeed dubious. Further, and as far as the "genuine connection" criterion is concerned, it is accepted that the Nottebohm dictum is nowadays a disproportionate restriction on the law of nationality. Domestic nationality regulations are among the strongest manifestations of state sovereignty. For this reason, the "genuine link" criterion was gradually abandoned[52]; it is now confirmed that nationality "shall be responsive to its diverse contemporary functions".[53] In other words, even if Russia's passportization policy is suspicious, the "genuine link" dictum is not the most proper means to tackle it. The element of extraterritoriality, and most importantly the temporal element (the fact that in the case of South Ossetia "the citizens on whose behalf the intervention was purportedly undertaken had in some cases been granted Russian citizenship just one month before the invasion"),[54] is far more important.

The mass issuance of Russian passports shortly before the invasion of Georgia remains an unresolved question in terms of public international law. Its employment as a tool of demographic alteration was part of the Russian policy which had as its ultimate goal the occupation of these territories. In terms of the forcible PNA doctrine, mass passportization is evidence how the two major limbs of sovereignty are interrelated. Nationality and territoriality cannot be fully detached, even though

[51] Jennings and Watts (1992), p. 874.

[52] Güven and Ribbelink (2016), p. 55.

[53] Sloane (2009), p. 60.

[54] Okowa (2008), p. 44.

their analysis is distinct. In this sense, mass naturalization predestined military developments.

4.2.5 *South Ossetia's and Abkhazia's Independence Claims as the Aftereffect of Kosovo*

The Five-Day War of 2008 brought to the surface the two regions' claim to self-determination, and subsequently secession from Georgia. These claims were put aside during the frozen period of the conflict (1992–2008).[55] In the aftermath of the invasion of Georgia, it became clear that Russia had sustained South Ossetia's and Abkhazia's claims for independence. The argumentative course it followed reiterated the rationale that had been followed with regards to Kosovo's declaration of independence.[56] That is, the South Ossetians and Abkhazians were targeted by the Georgian government and had suffered a systematic downgrade and violation of their human rights.[57] This proposition was coupled with the distinctiveness of the ethnic origin of the two groups from Georgians, as well as their possession of Russian passports, and used to cement Russia's secessionist rhetoric. It is quite interesting that the Russian discourse was not limited only to South Ossetia, where the conflict had erupted; it immediately expanded to cover the case of upper Abkhazia, although this was not an area affected by hostilities. This is the reason why the two areas' secession claims are examined together in international legal scholarship, and the Five-Day War is considered only as part of the bigger picture.

Russia attempted to parallel the cases of South Ossetia and Abkhazia with that of Kosovo and proclaimed that their populations were ethnic minorities which had long suffered systematic violations of their rights by the Georgian government. This narrative was conceived only a few months after Kosovo's declaration of independence, in February 2008. There is no doubt that both Russia and the two regions attempted to take advantage of the Kosovo momentum and the international community's turn to "remedial succession" as an exception to the principles of self-determination.[58] Yet this policy stumbled on at least three points.

First, it was noticed that the case of Kosovo was *sui generis*; states' acceptance of Kosovo's independence led the way an "exceptional legal regime" and could not set a precedent able to satisfy similar separatist claims. This was the view upheld by the ICJ in its 2010 Advisory Opinion regarding the Accordance with International Law of the Unilateral Declaration of Independence in Respect of Kosovo.[59] Although

[55] Nußberger (2009), p. 352.

[56] Hofmeister (2010), p. 161.

[57] Reference re Secession of Quebec, [1998] 2 S.C.R. 217, para 74; Vidmar (2010), pp. 37–56.

[58] Del Mar (2013), pp. 79–108.

[59] *Accordance with International Law of the Unilateral Declaration of Independence in Respect of Kosovo*, Advisory Opinion, I.C.J. Reports 2010, p. 403, para 100.

Russia followed the exact same line of argumentation in the cases of Abkhazia and South Ossetia, it did not align with the ICJ's justification on the case of Kosovo. In its written statement to the Court it held that:

> What remains to be analysed is whether there exists a possibility of secession where the State concerned does not "conduct itself in compliance with the principle of equal rights and self-determination of peoples" and thus does not possess a "government representing the whole population". Unilateral secession pursuant to the quoted provisions of the 1970 Declaration has been titled "remedial secession". Importantly, authors that advocate this right admit that it can be exercised only in extreme conditions, where violent acts of discrimination are continuously committed against the people in question and all the possibilities for a resolution of the problem within the existing State have been exhausted. Secession has been described as a measure of last resort, where the very existence of the people, or its characteristic features, are in danger.[60]

Evidently, Russia took a clear stance on the delicate balance between self-determination claims and territorial integrity; siding with numerous states, it upheld that general acceptance of remedial secession undermined the principle of territorial integrity. Russia's position regarding Kosovo's declaration of independence could be characterized as a 180-degree turn compared to its official statements on South Ossetia's and Abkhazia's secession from Georgia and the subsequent Decrees of Recognition it issued. However, this discrepancy in state practice was justified as a result of the circumstantial character of state creation. Nevertheless, it was a significant handicap in the rhetoric adopted on South Ossetia and Abkhazia.[61]

The second point of concern relates to Russia's alleged gross and systematic violation of the populations' rights in question. Trying to establish a legitimate claim of self-determination for South Ossetia and Abkhazia, Russia characterized Ossetians and Abkhazians as ethnic minorities within Georgia, for whom the level of respect for their human rights was constantly reduced. In addition, it brought up a claim of purported genocide, which it soon abandoned. Unlike the case of Kosovo, the threshold of human rights violations which could serve as the founding basis of remedial secession was not met. In terms of internal self-determination, the two districts enjoyed autonomous status for many years, while in both regions peacekeeping forces secured a level of relative stability. Moreover, if South Ossetians and Abkhazians were seen as minorities due to their ethnic origin, then this weakened the protection of nationals abroad justification of the use of force. If minority rights were to be attributed to these populations, then peaceful cohabitation would be a prerequisite.[62] Therefore, referenda, recognition of an autonomous status and peacekeepers would not be part of the territories' governance. In these terms, it could be

[60] Accordance with International Law of the Unilateral Declaration of Independence by the Provisional Institutions of Self-Government of Kosovo (Request for advisory opinion), Written Statement by the Russian Federation (16 April 2009) p. 30–31, para 86.

[61] Borgen (2009), p. 16.

[62] UN Subcommission on Prevention of Discrimination and Protection of Minorities (1979). Study on the Rights of Persons Belonging to Ethnic, Religious and Linguistic Minorities, by Francesco Capotorti. UN Doc E/CN.4/Sub.2/384/Rev.1.

argued that recourse to force by the Russian Federation fell within the context of humanitarian intervention.

Finally, another source of concern relates to the simultaneous declaration of independence of the two districts in the wake of the Five-Day War. The situation in Abkhazia was quite different from that in South Ossetia. Abkhazia's status was provided by a series of UNSC decisions which authorized peacekeeping forces onsite. In addition, the Five-Day War did not change in the slightest the situation in Abkhazia. Thus, there was no fundamental change of circumstances that would justify a claim to remedial secession, and so it was aptly pointed out that the "recognition of Abkhazia as an independent State by Russia might be considered as a 'windfall' in connection with the developments in South Ossetia".[63] After all, Abkhazia has long enjoyed a status of "maximal autonomy" within Georgia.[64]

Overall, the Five-Day War marked the starting point for the resumption of independence claims in the Caucasus region. However, South Ossetia's and Abkhazia's independence declaration did not have an international impact like that of Kosovo. No matter how many common features there might exist between the independence claims of the Caucasian districts and Kosovo, they did not follow a parallel course. Their territorial status was unchanging, since they were autonomous regions of the state of Georgia. Russia succeeded in consolidating the presence of its troops onsite, either in the context of peacekeeping or according to the provisions of peace accords by which Russia assumed the role of the guarantor of peace between the state of Georgia and South Ossetia and Abkhazia.[65] In addition, it enhanced its influence in the two districts through mass-passportization. Yet, it remained a question whether peace and stability in the Caucasus had been accomplished.

4.2.6 *Protection of Nationals Abroad in the Caucasus Region: A Reassessment*

From a legal viewpoint, the 2008 Five-Day War brought forward the fact that stable solutions were necessary for so-called "post-Soviet frozen conflicts".[66] PNA, either through forcible or diplomatic means, was of utmost importance for the Russian Federation's "near abroad" policy. For many, the current formation of Russia's foreign policy was anticipated as a long-term effect of the Soviet Union's dissolution. PNA was central to the policy of the Russian Federation since it was explicitly stipulated in its constitution.

Forcible PNA in the 2008 conflict brought to the fore the following consideration: how conferring nationality to massive groups of people gave rise to secession

[63] Nußberger (2009), p. 363.
[64] Hewitt (2013), p. 160.
[65] Black (2022), p. 1802.
[66] See Wittke (2023).

claims. Put simply, passportization facilitated separatist arguments in the Caucasus region. In retrospect, it has been asserted that Russia's invocation of the doctrine was part of a well-orchestrated state practice which aimed at the recognition of independence of the two regions. Therefore, the international community's skepticism over Russia's recourse to force for the protection of its nationals abroad was anticipated.

In this context, forcible PNA does not mark the detachment of sovereignty from territoriality, marking the significance of extraterritoriality, rather it annuls any understanding of territorial integrity, further directly breaching the principle of non-intervention. In addition, the preceding analysis has shown that, despite the doctrine's lack of clarity which leads to a case-by-case assessment, the doctrine's stable point of reference is the existence of nationals who face some sort of peril. The extraterritoriality of sovereignty for the sake of protection is a possibility only in the name of nationals; if the existence of the latter is not guaranteed then the doctrine's invocation is at least precarious. In addition, forcible PNA in the Caucasus region marks a shift in the concept of nationality and nationality ties. In the post-Charter era, it was not only borders and their inviolability that were fixed, but the notion of nationality took a particular meaning. Russian discourse brought in the spotlight the idea of compatriots and strong nationality ties, or allegiance between certain groups and a state other than that of their nationality. The question of who qualifies as the national of a state and when a state may identify itself as kin-state.

4.3 PNA and Crimea: The Emergence of a Pattern

A few years after the invasion of Georgia, Russia intervened in Ukraine's Crimea. Russia's legal justifications for recourse to force manifestly showed that the Five-Day War was not meant to be an isolated incident. Russia gradually unfolded its "near-abroad" policy. In this context, the forcible PNA doctrine played a key role in the formation of Russian state practice.

4.3.1 Crimea's Autonomous Status: Historical Aspects

The case of Crimea has many historical elements in common with South Ossetia and Abkhazia. A brief historical review demonstrates why the Crimean Peninsula was a disputed territory; throughout the years its territorial status was at the epicenter of national strategic objectives and vital interests.[67] At the time of the disintegration of the USSR, Crimea was populated by Tatars and Ukrainians, while

[67] Charap et al. (2021), p. 63.

there was also a strong Russian community[68]; thus, its national identity was not uncontested.[69] This multinational composition was utilized by Russia and Ukraine to make strong independence claims.

More specifically, in 1990 Ukraine conducted a referendum to decide on securing its independence from the Russian Federation. The Crimean Peninsula favored independence, but results demonstrated a strong division between citizens: while Ukraine opted for independence with 90% of its votes in favor, the results in Crimea differed and there was only a small 56% vote in favor.[70] A second referendum was conducted in early 1991 in Crimea and the population called for an autonomous republic within the Soviet Union. However, the result of the Crimean sovereignty referendum was not respected. More specifically, Crimea was at the time an oblast which was administratively part of the Ukrainian SSR. In this respect, although the Crimeans opted for their autonomy within the Soviet Union, the Ukrainian SSR, under whose administration they fell, granted them autonomy within the Ukrainian Republic on February 12, 1991.[71] Further, in 1992 the autonomous status of Crimea was expanded. This course of events pretty much followed that of Abkhazia and partly explains the concept of the "post-Soviet frozen conflicts".[72] On both occasions, a district which enjoyed wide autonomy in the USSR opted either for its independence or for autonomy within the Russian Federation, contrary to the will of the Soviet Republics of which they were a part.

From 1992 onwards the situation in Crimea was apparently calm. Yet the Russian community in Crimea continued demanding a greater status in Ukraine; they asked for equal representation within the Kyiv administration, proposing in effect the creation of a confederation. This demand was thought to have been satisfied in 1996 when Ukraine granted Crimea even more autonomous status, which allowed the peninsula to have its own parliament, government and constitution; as a counterweight, the Supreme Court of Ukraine reserved the power to control the constitutionality of Crimean legislation. More specifically, from 1992 to 1996 political tensions between the Ukrainian government and Crimean authorities were high. The two sides strove to achieve a *modus operandi* that would satisfy both Ukraine's demand for respect of its territorial integrity, as well as Crimea's claims in pursuance of enhancing its autonomous status.[73] However, Ukraine's constitutional amendment of 1996 provides in Art. 2 that Ukraine is a unitary state, and its

---

[68] Knott (2022). Retrieved, February 22, 2025, from https://www.lse.ac.uk/research/research-for-the-world/society/were-crimeans-really-pro-russian-before-annexation.

[69] Charron (2016), p. 226.

[70] Hilpold (2015), p. 243.

[71] On the Restoration of the Crimean Autonomous Soviet Socialist Republic, Bulleting of the Supreme Soviet of the Ukrainian SSR (VVR), 1991, No. 9, p. 84 (in Ukrainian). Retrieved, February 22, 2025, from https://zakon.rada.gov.ua/laws/show/712-12#Text.

[72] See, Pelliconi (26 January 2023), doi: 10.17176/20230126-081617-0.

[73] Kuzio (1994), pp. 743 et seq.

sovereignty extends throughout its entire territory.[74] This change, alongside constitutional provisions according to which the Crimean governmental bodies lost their governmental power and became representative bodies, fueled the tensions the years to come.[75]

The relationship between Ukraine and Russia fluctuated based on the levels of Russophilia of each Ukrainian government. Tensions arose again in 2013 on the event of the population's unrest against the Janukowytsch government in Kyiv. Violent incidents took place in Kyiv, resulting in casualties. By 2014, the government had been overthrown, and the Ukrainian president fled to Russia to find a safe haven. These events led to the definitive secession of Crimea from Ukraine.[76] Crimean separatist movements had the financial and political support and military backing of Russia. In March 2014, the Crimean parliament proceeded with two important actions. First, it declared Crimea's independence from Ukraine, and over a five-day period it conducted a referendum on Crimea's accession to Russia. Finally, on March 18, 2014, Crimea acceded to Russia. In the meantime, Ukraine formally proclaimed that it did not consent to Crimea's independence and accession to the Russian Federation and further underlined that the Crimean actions were in direct contradiction of the Ukrainian constitution. In addition, Ukraine accused Russia of intervening in its domestic affairs. Evidently, Crimea's unilateral declaration of independence followed Kosovo's example.[77] The UNGA backed Ukraine and adopted a resolution calling upon states not to recognize changes in the status of Crimea.[78]

It cannot be disputed that from 2014 onwards, Ukraine was effectively controlling the peninsula; thus, Crimea had *de facto* seceded from Crimea. For example, it is reported, *inter alia*, that "all flights connecting Crimea and continental Ukraine have been cancelled following the unlawful 'referendum'".[79] What is contested, though, is the validity of the 2014 referendum on Crimea's accession to Russia. The UNGA underlined the fact that the referendum of March 16, 2014, which was held in autonomous Crimea, breached Ukraine's sovereignty, political independence, unity and territorial integrity within its internationally recognized borders. Thereat, it underscored its invalidity.[80] The referendum attracted international attention: its legitimacy was considered precarious, as it was uncertain whether the population could freely express its will. It is alleged that when the referendum took place,

[74] Constitution of Ukraine (28 June 1996). Retrieved February 22, 2025, from https://rm.coe.int/constitution-of-ukraine/168071f58b.

[75] Tatarenko (2 April 2014). Retrieved, February 22, 2025, from https://verfassungsblog.de/the-legal-status-and-modern-history-of-crimean-autonomy/.

[76] Yue (2016), p. 182.

[77] Värk (2014), pp. 126–127.

[78] UNGA (1 April 2014). Territorial Integrity of Ukraine. UN Doc A/Res/68/262.

[79] UN OHCHR (15 May 2014). Report on the Human Rights Situation in Ukraine. Retrieved February 22, 2025, from https://www.ohchr.org/sites/default/files/Documents/Countries/UA/HRMMUReport15May2014.pdf, para 135.

[80] UNGA (1 April 2014), op. clause 5.

Russia already was in control of strategic points in Crimea and was giving substantial backing to separatist movements.

4.3.2 *The Crimean Status Referendum and Russian Intervention*

Acceptance, or non-acceptance, of the legitimacy of the 2014 status referendum in Crimea determined the two narratives that developed afterwards. On one hand, Russia claimed that Crimea's unilateral declaration of independence was neither in breach of general international law nor a violation of the territorial integrity of Ukraine. Echoing ICJ's 2010 Advisory Opinion on Kosovo, it claimed that Crimea could unilaterally declare its independence from Ukraine. In support of this argument, it highlighted that Crimea enjoyed wide autonomy from the 1990s onwards. The peninsula had its own government and was subject to little control by Ukraine's central government. Within this framework, a declaration of independence was most likely to occur if ever relations between the two (the state and the autonomous region) deteriorated.

This line of argumentation, adopted by Russia, directly rendered the Crimean status referendum a legitimate political process. By accepting the referendum's validity, Crimea's decision for incorporation in the Russian Federation immediately meant that it became part of Russia's territory. Therefore, Russian military presence on the peninsula was Russia's duty, at the invitation of the Crimean government. The permanent representative of Russia to the UNSC further explained this rationale, and mentioned that:

> We do not dispute the principle of the territorial integrity of States. It is indeed very important. It is also understandable that the enjoyment of the right to self-determination involving separation from an existing State is an extraordinary measure, applied when further coexistence within a single State becomes impossible. Moreover, as practice has demonstrated, in the majority of cases, the realization of peoples' right to self-determination is achieved without the agreement of the central authorities of the State.[81]

Russia emphasized people's right to self-determination and lowered the threshold of remedial secession. This did not exactly follow the Quebec secession test, according to which there must be gross and systematic violations of a group's human rights in order to render internal self-determination impossible; rather, it accepted that secession is possible when "further coexistence within a single State becomes impossible".[82] Overall, the Russian rhetoric undermined the principle of territorial integrity, even though Russia officially denied it.

On the other hand, most states and international organizations did not fall in line with the Russian argumentation, considering the conduct and results of the Crimea

---

[81] UN Doc S/PV.7138 (15 March 2014), p. 2.

[82] Bering (2017), p. 767.

status referendum to be illegitimate. Although there are few references to the legitimacy of Crimea's unilateral declaration of independence,[83] annexation to Russia was broadly deemed illegal. As a result, Russian effective control over the peninsula was considered occupation of Ukrainian territory. On April 1, 2014, the foreign ministers of the North Atlantic Treaty Organization (NATO)-Ukraine Commission condemned Russia's actions and called upon Russia

> to de-escalate by reducing its troops in Crimea to pre-crisis levels and withdrawing them to their bases; to reduce its military activities along the Ukrainian border; to reverse the illegal and illegitimate "annexation" of Crimea; to refrain from any further interference and aggressive actions in Ukraine; to respect the rights of the Ukrainian population including the Crimean Tatars; and to fulfil its international obligations and to abide by international law.[84]

The EU took this a step further, not merely condemning Russia but imposing import restrictions from the annexed territories of Crimea and Sevastopol.[85]

Russian military presence in the Crimean Peninsula and the subsequent occupation fell under the concept of the invasion of Ukraine, even though there was no recourse to actual force at the time.[86] That is, the intervention was consensual.[87] Russia invoked protection of its nationals in Crimea to supplement its legal argumentation.

4.3.3 PNA in Crimea

Russian policy on the protection of its compatriots abroad is best summarized in the following statement of its president, who stated that after the Soviet Union's disintegration:

> Millions of Russians went to bed in one country and woke up abroad. [...] Overnight, they were minorities in the former Soviet republics, and the Russian people became one of the biggest — if not the biggest — divided nations in the world.[88]

This excerpt explains Russia's "near-abroad" policy and is a strong indication of how Russia interpreted its constitutional duty to protect its compatriots abroad. Yet the concern with the situation in Crimea was that its population was trichotomized;

[83] Pellet (3 March 2022). Retrieved February 22, 2025, from https://www.ejiltalk.org/open-letter-to-my-russian-friends-ukraine-is-not-crimea/.

[84] NATO (1 April 2014). Retrieved February 22, 2025, from https://www.nato.int/cps/en/natolive/news_108499.htm.

[85] Council Regulation (EU) No 692/2014 of 23 June 2014 Concerning Restrictions on the Importing into the Union of Goods Originating in Crimea or Sevastopol, in Response to the Illegal Annexation of Crimea and Sevastopol (23 June 2014). Doc 32014R0692.

[86] Green (2014), p. 5.

[87] Buchan and Tsagourias (2017), p. 186.

[88] The New York Times (18 March 2014). Retrieved February 22, 2025, from https://www.nytimes.com/2014/03/19/world/europe/ukraine.html.

along with the Russian community there were also Ukrainians and ethnic Tatars. This fact heightened concerns about the referendum's results, which led to a 97% vote in favor of accession to Russia.[89]

It turned out that Russia had carefully extended its passportization policy to Crimea too. Straight after the 2008 Five-Day War a large-scale passportization of Crimea began, while it is estimated that only 2 weeks before the peninsula's annexation Russia had issued more than 143,000 passports to the citizens there.[90] Thus, it had been building its PNA claim for quite some time. The practice of nationals' creation remained after annexation and even became harsher, as Russia's passportization policy was no longer consensual. Crimean citizens who rejected a Russian passport and expressed their will to retain their Ukrainian nationality, became foreigners in their own homeland overnight, facing the risk of unlawful expulsion.[91] What is more, the terms of occupation became even stricter when Ukrainian citizens who did not possess Russian Federation passports or residence permits in Crimea were either required to complete migration paperwork[92] or were prohibited from entering the district.[93]

Thereat, mass-passportization is not the major point of concern in the case of Crimea. Its forced character is what matters the most. Russia's invocation of the forcible PNA doctrine did not meet the *jus ad bellum* prerequisites[94]; above this, is it seems to have missed the "nationals" part. More specifically, military presence and full control over the peninsula cannot be reconciled with the doctrinal preconditions of lawful recourse to force for PNA, whether it is considered an exception to the prohibition of the use of force or an aspect of self-defense.[95] However, even if this legal hurdle is overcome, then forcible PNA is an unstable claim, due to the absence of nationals themselves, taking into account that the population of Crimea did not merely consist of a Russian community.[96]

Evidently, the "near-abroad" Russian foreign policy was founded on two similar, circular arguments: (a) it invoked the forcible protection of its nationals abroad,

---

[89] UN News (27 March 2014). Backing Ukraine's territorial integrity, UN Assembly declares Crimea referendum invalid. Retrieved February 22, 2025, from https://news.un.org/en/story/2014/03/464812.

[90] Green (2014), p. 8.

[91] New York Open Society Institute (June 2018). Human Rights in the Context of Automatic Naturalization in Crimea, p. 4.

[92] US Department of State. 2016 Country Reports on Human Rights Practices: Ukraine. Retrieved February 22, 2025, from https://www.state.gov/reports/2016-country-reports-on-human-rights-practices/ukraine/.

[93] Human Rights Council (13 June–8 July 2022). Situation of Human Rights in the Temporarily Occupied Autonomous Republic of Crimea and the City of Sevastopol, Ukraine. (Report of the Secretary-General). UN Doc A/HRC/50/65, para 35; CoE (4 May 2022). Human Rights Situation in the Autonomous Republic of Crimea and the City of Sevastopol, Ukraine. SG/Inf(2022)15, p. 16, para 69.

[94] Olson (2014), p. 36.

[95] Dickinson (2017), p. 68.

[96] Bowring (2018), pp. 21–40.

rushing to their protection and then conferring nationality on individuals to substantiate the claim for their protection, or (b) it conferred nationality on citizens of a neighboring state so as to be able to claim that use of force was legitimate in their name. The first was the case of South Ossetia and Abkhazia, and the second variant was Crimea. Invoking the forcible PNA under these circumstances was diametrically opposed to *jus ad bellum* principles, while naturalization was an unsound procedure according to international human rights law norms, and general principles of nationality law. Interestingly enough, the international human rights regime has not yet tackled the issue of forcible non-consensual naturalization. On the contrary, international norms have so far dealt only with statelessness and the involuntary loss of people's citizenship.[97] What is more, any attempt to regulate the conferment of nationality on individuals, whether consensual or not, is hindered by state sovereignty argumentation which repeats the general proposition that it is a state's prerogative to decide when, to whom and under what conditions it will grant its citizenship.

Taking the above into consideration, it follows that one of the outcomes of the disintegration of the Soviet Union was that communities with allegiance to the then Russian Federation lost any official ties with it abruptly. Put simply, the number of expatriates or compatriots in the "near-abroad" rose sharply.[98] In this regard, mass-naturalization could be tolerated by international law, as long as it remained consensual and was not a pretext for territorial claims. In the Caucasus crisis, mass-passportization was not illegal *per se* from an international law perspective. In the 2014 Crimean crisis many voices expressed concerns regarding the mass-passportization which took place from 2008 until 2014; yet again, no action was or could be taken, since it was said to be a consensual process. The forced naturalization process which took place from 2014 onwards, though, was illegal, or at least problematic.[99] Automatic naturalization was a means to solidify Crimea's accession to Russia and justify the latter's military presence on the peninsula.[100] According to legal literature, forced naturalization

> denotes the *conferment of nationality against the will* of the individual concerned. Other than extraterritorial naturalizations, forced naturalizations do not necessarily address a bigger group of persons, but target a specific individual and do not only take place outside the territory of the state concerned. The practice of forced naturalizations seems questionable from an individual rights perspective, as it fails to respect the will of the individual concerned, thus interfering with the negative right not to be forcibly attributed a nationality.[101]

[97] See, Spiro (2 May 2023). Retrieved February 22, 2025, from https://globalcit.eu/weaponized-citizenship-should-international-law-restrict-oppressive-nationality-attribution/8/; New York Open Society Institute (2018), p. 52; Natoli (2010), pp. 416–417; UNGA (30 August 1961). 1961 Convention on the Reduction of Statelessness. U.N.T.S., vol. 989, p. 175.

[98] Wilson (2016), p. 166; Heinsch (2015), pp. 323–360.

[99] Santos Mariottini de Oliveira (2024). Retrieved February 22, 2025, from https://cadmus.eui.eu/handle/1814/77046.

[100] DeBenedictis (2022), p. 102.

[101] von Rütte (2022), p. 262.

Respectively, it was underlined that:

> While Russia is entitled to offer citizenship to whoever qualifies under its national law, irrespective of where they reside, a policy that seeks to coerce directly or indirectly, a population in occupied territory to assume Russian citizenship is not permitted under international law.[102]

Therefore, recourse to the forcible PNA doctrine was in every way manipulative.[103] It violated human rights norms, and it did not meet the prerequisites of *jus ad bellum* (furthermore, ever since Russia occupied Crimea it has been violating humanitarian law rules as well).

Crimea's annexation as the rationale or the result of the doctrine's invocation raises various concerns. The doctrine's necessary admittance of some form of extraterritoriality, or a minor breach of territoriality for the sake of nationals' protection is tolerated both doctrinally and legally. However, the Crimean example, and the Russian pattern that unfolded during the last decades, move to an extreme interpretation of the doctrine, disrespecting any idea of territorial integrity. What is more, it raises doubts regarding the concept of nationality. Even if once concedes, that the peninsula is largely inhabited by people who qualify for "Russian compatriots" according to Russia's legislation, then this does not amount to the prerequisites set for the invocation of forcible PNA. Although, doctrinal discussion revolved around territorial integrity, taking for granted what "nationals" stand for, there is no doubt that such an interpretation of "nationals" would not pass the forcible PNA threshold.

This view is consolidated, if we take into account all historical aspects of this conflict, pertaining to the *uti possidetis juris* principle.[104] That is, even if Crimean residents who were Russian nationals, or felt closer to the Russian Federation, this would not suffice for the doctrine's invocation, unless there was an imminent and tangible peril against them. The mere fact that the region's autonomous character was downgraded after Ukraine's constitutional amendment of 1996 does not qualify as a perilous condition for the residents of the peninsula. Thus, the doctrine is a misfit for the case of Crimea. The breach of sovereignty in this case, lies both in the violation of Ukraine's territorial integrity, as well as in the manipulation of the concept of nationality.

4.4 Forcible PNA and the Ongoing War against Ukraine

On February 24, 2022, Russia initiated military operations against Ukraine. The invasion of Ukraine did not come as a surprise to the international community. Russia employed similar arguments as those it used to justify the invasion of Georgia and the occupation of Crimea. The Russian Federation clarified that it would

[102] Gorbunova (2014), pp. 338–339.

[103] Tancredi (2014), pp. 10–11.

[104] Lalonde (2002), pp. 218–219.

renegotiate its role in the international plane and would reformulate its foreign policy after the Soviet Union's disintegration.[105] State practice was reflected in Putin's presidential address to Russian citizens the day on which the war against Ukraine was declared. More specifically, it was held, among others, that:

> We respect and will continue to respect all the newly formed countries of the former Soviet Union [...] But Russia cannot feel safe, develop and exist with a constant threat emanating from the territory of present-day Ukraine. Let me remind you that in 2000-2005 we used our military to push back against terrorists in the Caucasus, defended the integrity of our State and preserved Russia. In 2014, we supported the people of Crimea and Sevastopol. [...] The same is also happening now. [...] The People's Republics of Donbass appealed to Russia for help. In this regard, in accordance with Article 51 (chapter VII) of the Charter of the United Nations, I have decided to conduct a special military operation with the approval of the Federation Council of Russia and pursuant to the treaties on friendship and mutual assistance with the Donetsk People's Republic and the Lugansk People's Republic, as ratified by the Federal Assembly on 22 February this year. Its purpose is to protect people who have been subjected to abuse and genocide by the Kiev regime for eight years. And to this end, we will seek the demilitarization and de-Nazification of Ukraine, as well as the prosecution of those who have committed numerous bloody crimes against civilians, including citizens of the Russian Federation. However, our plans do not include the occupation of Ukrainian territories.[106]

This part of the presidential address encompassed all legal justifications brought up by Russia, while it determined in advance the goals of the invading state. More specifically, Russia repeated its commitment to its "near-abroad" policy. Military operations in Caucasus and Crimea were brought up as success stories and examples of Russia's consistent and well-framed state policy. From a legal viewpoint, the justifications adopted in the ongoing war against Ukraine bear many features in common with previous Russian military operations.[107] Once more, Russia invoked its inherent right to self-defense, pursuant to Art. 51 UNCh (a), its duty to intervene on humanitarian grounds (b), as well as the protection of Russian populations (c). In the 2022 invasion of Ukraine, two legal grounds were added: first, Russia claimed that it intervened in Ukraine to assist in the country's de-Nazification (d), and second, that it would achieve Ukraine's demilitarization and safeguard it, ensuring that it would not have access to nuclear weapons (e).

It goes without saying that Russia decided to take advantage of regions where Russian populations existed so as to establish territorial claims, even though there is explicit reference in the presidential address to the fact that Russia did not intend to occupy Ukrainian territories. Nevertheless, it shows that Russia aimed at the Donetsk and Lugansk provinces in the Donbass region in eastern Ukraine. From 2014, pro-Russian—and consequently anti-governmental—movements had grown in the region. Separatist movements had appeared, fueled by the Russian Federation. In this sense, their mention in the Russian presidential address was hardly accidental.

---

[105] Cavandoli and Wilson (2022), p. 405.

[106] UN Doc S/2022/154 (24 February 2022), p. 6.

[107] Pelliconi (2024a), p. 237.

This climate of civil unrest had existed in the Donbass region from 2014 onwards. The two provinces in eastern Ukraine came under the control of separatists shortly after Crimea's annexation. The claim for independence from the central Ukrainian government was expressed in 2014, when the Donbass rebels called upon Russia to intervene and safeguard their protection and send troops, at least in the form of peacekeepers. Thus, they envied regimes like Abkhazia and South Ossetia. After Crimea's status referendum, the two provinces held similar referenda, which resulted in favor of political independence from the Kyiv government. Although the results of the referenda where a strong indication of voters' will to separate from Ukraine, their outcome was not welcomed either by the international community or by Russia.[108]

Western countries immediately communicated their skepticism regarding their validity, given that these events took place simultaneously with Crimea's secession from Ukraine and its subsequent annexation by Russia. Therefore, they characterized the referenda as "pseudo-referenda". Russia officially took a neutral position with respect to these independence referenda. On one hand, it did not offer a positive response to the separatist movements' demands to incorporate into the Russian Federation. On the other hand, though, Russia asked for a peaceful process that would ultimately implement the results of the referenda. It further suggested that the best option for the region would be acquiring autonomous status in Ukraine.[109]

Due to upheaval in eastern Ukraine in the aftermath of the referenda, the Ukrainian government entered into a peace accord with the separatists of the Donbass, the so-called "Minsk Protocol" of September 2014.[110] This protocol did not ignore the people's will in Donetsk and Lugansk to accede to the Russian Federation. For this reason, the protocol was drafted under the auspices of the OSCE and was agreed between Ukraine and Russia. Thereat, the two regions' ties with the neighboring state were indirectly affirmed. The Minsk Protocol failed to ease tensions. After its signature, the two regions suffered from violent incidents which multiplied day by day. To halt the region's destabilization, the 13-point "Package of Measures for the Implementation of the Minsk Agreements" (Minsk II) was agreed in 2015.[111]

From 2015 onwards, until the outbreak of war in 2022, the Donbass region was the definition of a gray zone.[112] Normalcy and stability were not accomplished in the

---

[108] Kemp and Lyubashenko (2018), p. 344.

[109] Robinson (2016), p. 514.

[110] Protocol on the results of consultations of the Trilateral Contact Group with respect to the joint steps aimed at the implementation of the Peace Plan of the President of Ukraine, P. Poroshenko, and the initiatives of the President of Russia, V. Putin (Minsk Protocol, or Minsk I Agreement) (5 September 2014). Retrieved February 22, 2025, from https://www.peaceagreements.org/view/1363.

[111] Package of measures for the Implementation of the Minsk agreements (12 February 2015). Retrieved, February 22, 2025, from https://peacemaker.un.org/sites/peacemaker.un.org/files/UA_150212_MinskAgreement_en.pdf; UN Doc S/Res/2202(2015) (17 February 2015).

[112] Pettyjohn and Wasser (2019), pp. 10–11.

region, despite the agreements. It is reported that small-scale violence became part of people's everyday reality.[113] Yet this information cannot be fully verified, due to international observers' inability to reach the region and because of the contested reports coming from the conflicting parties. Despite the difficulty of establishing the factual background of civil unrest, it is undeniable that Ukraine's control over the region was not effective, while Russia's influence in the Donbass was sustained.

This short historical overview is exemplary of how Russia managed to exert its political and military influence in the "near-abroad". Unlike in the cases of Abkhazia, Crimea and South Ossetia, which already possessed autonomous status when conflicts erupted, the Donbass region became a troubled area within a few years. However, this reading of the conflict offers but a tiny explanation of what ensued in the 2022 war.

4.4.1 The Interchangeable Use of Legal Justifications by Russia

Russia's accumulation and interchangeable use of legal justifications for the 2022 war against Ukraine resulted in confusion. However, if one attempts to clarify Russia's discourse, everything converges on the fact that the goal of the Ukraine invasion was regime change. Russia proclaimed itself as the protector of Russian-speaking populations, as well as of all Ukrainian citizens against Nazification. In other words, humanitarian grounds pertained to the people's alleged oppression by a regime promoting Nazism.[114] This was the central tenet of Russia's rhetoric: the Ukrainian government was applying Nazi policies which put the state's people in peril and was wiping out minority populations.[115] Although this justification was manifestly unfounded, it was applied by Russia to demonstrate the prominent role it played in modern history to oust Nazism.[116] In addition, Russia took advantage of the UN's close eye cast all over the globe to report on policies or incidents that glorified Nazism, neo-Nazism and other practices that contributed to fueling contemporary forms of racism, racial discrimination, xenophobia and related intolerance.[117]

---

[113] OHCHR (3 March 2016). Report on the Human Rights Situation in Ukraine 16 November 2015 to 15 February 2016. Retrieved February 22, 2025, from https://www.ohchr.org/sites/default/files/Documents/Countries/UA/Ukraine_13th_HRMMU_Report_3March2016.pdf, p. 8, para 12; See also, Security Council Press Statement on Deterioration of Situation in Donetsk Region, Ukraine (31 January 2017). UN Doc SC/12700. Retrieved 22 February 2025, from https://press.un.org/en/2017/sc12700.doc.htm; UNGA (27 January 2015). Report of the Special Rapporteur on Minority Issues, Rita Izsák. UN Doc A/HRC/28/64/Add.1.

[114] Blitt (2024), p. 29.

[115] Starski and Arndt (2021), p. 787.

[116] Vorobiova (2022), p. 58.

[117] UN Human Rights Council (14 April 2023). Mandate of Special Rapporteur on contemporary forms of racism, racial discrimination, xenophobia and related intolerance. UN Doc A/HRC/Res/52/36.

In this sense, the Russian discourse linked Ukraine's domestic policies to those of extremist political parties that implemented discriminatory measures at a national or local level by targeting racial, ethnic or religious minorities based on ideas of hatred. Nevertheless, there was no actual suggestions that Ukraine's policies incorporated nationalistic elements equating to a modern form of Nazism.[118] This argumentation was rejected by the UN's Special Rapporteur on contemporary forms of racism, racial discrimination, xenophobia and related intolerance, who noted, with alarm, that

> the Russian Federation has sought to justify its military invasion and territorial aggression in Ukraine on the purported basis of eliminating neo-Nazism. This is a blatant instrumentalization of the serious human rights concerns raised by neo-Nazi mobilizations where they exist. The Special Rapporteur interprets resolution 76/149 as seeking the genuine protection of groups and individuals subject to human rights violations rooted in neo-Nazism. The use of neo-Nazism as a pretext to justify territorial aggression seriously undermines genuine attempts to combat neo-Nazism. The Special Rapporteur denounces and condemns in the strongest terms such pretextual use, including in relation to the unlawful breach of the sovereign territory of Ukraine and the humanitarian crisis that breach has caused.[119]

Therefore, drawing any potential connection between Ukraine's domestic legislation and policies to neo-Nazism was flatly refused by the UN.

If de-Nazification did not stand as an argument, then humanitarian grounds—either for the intervention or the attack which triggered Art. 51—need to be further explained. So far, it is clear that there is no such evidence that might substantiate either of these two clauses: humanitarian intervention or self-defense. As far as recourse to force pursuant to Art. 51 UNCh is concerned, Russia alleged that it was protecting itself from threats emanating from Ukraine, namely NATO's expansion and the claimed placement of Western nuclear weaponry in Ukraine.[120] Although these reasons might be considered an "existential threat to Russia", they do not meet the requirements set out by Art. 51 UNCh. As such, most writers consider them an application of the preemptive or preventive self-defense theory, whose validity is by and large doubted in international law.[121] Yet again, even if one accepts that preemptive self-defense has a strong standing in international law, then the Russian military actions do not fulfill the prerequisite of proportionality. Assuming that danger stems

[118] Longobardo (2022). Retrieved February 22, 2025, from https://papers.ssrn.com/sol3/papers.cfm?abstract_id=4214444.

[119] UN Human Rights Council (23 May 2022). Combating Glorification of Nazism, Neo-Nazism and Other Practices that Contribute to Fuelling Contemporary Forms of Racism, Racial Discrimination, Xenophobia and Related Intolerance. Report of the Special Rapporteur on Contemporary Forms of Racism, Racial Discrimination, Xenophobia and Related Intolerance, E. Tendayi Achiume. UN Doc A/HRC/50/61, p. 3; See also, UNGA, Note by the Secretary-General (10 August 2023). Contemporary Forms of Racism, Racial Discrimination, Xenophobia and Related Intolerance. UN Doc A/78/302, p. 8, para 21.

[120] Marten (2023), p. 209.

[121] Milanovic (24 February 2022). Retrieved February 22, 2025, from https://www.ejiltalk.org/page/2/?s=Russia+Ukraine+humanitarian+intervention.

either from Ukraine's neo-Nazi policies against Russian-speaking populations, or from the existence of the state's weaponization, then still none of this would justify the magnitude and duration of the ongoing war on Ukrainian soil.[122] Ultimately, this explains why most international analysts predicted at the beginning of the intervention in Ukraine that Russia would restrict itself to the Donbass region and not attack the rest of the country's territory by moving across the Dnipro river.[123] Overall, 3 years after the invasion of Ukraine, any notion of proportionality has been severely violated. Military operations have lasted longer than expected, military targets are hit all over the Ukrainian territory, while the above justifications have been put aside.

Finally, Russia justified its recourse to force on the grounds of humanitarian intervention, particularly in defense of the Donetsk and Lugansk provinces in the Donbass region. To substantiate this argument, Russia repeated the allegations it had made in relation to Abkhazia, South Ossetia and Crimea in the most precise way. At the very beginning of its intervention, it claimed that genocide had been perpetrated against the people of eastern Ukraine, a humanitarian concern for sure. However, international scholarship deemed this justification "alien" to international norms, given that turbulence in the area had existed from 2014 onwards and most of it could be attributed to separatists.[124]

Eventually, both legal justifications—an armed attack in the form of de-Nazification, or humanitarian grounds due to genocide against Russian-speaking populations—implied that Ukraine was in full control of the Donbass region. In effect, this proposition contradicted the Russian narrative according to which for a period of almost 8 years the Donetsk and Lugansk oblasts were not under Ukraine's effective control. In this sense, it nullifies the validity of the (pseudo)-referenda and the ensuing Minsk Agreements. Overall, the UN Secretary-General acknowledged that the Donbass conflict is "complex, with at least two permanently opposing narratives".[125]

4.4.2 Forcible PNA Unfolded

In the case of Ukraine, Russia claimed that the Donbass region was predominantly populated by Russian-speaking populations, for the sake of whom it intervened. The term "Russian speaking populations" was carefully chosen, as it encompassed both

[122] Pellet (2022).

[123] Pazzanese (17 February 2023). Retrieved February 22, 2025, from https://news.harvard.edu/gazette/story/2023/02/how-does-ukraine-war-end-experts-say-2023-could-prove-decisive-dangerous/.

[124] Weller (9 March 2022). Retrieved February 22, 2025, from https://www.cam.ac.uk/stories/weller-ukraine.

[125] UN Secretary-General (23 February 2022). Secretary-General Says Russian Federation's Recognition of 'Independent' Donetsk, Luhansk Violate Ukraine's Sovereignty, Territorial Integrity. UN Doc SG/SM/21153.

those who possessed Russian passports at the time of the invasion as well as those who did not, but who potentially favored the separatist movements.

Just as in the cases of South Ossetia, Abkhazia and Crimea, Russia proceeded with the mass-issuance of passports to Donbass citizens. The typical criterion for possessing a state's passport in order to be considered a national of that state was critical to the Russian intervention in Ukraine, too. However, unlike on previous occasions, Russia expanded its passportization policy. From 2014 onwards, when the separatist movements in the two former Soviet oblasts declared their will to accede to Russia, passportization had officially begun. In this regard, Russia had ample time to ensure that most Donbass citizens would possess a Russian passport by the time of intervention. More specifically, it is reported that the phase of intensive passportization of the soon-to-be-annexed areas started from 2019. The data provided by Donbass' de facto authorities suggests that

> 635,000 Russian passports were issued to Donbas residents between April 2019 and the end of January 2022, amounting to somewhere between a third and a fourth of the population [...] By 2020, these citizens were granted the right to vote in the Russian constitutional plebiscite, and in 2021 they could vote for the 2021 Duma elections from polling stations in Rostov oblast, Russia.[126]

As has already been mentioned, the mass-conferment of a state's nationality to aliens is not per se a breach of the law of nationality, but most of a legal grey area. If, though, it is tallied alongside territorial claims then it signifies the instrumentalization of this process. Passportization is a term which already carried a negative connotation, and the Russian policy during the last decades seems to have worsened its meaning. For this reason, it is suggested that the term stands for "a securitized version of fast-track preferential, extraterritorial naturalization targeted at breakaway territories such as the Donbas".[127]

The issuance of Russian passports to Donbass citizens from 2014 to 2022 was reported to be a consensual process. After Ukraine's invasion, though, there were concerns that Russian authorities were compelling citizens to accept passports.[128] If these reports are proven true then two implications arise. First, if Russian authorities can forcibly compel Ukrainian citizens to accept Russian citizenship, then they can exercise effective control over the territories in which they enforce this practice. In effect, this denotes that Russia occupies part of Ukraine. Second, the forcible conferment of nationality is only one means that Russia employs to alter the demographics of eastern Ukraine. More specifically, passportization is only one strand of Russia's attempt to depopulate Ukraine. So far, there have been testimonies that Russian authorities have proceeded with the forcible expulsion of all those who refuse Russian citizenship. So far, international media mentions that on April 27,

[126] Bækken (2024), pp. 42–43.

[127] Burkhardt et al. (2022), p. 7.

[128] Santora (2 May 2023). Retrieved, 22 February 2025, from https://www.nytimes.com/2023/05/02/world/europe/russia-ukraine-civilians.html#:~:text=Russia%20is%20ramping%20up%20pressure,of%20a%20widely%20expected%20counteroffensive.

2023, Russia issued a decree which provided for a simplified, fast-track procedure for the issuance of Russian passports to the residents of four Ukrainian regions, namely Donetsk, Lugansk, Zaporizhia and Kherson.[129] According to this decree, Ukrainian citizens in possession of passports issued by the "republics" of Donetsk and Lugansk who fail to obtain Russian passports in 1 year's time following the decree's issuance will be considered foreign nationals.

Evidently, Ukrainians who have been living in these regions for decades now find themselves facing the extreme danger of being deported from their homeland. Besides, Russian authorities exert pressure on citizens in multiple ways to comply with this legislative framework. All those who do not wish to acquire Russian nationality, or who hesitate to do so, are under the microscope of the Russian authorities. Discrimination against them is almost certain, while their access to public services is in doubt.[130] In addition, anyone resisting the Russian occupation of the Donbass faces the peril of enforced disappearance.[131] It has been testified that civilians who have not taken direct part in the hostilities have gone unaccounted for, lost without trace overnight.[132] Finally, Russia is also accused of the forcible transfer of children from Ukraine to the Russian mainland. According to the information available, children whose parents have been lost on the battlefield have been taken by the Russian military to Russia on the pretext that they will receive proper education and training.[133]

In this context, it appears that conferment of Russian nationality to citizens of eastern Ukraine, irrespective of their potential ties to Russia or the language they speak, is a matter of major importance to the occupying power. Citizens' acceptance of these terms set by Russia is a prerequisite for their well-being; otherwise, their fundamental rights and freedoms are in jeopardy. These practices, taken together, exceed by far the concept of forced or non-consensual naturalization.[134] Russia's

---

[129] Decree of the President of the Russian Federation (27 April 2023). Retrieved February 22, 2025, from http://publication.pravo.gov.ru/Document/View/0001202304270013.

[130] See, Kvitka (16 May 2023). Retrieved, February 22, 2025, from https://www.hrw.org/news/2023/05/16/russia-threatens-ukrainians-who-refuse-russian-citizenship.

[131] By March 31, 2023, the UN has documented 621 cases of enforced disappearance and arbitrary detention. OHCHR (31 March 2023). Retrieved February 22, 2025, from https://www.ohchr.org/en/statements/2023/03/ukraine-high-commissioner-turk-details-severe-violations-and-calls-just-peace.

[132] CoE, Commissioner for Human Rights (29 August 2022). Statement on the Occasion of the International Day of Victims of Enforced Disappearances. Retrieved, February 22, 2025, from https://www.coe.int/en/web/commissioner/-/statement-on-the-occasion-of-the-international-day-of-victims-of-enforced-disappearances.

[133] European Parliament Briefing. Russia's War on Ukraine, Forcibly Displaced Ukrainian Children. Retrieved February 22, 2025, from https://www.europarl.europa.eu/RegData/etudes/BRIE/2023/747093/EPRS_BRI(2023)747093_EN.pdf; PACE (30 October 2023). Deportations and Forcible Transfers of Ukrainian Children and Other Civilians to Russian Federation or to Ukrainian Territories Temporarily Occupied: Create Conditions for their Safe Return, Stop these Crimes and Punish the Perpetrators. Res 2495(2023).

[134] Pelliconi (8 September 2024b). Retrieved February 22, 2025, from https://www.e-ir.info/2024/09/08/unexceptional-exceptionalism-the-use-of-force-by-great-powers-and-international-instability/.

aggressive policy on passportization is the means to achieve the so-called "Russification" of eastern Ukraine. At this point, it shall be mentioned that the term "Russification" predates the 2022 war in Ukraine. It is recorded as an established Soviet practice, given that on several occasions the central government of the Soviet Union encouraged the immigration of ethnic Russians into Soviet republics to fortify their Russian identity.[135] Ukraine has suffered Russification policies before the 2022 aggression. Nevertheless, it managed to sustain its national identity.[136]

4.5 Russia's Hegemonic Use of the Forcible PNA Doctrine

An assessment of Russia's interpretation of the forcible PNA doctrine leads to two safe conclusions. From 2008 onwards, the Russian Federation has decided to employ the doctrine to enforce its near-abroad policy and to defrost territorial claims which stemmed from the Soviet Union's disintegration. In this context, the forcible PNA has been employed on three occasions over the last 15 years and the emergence of a pattern is definite. The Russian motive can be broken down into two propositions.

First, Russia mingles the forcible PNA with territorial claims (independence of autonomous areas, or incorporation into Russia). In retrospect, the forcible PNA comes as a direct breach of the principle of territorial integrity. The use of the doctrine in such a way ruptures all developments which have taken place from 1945 onwards. Both the international normative framework and state conduct converge to the point that the forcible PNA must meet the requirements set by the UNCh. As such, it cannot pose a threat to states' territorial integrity, while it is also asserted that it must align with the prerequisites set by the law of self-defense. This convergence led eventually to NEOs and the recent UN practice which seems to tolerate the doctrine on certain occasions. Russia's policy, though, runs contrary to the above and discards legal developments. The Russian use of the doctrine echoes the hegemonic and imperialistic use of it in the pre-Charter era by civilized nations, further disrupting any sense of continuity in international law. Russia has revived the concept of "non-Western imperialism",[137] as it has managed to destabilize and change the legal status in the areas in which it has intervened.

The second distinctive aspect of the Russian policy pertains to the notion of nationals. On all previous occasions when states have resorted to force in the name of their nationals, military operations have usually applied to distinct groups of people that reside in a third state. Given that Russia has employed the doctrine to

[135] Molodikova (2024), p. 241.

[136] Coleman (2021–2022), pp. 120–121.

[137] Kotova and Tzouvala (2022), doi:10.1017/ajil.2022.48; Pelliconi (2024), p. 256; Pervou (2024), p. 275.

ground its territorial claims, it appears that the concept of "nationals" needs be redefined. The question "whose nationals" is a central feature of all Russian interventions. Russian interventions were followed by the mass-issuance of passports both in Georgia and in Ukraine. This process took place in order to ensure that the intervention in the name of nationals did indeed have such a character and to confirm the significance of a typical dimension of nationality, that is passports. Russia initially claimed that all disputed areas were populated by people with allegiance to Russia: either Russian-speaking populations, or people who felt that they were closer to Russia than to their state of nationality and/or residence.

Therefore, the prerequisite of nationality did not necessarily exist, in its most strict form, when military operations started. The mass-issuance of passports has been an easier way to create official ties between an intervening state and citizens and it was thus preferred.[138] Otherwise, one would expect that more elaborate claims of self-determination should have been put forth. This approach affirms that nationality is not an abstract term, rather it holds a prominent role in states' territorial affairs.[139] Overall, the Russian policy of conferring Russian nationality *en masse* on persons residing outside Russia "is in many respects exorbitant and risks to violate various principles of international law",[140] and most specifically people's right to hold, deny or change their nationality.[141]

The Russian pattern in all these three examples does not only prove that the nationality link was not the tip of the spear that triggered these wars. Even if one accepts that nationality is not a typical aspect of forcible PNA, then allegiance between people and the protecting state needs to be there for the doctrine's legitimate invocation. Lack of formal nationality ties has time and again occupied legal debate on various circumstances. The Russian example differs though, since Russia used demographic politics to substantiate its forcible PNA claim. Except for these considerations, the differentiating element, which is common in all three Russian invocations of the doctrine, is that it brought up forcible PNA for large populations. The populations that Russia is seeking to protect through these military operations are large and so its policy cannot be compared to small-scale raids, evacuation operations or rescue missions. In this context, forcible PNA becomes a synonym to military intervention, availed of any legal justification. This reading of forcible PNA relativizes even more the doctrine's content. Forcible protection of large populations means that military operations will be extensive by way of analogy. This admission shows the doctrine's extreme limits. If the protection of large groups is at stake, then the forcible PNA doctrine is not suitable, otherwise this would contravene any sense of territoriality and sovereignty.

---

[138] Spiro (2023); Ganohariti (2021), pp. 1–8.

[139] Gray (2018), p. 724; Harzl (2021), p. 82.

[140] Peters (9 May 2019). Retrieved, February 22, 2025, from https://www.ejiltalk.org/passportisation-risks-for-international-law-and-stability-part-one/.

[141] Art. 15 UDHR provides that "Everyone has the right to a nationality. No one shall be arbitrarily deprived of his nationality nor denied the right to change his nationality." UNGA (10 December 1948). Universal Declaration of Human Rights (UDHR), 217 A (III).

4.6 Conclusions

The Russian policy regarding the protection of Russian compatriots residing in former autonomous Soviet oblasts is consistent. Military operations after the mass issuance of passports with the legal justification of forcible PNA is easily traced. Apart from this descriptive analysis, the above analysis offers interesting insights regarding the concept of state sovereignty. The Russian example of the doctrine's invocation made it clear that the doctrine is tolerated by the international legal order only as long as the principle of territoriality is not utterly violated. Criticism of the Russian discourse is not the outcome of a pro-Western reading of international law; rather, it is directly related to Russia's attempt to base its territorial claims on the doctrine. Although Russia's specious invocation of the doctrine questioned its legitimacy under international law once more, this is not the major issue of concern. The doctrine's legitimacy depends on the fine balance between the principles of territoriality and nationality (or more precisely the principle of active personality). Russia's conduct can be characterized as hegemonic, for it repudiates the central role territoriality plays in the international legal regime.

The UN Charter's prohibition of the use of force is not only cardinal for the maintenance of international peace and security, but is also a constant reminder of how this system is grounded on territoriality. As a matter of fact, in the post-Charter era territoriality and the standardization of borders since the completion of decolonization have been the pillars of the international legal regime. It is no exaggeration to suggest that territoriality has prevailed over nationality. Sovereignty and territorial integrity have gradually attained the same meaning, both considered sacrosanct by the international legal order.[142] Thus, the Russian invocation of the doctrine over the last years has reintroduced the question of the fine balance between territoriality and active personality. The Vattelian perception of sovereignty is more relevant than ever, given that nationality has long been ignored by legal theory. It is no surprise that mass passportization and forced naturalization are not stipulated as practices contrary to international law. Therefore, the Russian paradigm has brought back to the legal debate the significance of nationality when associated with territorial claims and military operations. This degradation of the meaning of nationality for these legal domains is not a surprise, given that emphasis was put on doctrines like humanitarian intervention, where the nationality element is indifferent. At the same time, forcible PNA was invoked by states but on a smaller scale.

The Russian discourse unfolding during the last decades shakes the foundations of the legal regime on the use of force. One would expect that this proposition refers to its territorial claims, however the illegality of these claims is easy to establish. The major points of concern are two. First, how this practice opens Pandora's box, as it manifestly disrespects the *uti possidetis* principle. Second, the Russian

[142] UN Secretary-General Press Release (17 March 2022). Sovereignty, Territorial Integrity 'Sacrosanct', Secretary-General Tells Forum of Small States, Stressing Borders Cannot Be Withdrawn at Great-Power Whim. UN Doc SG/SM/21188.

example questions forcible PNA's very essence. The Russian government invoked the doctrine for large diasporic populations, substantially moderating it. Military intervention in the name of nationals was always part of state discourse, but it never referred to such large groups of people. If this quantitative change is accepted, then forcible PNA shall be interpreted according to it. Forcible protection of entire regions requires full scale military operations; thus, the doctrine would not be just an exception to the prohibition to use force in international law. This is why the Russian discourse over the last years is deemed a source of discontinuity in international law.[143]

UN Documentation

UNSC

UN Doc S/2022/154 (24 February 2022).
Security Council Press Statement on Deterioration of Situation in Donetsk Region, Ukraine (31 January 2017). UN Doc SC/12700. Retrieved February 22, 2025, from https://press.un.org/en/2017/sc12700.doc.htm.
UN Doc S/Res/2202(2015) (17 February 2015).
UN Doc S/PV.7138 (15 March 2014).
UNSC (28 August 2008). The Situation in Georgia. UN Doc S/PV.5969.
UN Doc S/PV.5961 (19 August 2008).
UN Doc S/PV.5953 (10 August 2008).
UNSC (8 August 2008). Security Council Hears Conflicting Russian, Georgian Views on Worsening Crisis. UN Doc SC/9418.
UN Doc S/PV.5952 (8 August 2008).
UN Doc S/PV.5951 (8 August 2008).
UN Doc S/1994/583 (17 May 1994).
UN Doc S/Res/858(1993) (24 August 1993).
UN Doc S/Res/854(1993) (6 August 1993).
UN Doc S/Res/849(1993) (9 July 1993).

UNGA

UNGA, Note by the Secretary-General (10 August 2023). Contemporary Forms of Racism, Racial Discrimination, Xenophobia and Related Intolerance. UN Doc A/78/302.

[143] Kanetake et al. (2024), p. 229.

UNGA (27 January 2015). Report of the Special Rapporteur on minority issues, Rita Izsák. UN Doc A/HRC/28/64/Add.1.
UNGA (1 April 2014). Territorial Integrity of Ukraine. UN Doc A/Res/ 68/262.
UNGA (24 October 1970). Declaration on Principles of International Law Concerning Friendly Relations and Co-operation Among States in Accordance with the Charter of the United Nations. UN Doc. A/RES/2625 (XXV).
UNGA, Thirty-Third Session, 1679th Plenary Meeting (3 October 1968). UN Doc A/PV.1679.
UNGA (30 August 1961). 1961 Convention on the Reduction of Statelessness. U.N.T.S., vol. 989, p. 175.
UNGA (10 December 1948). Universal Declaration of Human Rights (UDHR), 217 A (III).

Other

UN Human Rights Council (14 April 2023). Mandate of Special Rapporteur on contemporary forms of racism, racial discrimination, xenophobia and related intolerance. UN Doc A/HRC/Res/52/36.
OHCHR (31 March 2023). On Ukraine, High Commissioner Türk Details Severe Violations and Calls for a Just Peace. Retrieved February 22, 2025, from https://www.ohchr.org/en/statements/2023/03/ukraine-high-commissioner-turk-details-severe-violations-and-calls-just-peace.
UN Secretary-General Press Release (17 March 2022). Sovereignty, Territorial Integrity 'Sacrosanct', Secretary-General Tells Forum of Small States, Stressing Borders Cannot Be Withdrawn at Great-Power Whim. UN Doc SG/SM/21188.
UN Secretary-General (23 February 2022). Secretary-General Says Russian Federation's Recognition of 'Independent' Donetsk, Luhansk Violate Ukraine's Sovereignty, Territorial Integrity. UN Doc SG/SM/21153.
Human Rights Council (13 June – 8 July 2022). Situation of Human Rights in the Temporarily Occupied Autonomous Republic of Crimea and the City of Sevastopol, Ukraine. (Report of the Secretary-General). UN Doc A/HRC/50/65.
UN Human Rights Council (23 May 2022). Combating Glorification of Nazism, Neo-Nazism and Other Practices that Contribute to Fuelling Contemporary Forms of Racism, Racial Discrimination, Xenophobia and Related Intolerance. Report of the Special Rapporteur on Contemporary Forms of Racism, Racial Discrimination, Xenophobia and Related Intolerance, E. Tendayi Achiume. UN Doc A/HRC/50/61.
OHCHR (3 March 2016). Report on the Human Rights Situation in Ukraine 16 November 2015 to 15 February 2016. Retrieved February 22, 2025, from https://www.ohchr.org/sites/default/files/Documents/Countries/UA/Ukraine_13th_HRMMU_Report_3March2016.pdf.

UN News (27 March 2014). Backing Ukraine's territorial integrity, UN Assembly declares Crimea referendum invalid. Retrieved February 22, 2025, from https://news.un.org/en/story/2014/03/464812.

United Nations Office for the Coordination of Humanitarian Affairs (OCHA) (15 August 2008). Background: Six-point peace plan for the Georgia-Russia conflict. Retrieved February 22, 2025, from https://reliefweb.int/report/georgia/background-six-point-peace-plan-georgia-russia-conflict.

UN Subcommission on Prevention of Discrimination and Protection of Minorities (1979). Study on the Rights of Persons Belonging to Ethnic, Religious and Linguistic Minorities, by Francesco Capotorti. UN Doc E/CN.4/Sub.2/384/Rev.1.

International Law Commission (1952). Report on Nationality, Including Statelessness by Mr. Manley O. Hudson, Special Rapporteur, Nationality Including Statelessness, UN Doc A/CN.4/50.

CoE

PACE (30 October 2023). Deportations and Forcible Transfers of Ukrainian Children and Other Civilians to Russian Federation or to Ukrainian Territories Temporarily Occupied: Create Conditions for their Safe Return, Stop these Crimes and Punish the Perpetrators. Res 2495(2023).

CoE, Commissioner for Human Rights (29 August 2022). Statement on the Occasion of the International Day of Victims of Enforced Disappearances. Retrieved February 22, 2025, from https://www.coe.int/en/web/commissioner/-/statement-on-the-occasion-of-the-international-day-of-victims-of-enforced-disappearances.

CoE (4 May 2022). Human Rights Situation in the Autonomous Republic of Crimea and the City of Sevastopol, Ukraine. SG/Inf(2022)15.

IIFFMCG, Report Vol. II (September 2009). Retrieved February 22, 2025, from http://www.ceiig.ch/pdf/IIFFMCG_Volume_II.pdf.

IIFFMCG, Report Vol. I (September 2009). Retrieved February 22, 2025, from https://www.echr.coe.int/Documents/HUDOC_38263_08_Annexes_ENG.pdf.

PACE (30 September – 2 October 2008). The Consequences of the War between Georgia and Russia. Res1633(2008).

EU

Council Regulation (EU) No 692/2014 of 23 June 2014 Concerning Restrictions on the Importing into the Union of Goods Originating in Crimea or Sevastopol, in Response to the Illegal Annexation of Crimea and Sevastopol (23 June 2014). Doc 32014R0692.

European Parliament Briefing. Russia's War on Ukraine, Forcibly Displaced Ukrainian children. Retrieved February 22, 2025, from https://www.europarl.europa.eu/RegData/etudes/BRIE/2023/747093/EPRS_BRI(2023)747093_EN.pdf.

Council of the European Union (2 December 2008). Concerning an Independent International Fact-Finding Mission on the Conflict in Georgia. Council Decision 2008/901CFSP.

Jurisprudence

ICJ

Application of the International Convention on the Elimination of All Forms of Racial Discrimination (Georgia v. Russian Federation), Preliminary Objections, Judgment, I.C.J. Reports 2011, p. 70.

Accordance with International Law of the Unilateral Declaration of Independence in Respect of Kosovo, Advisory Opinion, I.C.J. Reports 2010, p. 403.

Accordance with International Law of the Unilateral Declaration of Independence by the Provisional Institutions of Self-Government of Kosovo (Request for advisory opinion), Written Statement by the Russian Federation (16 April 2009).

Nottebohm Case (second phase), Judgment of April 6th, 1955: ICJ Reports 1955, p. 4.

ECtHR

Georgia v. Russia (II), App. No 38263/08 (ECtHR, 21 January 2021).

Georgia v. Russia (I), App. No 13255/07 (ECtHR, 3 July 2014).

Miscellaneous

Decree of the President of the Russian Federation (27 April 2023). On the Specifics of the Legal Status of Certain Categories of Foreign Citizens and Stateless Persons in the Russian Federation. No. 307. Retrieved, February 22, 2025, from http://publication.pravo.gov.ru/Document/View/0001202304270013.

OSCE, Group of Friends of Georgia (2 September 2022). Russia's 2008 Military Invasion of Georgia. Retrieved February 22, 2025, from https://www.gov.uk/government/speeches/russias-2008-military-invasion-of-georgia-joint-statement-to-the-osce.

US Department of State. 2016 Country Reports on Human Rights Practices: Ukraine. Retrieved February 22, 2025, from https://www.state.gov/reports/2016-country-reports-on-human-rights-practices/ukraine/.

Package of measures for the Implementation of the Minsk agreements (12 February 2015). Retrieved February 22, 2025, from https://peacemaker.un.org/sites/peacemaker.un.org/files/UA_150212_MinskAgreement_en.pdf.

Protocol on the results of consultations of the Trilateral Contact Group with respect to the joint steps aimed at the implementation of the Peace Plan of the President of Ukraine, P. Poroshenko, and the initiatives of the President of Russia, V. Putin (Minsk Protocol, or Minsk I Agreement) (5 September 2014). Retrieved February 22, 2025, from https://www.peaceagreements.org/view/1363.

Reference re Secession of Quebec, [1998] 2 S.C.R. 217.

Constitution of Ukraine (28 June 1996). Retrieved February 22, 2025, from https://rm.coe.int/constitution-of-ukraine/168071f58b.

Russian Federation 1993 (rev. 2014) (Constitution of the Russian Federation). Retrieved February 22, 2025, from https://www.constituteproject.org/constitution/Russia_2014.

Agreement of Principles of Settlement of the Georgian – Ossetian Conflict (Sochi Agreement) (24 June 1992). Retrieved, February 22, 2025, from https://peacemaker.un.org/sites/default/files/document/files/2024/05/ge20ru920624agreemenonprinciplesofsettlementgeorgianossetianconflict.pdf.

On the Restoration of the Crimean Autonomous Soviet Socialist Republic, Bulleting of the Supreme Soviet of the Ukrainian SSR (VVR), 1991, No. 9, p. 84 (in Ukrainian). Retrieved, February 22, 2025, from https://zakon.rada.gov.ua/laws/show/712-12#Text.

References

Books

Amnesty International (2008) Civilians in the line of fire, the Georgia-Russia conflict. Amnesty International Publications

Charap S et al (2021) Russia's military interventions, patterns, drivers, and signposts. Rand

Crawford J (2006) The creation of states in international law, 2nd edn. Oxford University Press

DeBenedictis K (2022) Russian "Hybrid Warfare" and the Annexation of Crimea. The modern application of soviet political warfare. Bloomsbury

Hewitt G (2013) Discordant neighbors, a reassessment of the Georgian-Abkhazian and Georgian-South Ossetian conflicts. Brill

Jennings R, Watts A (1992) Oppenheim's international law, Vol. I, 9th edn. Longman House

Kushnir O (2018) Ukraine and Russian Neo-Imperialism, the Divergent Break. Lexington Books

Lalonde S (2002) Determining boundaries in a conflicted world, the role of Uti Possidetis. McGill-Queen's University Press

Pettyjohn SL, Wasser B (2019) Competing in the Gray Zone, Russian Tactics and Western Responses. Rand

Suny RG (1994) The making of the Georgian Nation, 2nd edn. Indiana University Press

von Rütte B (2022) The human right to citizenship within international and regional human rights law. Brill
Wittke C (ed) (2023) Post-soviet conflict potentials. Routledge

Articles

Allison R (2009) The Russian case for military intervention in Georgia: international law, norms and political calculation. Eur Secur 18(2):173–200
Bering J (2017) The prohibition of annexation: lessons from Crimea. New York Univ J Int Law Policy 49(3):747–832
Black M (2022) Waging war: exercising the right to self-Defense in disputed territories. Cornell Law Rev 108(7):1793–1820
Blitt RC (2024) Justifying aggression: Russia's 2020 constitutional amendments and the invasion of Ukraine. Vanderbilt J Transnatl Law 57(1):1–90
Bloed A (2006) Russia and Georgia disagree on Russian peacekeepers. Hels Monit 17(2):193–195
Borgen CJ (2009) The language of law and the practice of politics: great powers and the rhetoric of self-determination in the cases of Kosovo and South Ossetia. Chic J Int Law 10(1):1–33
Buchan R, Tsagourias N (2017) The crisis in Crimea and the principle of non-intervention. Int Commun Law Rev 19(2–3):165–193
Bækken H (2024) Forging frontline Russians, militarized patriotism and identity policy in the occupied Donbas̆. Communis Post-Commun 58(1):28–52
Cannizzaro E (2001) The role of proportionality in the law of international countermeasures. Eur J Int Law 12(5):899–916
Cavandoli S, Wilson G (2022) Distoring fundamental norms of international law to resurrect the Soviet Union: the international law context of Russia's invasion of Ukraine. Netherlands Int Law Rev 69:383–410
Charron A (2016) Whose is crimea? Contested sovereignty and regional identity. Region 5(2):225–256
Chatham RP (2011) Defense of nationals abroad: the legitimacy of Russia's invasion of Georgia. Florida J Int Law 23(1):75–102
Coleman D (2021–2022) The depopulation of Ukraine—a recurrent disaster revisited. Finnish Yearb Popul Res 55:115–136
Criddle EJ (2015) Standing for human rights abroad. Cornell Law Rev 100(2):269–334
Dickinson D (2017) The crisis in Crimea: does the 2014 military intervention in and subsequent annexation of Crimea by The Russian Federation constitute violation of the prohibition on the use of force enshrined within article 2(4) of the UN Charter. Bristol Law Rev 4:54–72
Franck TM (2008) On proportionality of countermeasures in international law. Am J Int Law 102(4):715–767
Franck TM, Weisband E (1970) The Johnson and Brezhnev doctrines: the law you make may be your own. Stanford Law Rev 22(5):979–1014
Goodman RM (1969) The invasion of Czechoslovakia: 1968. Int Lawyer 4(1):42–79
Gorbunova Y (2014) Human rights abuses in Crimea under Russia's occupation. Secur Human Rights 25(3):328–340
Götz E (2022) Near abroad: Russia's role in post-soviet Eurasia. Eur Asia Stud 74(9):1529–1550
Green JA (2014) Annexation of Crimea: Russia, passportisation and the protection of nationals revisited. J Use Force Int Law 1(1):3–10
Hafkin G (2010) The Russo-Georgian war of 2008: developing the law of unauthorized humanitarian intervention after Kosovo. Boston Univ Int Law J 28(1):219–239
Heinsch R (2015) Conflict classification in Ukraine: the return of the "Proxy War"? Int Law Stud 91(1):323–360

Hewitt G (2008) Abkhazia and Georgia: time for a reassessment. Brown J World Aff 15(2):185–196
Hilpold P (2015) Ukraine, Crimea and new international law: balancing international law with arguments drawn from history. Chinese J Int Law 14(2):237–270
Hofmeister H (2010) "Don't mess with Moscow"—legal aspects of the 2008 Caucasus conflict. San Diego Int Law J 12(1):147–173
Kanetake M, Prevost D, Wouters J (2024) The Russia-Ukraine war and (dis)continuity in international law. Neth Int Law Rev 71(2):227–231
Kostelyanets SV (2019) Russia's peace initiatives in the MENA region: evaluation and prospects. Asian J Middle Eastern Islamic Countr 13(4):534–555
Kotova A, Tzouvala N (2022) In Defense of comparisons: Russia and the transmutations of imperialism in international law. Am Soc Int Law. https://doi.org/10.1017/ajil.2022.48
Kuzio T (1994) The crimea and European security. Eur Secur 3(4):733–774
Longobardo M, Wallace S (2022) The 2021 ECtHR decision in *Georgia v Russia (II)* and the application of human rights law to extraterritorial hostilities. Israel Law Rev 55(2):145–177
Natoli K (2010) Weaponizing nationality: an analysis of Russia's passport policy in Georgia. Boston Univ Int Law J 28(2):389–417
New York Open Society Institute (June 2018) Human Rights in the Context of Automatic Naturalization in Crimea
Nußberger A (2009) The war between Russia and Georgia—consequences and unresolved questions. Goettingen J Int Law 1(2):341–364
Okowa P (2008) The Georgia v. Russia case: a commentary. Hague Just J 3(3):41–50
Olson PM (2014) The lawfulness of Russian use of force in Crimea. Military Law Law War Rev 53(1):17–44
Pelliconi AM (26 January 2023) Self-determination as faux remedial secession in Russia's annexation policies: when the devil wears justice. Völkerrechtsblog, https://doi.org/10.17176/20230126-081617-0
Pelliconi AM (2024a) Self-defence as remedial self-determination: continuity in Russian narratives to justify imperialism and the use of force. Neth Int Law Rev 71(2):233–260
Pervou I (2024) Forcible protection of nationals abroad: the doctrine's hegemonic use. Neth Int Law Rev 71(2):261–279
Petro NN (2009) The legal case for Russian intervention in Georgia. Fordham Int Law J 32(5):1524–1549
Reisman WM (1988) Old wine in new bottles: the Reagan and Brezhnev doctrines in contemporary international law and practice. Yale J Int Law 13(1):171–198
Robinson P (2016) Russia's role in the war in Donbass, and the threat to European security. Eur Politics Soc 17(4):506–521
Rostow N (1981) Law and the use of force by states: the Brezhnev doctrine. Yale J World Public Order 7(2):209–243
Shanahan Cutts NM (2007) Enemies through the gates: the Russian violations of international law in the Georgia / Abkhazia conflict. Case Western Reserv J Int Law 40(1):281–310
Sicilianos L-A (2017) L' Articulation entre Droit International Humanitaire et Droits de l'Homme dans la Jurisprudence de la Cour Europeene des Droits de l'Homme. Swiss Rev Int Eur Law 27(1):3–18
Sloane RD (2009) Breaking the genuine link: the contemporary international legal regulation of nationality. Harv Int Law J 50(1):1–60
Starski P, Arndt F (2021) The Russian aggression against Ukraine—Putin and his 'legality claims'. Max Planck Yearb United Nations Law 25:756–796
Tagliavini H (2011) The august 2008 conflict in Georgia. Proc Ann Meet Am Soc Int Law 105:89–94
Tancredi A (2014) The Russian annexation of the Crimea: questions relating to the use of force. Quest Int Law 6:5–34
Tokarev A, Margoev A, Prikhodchenko A (2021) The statehood of Eurasia's de facto states: an empirical model of engagement by great powers and patrons. Caucasus Surv 9(2):93–119

Värk R (2014) The advisory opinion on Kosovo's declaration of Independence: hopes, disappointments and its relevance to Crimea. Polish Yearb Int Law 34:115–131
Vidmar J (2010) Remedial secession in international law. St Antony's Int Rev 6(1):37–56
Vorobiova A (2022) The "lessons of Nuremberg": their use and abuse in the current Russia-Ukraine war. Polish Yearb Int Law 44:55–82
Wilson G (2016) Secession and intervention in the former soviet space: the Crimean incident and Russian interference in its 'near abroad'. Liverpool Law Rev 37(3):153–176
Yue H (2016) Crimea's Independence from Ukraine and incorporation into Russia: the unlawfulness of Russia's use of force. Beijing Law Rev 7(3):181–191

Book Chapters

Bowring B (2018) Who are the "Crimea People" or "People of Crimea"? The fate of the Crimean Tatars, Russia's legal justification for annexation, and Pandora's Box. In: Sayapin S, Tsybulenko E (eds) The use of force against Ukraine in international law, Jus Ad Bellum, Jus In Bello, Jus Post Bellum. Springer, pp 21–40
Del Mar K (2013) The myth of remedial secession. In: French D (ed) Statehood and self-determination, reconciling tradition and modernity in international law. Cambridge University Press, pp 79–108
Ganohariti R (2021) Politics of passportization and territorial conflicts. In: Richmond OP, Visoka G (eds) The Palgrave Encyclopedia of peace and conflict studies. Cham, Springer International Publishing, pp 1–8
Gray C (2018) The conflict in Georgia—2008. In: Ruys T, Corten O (eds) The use of force in international law, a case-based approach. Oxford University Press, pp 712–728
Güven O, Ribbelink O (2016) The protection of nationals abroad: a return to old practice? In: Paulussen C et al (eds) Fundamental rights in international and European law, public and private law perspectives. TMC Asser Press, pp 45–72
Harzl BC (2021) The arrow of passports in the quiver of Russia: eastern Ukraine, Abkhazia and South Ossetia in perspective. In: Harzl BC, Petrov R (eds) Unrecognized entities, perspectives in international, European and constitutional law. Brill, pp 54–83
Kemp G, Lyubashenko I (2018) The conflict in Ukrainian Donbas: international, regional and comparative perspectives on the Jus Post Bellum options. In: Sayapin S, Tsybulenko E (eds) The use of force against Ukraine in international law, Jus Ad Bellum, Jus In Bello, Jus Post Bellum. Springer, pp 329–354
Marten K (2023) NATO enlargement: evaluating its consequences in Russia. In: Goldgeier J, Itzkowitz-Shifrinson JR (eds) Evaluating NATO enlargement, from cold war victory to the Russia-Ukraine war. Palgrave Macmillan, pp 209–250
Molodikova I (2024) Eurasian migration towards Russia: old and new regional dynamics in the era of globalization. In: Triandafyllidou A (ed) Handbook of migration and globalization. Edward Elgar, pp 234–253

Online Material

Burkhardt F et al (2022) Passportization, Diminished Citizenship Rights, and the Donbas Vote in Russia's 2021 Duma Elections. Harvard University, Ukrainian Research Institute, TCUP Report. Retrieved February 22, 2025, from https://www.ssoar.info/ssoar/handle/document/76864

Human Rights Watch (13 January 2009) Up in Flames, Humanitarian Law Violations and Civilian Victims in the Conflict over South Ossetia. Retrieved, February 22, 2025, from https://www.hrw.org/report/2009/01/23/flames/humanitarian-law-violations-and-civilian-victims-conflict-over-south

Knott E (2022) Were Crimeans Really pro-Russian before Annexation?. Retrieved February 22, 2025 https://www.lse.ac.uk/research/research-for-the-world/society/were-crimeans-really-pro-russian-before-annexation

Kvitka K (16 May 2023) Russia Threatens Ukrainians Who Refuse Russian Citizenship, Russian Occupation Authorities Depriving Residents of Their Rights. Human Rights Watch. Retrieved February 22, 2025, from https://www.hrw.org/news/2023/05/16/russia-threatens-ukrainians-who-refuse-russian-citizenship

Longobardo M (2022) Legal Perspectives on the Role of the Notion of "Denazification" in the Russian Invasion of Ukraine under *Jus contra Bellum* and *Jus in Bello*. *Revue Belge de Droit International*. Retrieved, February 22, 2025, from https://papers.ssrn.com/sol3/papers.cfm?abstract_id=4214444

Maco J (29 January 2016) Nationalism, Soviet Legacies and Majority-Minorities Dynamic amid the Establishment of the Independent State of Georgia. Security Outlines. Retrieved February 22, 2025, from https://www.securityoutlines.cz/nationalism-soviet-legacies-and-majority-minorities-dynamic-amid-the-establishment-of-the-independent-state-of-georgia/

Milanovic M (24 February 2022) What is Russia's Legal Justification for Using Force against Ukraine?. EJIL:Talk!. Retrieved February 22, 2025, from https://www.ejiltalk.org/page/2/?s=Russia+Ukraine+humanitarian+intervention

NATO (1 April 2014) Statement of the NATO-Ukraine Commission. Retrieved February 22, 2025, from https://www.nato.int/cps/en/natolive/news_108499.htm

Pazzanese C (17 February 2023) One year later: How does Ukraine war end?. The Harvard Gazette. Retrieved, February 22, 2025, from https://news.harvard.edu/gazette/story/2023/02/how-does-ukraine-war-end-experts-say-2023-could-prove-decisive-dangerous/

Pellet A (3 March 2022) Open Letter to my Russian Friends: Ukraine is Not Crimea. EJIL:Talk!. Retrieved February 22, 2025, from https://www.ejiltalk.org/open-letter-to-my-russian-friends-ukraine-is-not-crimea/

Pelliconi AM (8 September 2024b) Unexceptional exceptionalism: the use of force by great powers and international instability. E-Int Relat. Retrieved February 22, 2025, from https://www.e-ir.info/2024/09/08/unexceptional-exceptionalism-the-use-of-force-by-great-powers-and-international-instability/

Peters A (9 May 2019) Passportisation: Risks for International Law and Stability – Part I. EJIL: Talk!. Retrieved February 22, 2025, from https://www.ejiltalk.org/passportisation-risks-for-international-law-and-stability-part-one/

Reuters (8 August 2008) Medvedev Vows to Protect Compatriots in South Ossetia. Retrieved February 22, 2025, from https://www.reuters.com/article/idUSL8661071

Santora M (2 May 2023) Russia Ramps up Pressure on Civilians in Occupied Ukraine. NYTimes. Retrieved, February 22, 2025, from https://www.nytimes.com/2023/05/02/world/europe/russia-ukraine-civilians.html#:~:text=Russia%20is%20ramping%20up%20pressure,of%20a%20widely%20expected%20counteroffensive

Santos Mariottini de Oliveira V (2024) Russia's 'Passportization' and the Pitfalls of 'Personal Annexation' in the Post-Soviet Space: Recasting the Limits of Nationality Attribution in International Law. EUI, LAW, AEL, Working Paper, 2024/18, European Society of International Law (ESIL) Paper. Retrieved February 22, 2025, from https://cadmus.eui.eu/handle/1814/77046

Spiro P (2 May 2023) Weaponized Citizenship: Should International Law Restrict Oppressive Nationality Attribution?. EUI Global Citizenship Observatory. Retrieved February 22, 2025, from https://globalcit.eu/weaponized-citizenship-should-international-law-restrict-oppressive-nationality-attribution/8/

Tatarenko A (2 April2014) The Legal Status and Modern History of Crimean Autonomy. Verfassungsblog. Retrieved, February 22, 2025, from https://verfassungsblog.de/the-legal-status-and-modern-history-of-crimean-autonomy/

The New York Times (18 March 2014) Putin Reclaims Crimea for Russia and Bitterly Denounces the West. Research, February 22, 2025, from https://www.nytimes.com/2014/03/19/world/europe/ukraine.html

Weller M (9 March 2022) A Perversion of Both the Facts and the Law", Russian Attempts to Invoke International Law Dismantled. University of Cambridge. Retrieved, February 22, 2025, from https://www.cam.ac.uk/stories/weller-ukraine

Chapter 5
Forcible PNA and the Human Element

5.1 Forcible PNA: Reconceptualizing Sovereignty

The forcible PNA is a dubious doctrine in international law, as it reflects an obsolete structure of international society before nation-states were well established. Despite the prevalence of territoriality over nationality, as the Westphalian model requires,[1] the latter is still of importance for the formation of states and the international legal order. The principle of active personality is the legal foundation of most constitutional democracies, expressed through the concept of "popular sovereignty", according to which all powers derive from the people and exist for them.[2]

People are the source of political power according to most constitutional orders all over the globe, and in effect they can be the source of political change and state claims. Following this course of thinking, the principle of nationality can never be substituted for territoriality. The interplay between the two is unavoidable and the forcible PNA stands in between. This is why it is broadly apprehended that

> the nationality principle is among the most firmly established bases for jurisdiction recognized by international law. [...] The concept of active personality jurisdiction draws on the conception of a State as a group of persons, wherever located, who are subject to a common authority [...] active personality jurisdiction is in fact a compensation for the diplomatic protection that the state offers to its nationals abroad (the so-called "allegiance theory").[3]

Thus, the nationality principle plays a cardinal role for the internal formation of a state and its political governance. The idea that nationals form a common authority, wherever they might be, creates a standing claim for their protection.

---

[1] Pal (2021), p. 35; Raustiala (2009), pp. 11–12; Barreto (2017), p. 160.

[2] Lee (2016).

[3] Ryngaert (2015), p. 106.

© The Author(s), under exclusive license to Springer Nature Switzerland AG 2025

I. Pervou, *Protecting Nationals Abroad and the Reconceptualization of Sovereignty*, Studies in the History of Law and Justice 32,
https://doi.org/10.1007/978-3-032-05231-5_5

The potential clash between territoriality and nationality as distinct grounds of sovereignty had come to be thought of as a matter of no further interest, but there have been recent shifts in the international plane which prove the opposite. Over the last decades, the voices supporting the idea that the concept of the sovereign nation-state no longer covers the needs of the international system have multiplied.[4] In general, globalization has affected the notion of sovereignty and has been gradually degrading territoriality, given that people are not so closely attached to nation-states. This proposition has been captured by the phrase "postnational constellation" and it also denotes how people today perceive themselves as "world citizens".[5] In the words of Kofi Annan:

> State sovereignty, in its most basic sense, is being redefined—not least by the forces of globalisation and international co-operation. States are now widely understood to be instruments at the service of their peoples, and not vice versa.[6]

Fluctuations and continuous alterations in the content and meaning of the two principles are not only matters of theoretical interest. On the contrary, they shape states' policies and, in effect, legal arguments and doctrinal perceptions. The recent Joint Statement of Russia and China supports this proposition. The two countries state, among others, that they

> reaffirm their strong mutual support for the protection of their core interests, state sovereignty and territorial integrity, and oppose interference by external forces in their internal affairs.[7]

This statement does not deviate at first sight from their fixed position that their respect for sovereignty extends to territorial integrity and as such clearly forbids interference in their domestic affairs. A position that China upheld regarding the Ukrainian conflict too.[8]

However, a more careful and systematic reading of the Joint Statement leaves room for other considerations. The following excerpts are enlightening in this regard, as it is stated that:

> The Russian side reaffirms its support for the One-China principle, confirms that Taiwan is an inalienable part of China, and opposes any forms of independence of Taiwan. Russia and China stand against attempts by external forces to undermine security and stability in their common adjacent regions, intend to counter interference by outside forces in the internal

[4] Kumar (2008), p. 252.

[5] Habermas (2001), p. 107.

[6] Annan (18 September 1999). Retrieved February 22, 2025, from https://www.un.org/sg/en/content/sg/articles/1999-09-18/two-concepts-sovereignty.

[7] Joint Statement of the Russian Federation and the People's Republic of China on the International Relations Entering a New Era and the Global Sustainable Development (4 February 2022). Retrieved February 22, 2025, from http://www.en.kremlin.ru/supplement/577.

[8] Ministry of Foreign Affairs of the People's Republic of China (24 February 2024). Retrieved February 22, 2025, from https://www.fmprc.gov.cn/mfa_eng/zxxx_662805/202302/t20230224_11030713.html.

> affairs of sovereign countries under any pretext, oppose colour revolutions, and will increase cooperation in the aforementioned areas.[9]

Apart from China's and Russia's agreement to back up each other's territorial claims and statehood perceptions, this Joint Statement is more than a shared understanding of the international legal system. Russia's support for the One-China principle comes as a trade-off for the states' commitment to resist "attempts by external forces to undermine security and stability in their common adjacent regions".[10] It is therefore implied that the two states perceive themselves as guardians of regional peace and security, carrying the burden to protect adjacent regions from external interference. Apart from the obvious hegemonic character of this comment, it is significant how it contravenes the previous line. Put simply, territorial integrity and sovereignty are of utmost importance if it is ours. In other words, these rules are not absolute and according to the two states there is space for improvement when democratic values are at stake. Yet again, the interpretation of these democratic standards relies on the interpreter's viewpoint; as such, the Joint Statement also provides that:

> Certain States' attempts to impose their own "democratic standards" on other countries, to monopolize the right to assess the level of compliance with democratic criteria, to draw dividing lines based on the grounds of ideology, including by establishing exclusive blocs and alliances of convenience, prove to be nothing but flouting of democracy and go against the spirit and true values of democracy. Such attempts at hegemony pose serious threats to global and regional peace and stability and undermine the stability of the world order. [...] The sides call on the international community to respect cultural and civilizational diversity and the rights of peoples of different countries to self-determination.[11]

Evidently, an overall reading of the Joint Statement reveals that respect for sovereignty and territorial integrity, which is proclaimed at the forefront of the statement in unequivocal terms, is not that absolute after all. References to "cultural and civilizational diversity", as well as to "the rights of peoples of different countries to self-determination", are inevitably translated in legal terms into collective self-determination and remedial secession. Considering that self-determination due to cultural and civilizational diversity has long ago been exhausted and left behind in international law, the argument that peoples of different countries are entitled to self-determination due to cultural and civilizational diversity can be directly correlated with Russia's "near-abroad policy". According to the Joint Statement this approach is imposed by the need for democratic governance.[12] On a second reading, the Statement embraces interventions on democratic or humanitarian grounds, and the two states have expressed their intention to effortlessly take on the role of local stability guarantors.[13]

[9] Joint Statement of the Russian Federation and the People's Republic of China on the International Relations Entering a New Era and the Global Sustainable Development (4 February 2022).

[10] European Parliament (Briefing) (May 2023). Retrieved, February 22, 2025, from https://www.europarl.europa.eu/RegData/etudes/BRIE/2022/729349/EPRS_BRI(2022)729349_EN.pdf, p. 8.

[11] Idem.

[12] Kim (2023), p. 99.

[13] Baum (2020), p. 270.

The Joint Statement's analysis validates the proposition that the concept of protecting one's nationals abroad has not been invoked as a subsidiary legal basis during recent interventions. On the contrary, it is expected to hold a central role in the two states' foreign policy in the future. From this viewpoint, the statement normalizes the doctrine of the forcible PNA: military intervention is highly probable wherever the intervening state deems that third states fall short of their democratic standards, putting cultural and civilizational diversity in peril. If this reading is accepted, then doctrinal developments on the forcible protection of nationals abroad from 1945 onwards will be disregarded.

All in all, institutional transformations of the international legal system conjoined with recent policy shifts lead to two safe conclusions: sovereignty is a multidimensional concept subject to spatiotemporal changes;[14] however, all and any interpretations of it come down to two constitutive elements, territoriality and nationality. No matter how sovereignty is understood, these two jurisdictional bases are foundational, simply because a sovereign cannot exist without territory and people. The forcible PNA doctrine evaluates a threat against a sovereign's nationals more highly than another sovereign's territorial integrity. As such, it is perceived a ticking bomb lying at the basis of the international legal structure, for it primarily contravenes the principle of territorial integrity. If insincere invocations of the doctrine are to be added to this inherent conundrum, then we can better understand why the doctrine does not meet wide acceptance and is only tolerated by the UN Charter at best.

5.2 Forcible PNA: Redefining Nationals

Legal research has been focusing on striking a fair balance between the doctrine's employment and territoriality. Ultimately, elaboration on the concept of "nationals" has been sidestepped. The preceding analysis has shown that the prerequisite of nationality is essential and not a mere formality, although it is proved by, and exhausted in formal elements. More specifically, dismissal of the "genuine link" criterion and the acknowledgement that conferment of nationality relies on states' absolute discretion, must be combined with the need for official documentation such as passports to verify that military intervention does indeed take place on behalf of nationals. That is, recourse to force for the protection of nationals abroad cannot be invoked unless there is a definite nationality link between the intervening state and the populations in jeopardy. This rough scheme regarding the proof of national ties partly explains why passports, or other similar documents, are key for the doctrine's invocation. There are several questions, though, which remain unanswered.

---

[14] See, UNGA (21 December 1965). Declaration on the Inadmissibility of Intervention in the Domestic Affairs of States and the Protection of Their Independence and Sovereignty. UN Doc A/Res/20/2131.

The international community's legal interest in domestic legislative frameworks on nationality has reasonably focused up till now on the potential loss of nationality and on whether non-conferment leads to discriminatory treatment.[15] By way of contrast, military operations for PNA, both before and after the UN Charter, were not doubted on grounds of the existence of nationals, with the exception of the later Russian incidents. International scrutiny focused on recourse to force and compliance with the respective requirements and not on the verification of alleged nationality ties. After all, the fact that states initiated such costly operations, both in financial and human resources terms, sufficed to establish their legitimacy; a state's decision to expend resources and organize such an operation created the belief that national ties were not in question. National ties between subjects of protection and the intervening state were not disputed; thus, they remained a strand requiring no legal analysis. What is more, such operations or raids were executed in non-amiable or hostile environments, and thus it was extremely difficult for national authorities to carefully check if formal conditions establishing whether someone should be considered a national were indeed met. There was an expedited inspection of passports or other documentation on all such occasions. In light of the recent events, though, it is recalled that national ties are the bottom line for the doctrine's invocation.

A brief historical review shows that legislative frameworks were based on a fictional split between those who bore a state's nationality and the rest. By way of extrapolation, someone residing in a state without being a national of it was deemed a foreigner or an alien. This distinction was deemed necessary, as it simplified a state's expected behavior. There were two different sets of state obligations, one vis-à-vis its nationals, and another regarding aliens. This distinction is envisaged in the UN Declaration on the Human Rights of Individuals who are not nationals of the country in which they live, which provides the minimum standard of protection they shall receive by the state where they are present.[16]

These steps had a positive impact during the early years of the UN, as they constituted original attempts to ensure human rights protection at a point when the international human rights regime was in its infancy. Yet despite its good intentions, this dichotomy was oversimplistic from its very birth and did not correspond to the status of many. Terms like "expatriates" or "compatriots" were used to explain people's various conditions in relation to the state of their residence. These terms played a crucial role in shaping states' domestic and foreign policies, albeit they were extra-legal. Most researchers agree that there can be no clear and unambiguous definitions of them.

For example, Fetcher notices that

[15] UNGA (30 August 1961) Convention on the Reduction of Statelessness. UNTS 989, p. 175; UNGA (28 September 1954). Convention Relating to the Status of Stateless Persons. UNTS 360, p. 117.

[16] UNGA (13 December 1985). Declaration on the Human Rights of Individuals Who Are Not Nationals of the Country in Which They Live. UN Doc A/RES/40/144.

> the word 'expatriate' is recognized across the spectrum of different foreign nationalities [despite the fact that] the term 'expatriate' is socially contested, politically and morally charged, ambiguous and is linked to particular notions of ethnicity and class...[a] pertinent reason to employ the term is its prominence in discourse among foreigners, whether through positive identification or emphatic dissociation.[17]

An expatriate is broadly defined as a person living "somewhere other than in their home country—'home' being determined by their passport and citizenship – thus undertaking a 'change in their dominant place of residence'".[18] The term reappeared in former colonies' correspondence as a way to identify their citizens who had long resided in another country due to labor ties, usually in corporations whose interests were closely related to their state of citizenship. Evidently, an expatriate falls within the traditional understanding of a "national abroad"; as such, the term came up in the Suez Canal crisis, as well as in the most recent unrest in Libya.

On the other side, though, the concept of "compatriot" is much more challenging from an international law perspective. The traditional meaning of the term is "a person from the same country as someone else" and thus could be perfectly synonymous with a national or an expatriate, given that it does not signify any special characteristic of the person being referred to. Recent state practice, though, has employed the term to mean "someone who belongs to the same group": i.e., that is not necessarily a co-national. The most prominent example is in Russian discourse, according to which compatriots (*sootechestvenniki*) are the citizens of countries which hold close ties with Russia, such as Belarus, or parts of Moldova, or even 'Russian speakers beyond the historic homeland'.[19] In this context, a compatriot is the citizen of any country who feels close to another in terms of their national identity. If compatriots are defined in such a broad manner, then the concept includes anyone with some sort of ties to a state other than that of their nationality. This reading would prove detrimental for the international legal order if states decided to extend it to cover larger groups of people who shared common nationality elements with another nation-state, such as language or religion. Not to mention that it would contravene various international law rules pertaining to the laws of self-determination and human rights protection, re-questioning the status of minorities or other groups.

In other words, this interpretation takes advantage of shared ethnicity, language or religion, and most importantly people's (self)-identification that they belong to a group closer to a third state than to the one of their citizenship, contrary to the rules of public international law over time.[20] By perceiving groups that share the elements of common language and self-identification that show proximity to a third-kin state

---

[17] Fechter (2007), p. 6.

[18] McNulty and Brewster (2017), p. 23.

[19] Pearce (2020), p. 35.

[20] UNGA (3 February 1992). Declaration on the Rights of Persons Belonging to National or Ethnic, Religious and Linguistic Minorities. UN Doc A/RES/47/135; UN Subcommission on Prevention of Discrimination and Protection of Minorities (1979). Study on the Rights of Persons Belonging to Ethnic, Religious and Linguistic Minorities, by Francesco Capotorti. UN Doc E/CN.4/Sub.2_384_Rev.1.

as 'compatriots', whether there is official recognition of a group as a minority or not,[21] states would be able to overturn the very underpinnings of the international legal order, further provoking a series of unpredictable reactions.

This is the main reason why Russia opted for mass-passportization in all previously analyzed occasions and did not openly speak of compatriots, even though it had made amendments to its constitution for this purpose. Forcible PNA relies, above all, on the existence of nationality ties between the intervening state and the population in peril; and these ties must be typically and formally proven, as otherwise this action would shake the foundations of the international plane. The position that passportization is an inevitable part of current Russian policy is not that popular, given that most researchers give the big picture, which includes other means of demographic engineering and depopulation too. Passportization is a safe option in this sense, for it provides the typical requirements for the application of forcible PNA.

Overall, the questions "what nationals" and "whose nationals" are ones that matter more in the invocation of the doctrine. *Jus ad bellum* rules have shaped all criteria and prerequisites that states should follow when they resort to force. The distinctive element of this doctrine is that a state's nationals are in jeopardy while residing abroad. Thus, this element must be narrowly construed as a guarantee that the doctrine is not manipulated by states, or, better, that mass-passportization is a hint of its wrongful use. However, even this view, although correct in its essence and according to international law principles, is not popular among states. Passportization, even when massive and at a rapid pace, is dubious but within the limits of legitimacy. States' prerogative to confer their nationality to anyone, according to their national interests, is a matter which falls within their absolute discretion. Hence, the element of nationality is a typical and unexceptional requirement for the doctrine's invocation.

5.3 Forcible PNA and Diplomatic Protection: The Space in Between

Part of the preceding analysis focuses on how diplomatic protection and the forcible protection of nationals abroad are two sides of the same coin, given that they share the same rationale: a state's need to protect its nationals found under another jurisdiction. The question that needs to be addressed is whether these two institutions suffice to justify a state's protection of its nationals abroad. Is there anything else a state may do except for extend diplomatic protection or begin an evacuation operation in situations where its nationals face an imminent threat? This question might seem inappropriate, if we accept that the two institutions cover the spectrum of a state's possible options. However, both institutions come with a considerable

[21] Spiliopoulou Åkermark (1996), pp. 52–54.

limitation: neither are applicable for occasions where large populations of a state's nationals abroad are threatened. On one hand, diplomatic protection cannot satisfy claims pertaining to large populations, while on the other, evacuation and rescue operations are limited by their operational capabilities.

The quantitative criterion is deemed outdated when a legal analysis is at hand; however, protection of nationals abroad is an exception to this general trend. Neither institution is meant to be applied, and correctly so, in cases where the existence and fundamental rights of large populations are threatened. To demonstrate this proposition, we can consider how diasporas are treated in international law, and if the protective shield of the two institutions is sufficient for this purpose. The concept of "diaspora" is one of the least explored in international law. The term refers to the phenomenon where:

> Groups of persons of the same ethno-national origin who themselves, or their ancestors, voluntarily or under coercion migrated from one place to another, or to several other places, settled in these other places, and maintain their identity and various kinds of contacts with their place of origin.[22]

It is of course another extra-legal concept, and a definition which does not shed light on the legal aspects of the term; instead, it blurs the lines. The term might well cover a recognized minority, or any other group which holds ties with its place of origin, such as "naturalized foreigners", or "compatriots". Thereat, it refers to any group of people who identify themselves as being close to another country, irrespective of their citizenship. They may have acquired the nationality of their state of residence, possess double citizenship, or remain nationals of their state of origin; and all three may coexist.

As a phenomenological concept, a diaspora does not fit the protection of nationals abroad doctrine, as it does not meet the strict requirement of citizenship. At the same time, protection of diasporic populations cannot be always achieved through diplomatic means. For example, in several historical cases diasporas were found amidst conflicting parties, trapped in the midst of hostilities. In such cases, the means that their state of origin had to extend its protection to them were not clearly defined in international law. The decision to conduct an evacuation or rescue operation was left to the state's discretion, and the same applied to the diplomatic means it chose to employ to ensure their safety or repatriation. Their state of origin could choose either of the two, according to its economic and human resources, its political interests and its international relations. Again, everything was left to its discretion; taking no action was an option too. There are recent examples which support these propositions. During the early nineties the upheaval in Upper Abkhazia put the Greek diaspora in jeopardy. The Greek state opted to rescue and repatriate them, and it so proceeded with operation "Golden Fleece". The operation was designed on the basis that these people had close historical ties with Greece, irrespective of the fact that most of them did not possess Greek passports. By way of analogy, the same

[22] Encyclopedia Princetoniensis. Retrieved February 22, 2025, from https://pesd.princeton.edu/node/256.

conditions exist in the ongoing war against Ukraine. Although the details of the current circumstances have not yet been revealed, it is not contested that a large Greek diaspora of approximately 200,000 people reside around Mariupol. It has not come to light which diplomatic means Greece employed to guarantee those people's safety; what it is known, though, is that an extremely small percentage of them (around 200 people) managed to repatriate after the coordinated attempts of the Greek Ministry of Foreign Affairs. Evidently, different treatment applied on these two distinct occasions: diasporic protection does not perfectly align with the protection of nationals abroad doctrine. Nevertheless, diasporic protection also depends on the state's absolute discretion.[23]

Reference to diasporic protection shows the limits of the forcible PNA doctrine. Apart from the strict typical requirement of the existence of nationality and not merely nationality ties, it is evident by way of extrapolation, that states invoke the doctrine for the protection of certain groups. The quantitative criterion is helpful in understanding the doctrine's practical limits, but state practice is illuminating, regarding the type and means of protection they choose regarding diasporas. The course of history affirms that forcible PNA is case specific and does not pertain to wide diasporic populations found in peril. Forcible PNA is not a fit-for-all doctrine of protection. Although its typification and doctrinal understanding has proven difficult, there are certain limitations. It refers to targeted groups facing imminent threat, instead of wider populations that may be entrapped in unregulated circumstances.

5.4 Forcible PNA and Sovereignty: A Matter of Control

The above analysis reveals that there can be no straightforward answer regarding the legality of the doctrine's invocation. Forcible PNA relies on a series of parameters which constitute a unique mosaic. The factual background of each case directly affects whether the doctrine has a solid legal justification or not. Sovereignty is not a static term. The concept is fluid, and its understanding has changed many times throughout history. This proposition is not self-evident; it is verified by the fact that both territoriality and nationality are notions which fluctuated during time too. On the one hand, territoriality is *prima facie* a settled concept. Yet, there is no consensus on which actions constitute a breach of it, and how it is effectively protected under international law. However, it is true that in the post-Charter era, territoriality was

[23] Dionyssis Kalamvrezos (9 August 2003). The Anniversary of Operation Golden Fleece to Evacuate Diaspora Greeks from War in Abkhazia. Retrieved February 22, 2025, from https://www.ekathimerini.com/news/16335/the-anniversary-of-operation-golden-fleece-to-evacuate-diaspora-greeks-from-war-in-abkhazia/; Reuters (21 March 2022). 'What I Saw, I Hope No one Will Ever See' Says Greek Diplomat Returning from Mariupol. Retrieved February 22, 2025, from https://www.reuters.com/world/europe/what-i-saw-i-hope-no-one-will-ever-see-says-greek-diplomat-returning-mariupol-2022-03-20/.

institutionally and legally consolidated. On the other hand, the legal framework regarding nationality is far more nebulous. International law has not paid enough attention to the legal framework regarding nationality, considering it as part of each national legal order. The recent invocations of forcible PNA point to this legal lacuna and underline how the tectonic changes brought by globalization affect the nucleus of the nationality concept.

The remaining question to be answered is which are those constituents of sovereignty that matter when the forcible PNA doctrine is invoked by states. If both territoriality and nationality are occasionally relativized, then another more stable concept is necessary, to explain forcible PNA. From this point of view, states willing either to justify their reference to forcible PNA, or to outlaw it, must delve into the essence of state sovereignty and analyze why the doctrine is intrinsically connected to it. Following a hard-power way of thinking, sovereignty exists where control is and is absent if there are no such mechanisms.

The idea of control has time and again been employed by states to substantiate extraterritoriality claims, or by international organs, to expand state responsibility.[24] However, control has not come into the forcible PNA discussion so far. To verify if a state has a justified case to invoke forcible PNA both territoriality and nationality do not suffice; because technically the doctrine is a breach of the former, while the latter can be easily manipulated. An alternative course of thinking would be support that there is a claim for forcible PNA where there is control over a group of people, like there is over nationals. This would justify PNA in cases involving expatriates, compatriots etc. However, this view is vehemently rejected as it would become the Trojan Horse of territoriality. If control over nationals residing abroad is the underlying value of forcible PNA, then the Russian discourse would totally be in order, or historical examples resembling it, like the Turkish invasion of Northern Cyprus. The concept of control fits in most cases where forcible PNA was used, but it indeed echoes hegemonic, pro-Charter policies.

Overall, although state sovereignty, territoriality and nationality are well established ideas in legal doctrine, the assessment over their breach is not an easy task. Forcible PNA is a doctrine touching upon them all, putting under the microscope the exceptional characteristics of each case. Although state practice and doctrinal discussion have developed over the doctrine's outer limits, recent practice demonstrates that legal debate is so far inconclusive, primarily because there are gray areas regarding the concept of nationality. Adversely, current developments point at the importance of the human element for the doctrine's invocation and application. Thus, there is a gradual shift from sovereignty to humanity,[25] or a more humanistic reading of sovereignty.

[24] Talmon (2009), p. 494.

[25] Peters and Sparks (2024), pp. 14–15.

UN Documentation

UNGA (3 February 1992). Declaration on the Rights of Persons Belonging to National or Ethnic, Religious and Linguistic Minorities. UN Doc A/RES/47/135.
UNGA (13 December 1985). Declaration on the Human Rights of Individuals Who Are Not Nationals of the Country in Which They Live. UN Doc A/RES/40/144.
UN Subcommission on Prevention of Discrimination and Protection of Minorities (1979). Study on The Rights of Persons Belonging to Ethnic, Religious and Linguistic Minorities, by Francesco Capotorti. UN Doc E/CN.4/ Sub.2_384_Rev.1.
UNGA (21 December 1965). Declaration on the Inadmissibility of Intervention in the Domestic Affairs of States and the Protection of Their Independence and Sovereignty. UN Doc A/Res/20/2131.
UNGA (30 August 1961). Convention on the Reduction of Statelessness. UNTS 989, p. 175.
UNGA (28 September 1954). Convention Relating to the Status of Stateless Persons. UNTS 360, p. 117.

Miscellaneous

Encyclopedia Princetoniensis. Diaspora. Retrieved February 22, 2025, from https://pesd.princeton.edu/node/256.

References

Books

Fechter A-M (2007) Transnational lives, expatriates in Indonesia. Routledge
Habermas J (2001) The postnational constellation, political essays (trans. & ed. Max Pensky), Polity
Lee D (2016) Popular sovereignty in early modern constitutional thought. Oxford University Press
Pal M (2021) Jurisdictional accumulation, an early modern history of law, empires, and capital. Cambridge University Press
Pearce JC (2020) The use of history in Putin's Russia. Vernon Press
Raustiala K (2009) Does the constitution follow the flag? The evolution of territoriality in American law. Oxford University Press
Ryngaert C (2015) Jurisdiction in international law, 2nd edn. Oxford University Press
Spiliopoulou Åkermark A (1996) Justifications of minority protection in international law. Kluwer International

Articles

Baum TJ (2020) The responsibility of power: shifts in Chinese conceptualization of the legitimacy of overseas intervention to protect nationals abroad. Global Change Peace Secur 32(3):259–273
Kim PM (2023) The limits of the no-limits partnership, China and Russia can't be split, but they can be thwarted. Foreign Aff 100(2):94–105
Talmon S (2009) The responsibility of outside powers for acts of secessionist entities. Int Comp Law Quart 58(3):493–517

Book Chapters

Barreto J-M (2017) Cerberus: rethinking Grotius and the Westphalian System'. In: Koskenniemi M, Rech W, Fonseca MJ (eds) International law and empire, historical explorations. Oxford University Press, pp 149–176
Kumar CR (2008) Corruption and transparency in governance and development: reinventing sovereignty for promoting good governance. In: Jacobsen T, Sampford C, Thakur R (eds) Re-envisioning sovereignty, the end of Westphalia? Routledge, pp 251–266
McNulty Y, Brewster C (2017) The concept of business expatriates. In: McNulty Y, Selmer J (eds) Research handbook of expatriates. Edward Elgar, pp 21–60
Peters A, Sparks T (2024) Introduction: the history and theory of the individual in international law. In: Peters A, Sparks T (eds) The individual in international law. Oxford University Press, pp 1–30

Online Material

Annan K (18 September 1999) Two concepts of sovereignty. Retrieved, February 22, 2025, from https://www.un.org/sg/en/content/sg/articles/1999-09-18/two-concepts-sovereignty
European Parliament (Briefing) (May 2023). China-Russia Relations: A Quantum Leap?. Retrieved February 22, 2025, from https://www.europarl.europa.eu/RegData/etudes/BRIE/2022/729349/EPRS_BRI(2022)729349_EN.pdf
Joint Statement of the Russian Federation and the People's Republic of China on the International Relations Entering a New Era and the Global Sustainable Development (4 February 2022). Retrieved February 22, 2025, from http://www.en.kremlin.ru/supplement/5770
Kalamvrezos D (9 August 2003). The Anniversary of Operation Golden Fleece to Evacuate Diaspora Greeks from War in Abkhazia. Retrieved February 22, 2025, from https://www.ekathimerini.com/news/16335/the-anniversary-of-operation-golden-fleece-to-evacuate-diaspora-greeks-from-war-in-abkhazia/
Ministry of Foreign Affairs of the People's Republic of China (24 February 2024) China's Position on the Political Settlement of the Ukraine Crisis. Retrieved February 22, 2025, from https://www.fmprc.gov.cn/mfa_eng/zxxx_662805/202302/t20230224_11030713.html
Reuters (21 March 2022) 'What I Saw, I Hope No One Will Ever See' Says Greek Diplomat Returning From Mariupol. Retrieved February 22, 2025, from https://www.reuters.com/world/europe/what-i-saw-i-hope-no-one-will-ever-see-says-greek-diplomat-returning-mariupol-2022-03-20/

Chapter 6
Conclusions

Forcible PNA is a doctrine inextricably linked to state sovereignty. For many years, it was neglected by international law, in an attempt to secure sovereignty and leave territorial integrity untouched. For this reason, the doctrine was deemed obsolete, echoing older times, not fitting the current international legal order. Although these propositions are true in their essence and forcible PNA was considered marginally at the limits of international law, state practice demonstrates the doctrine's validity. Recurrence of its invocation by states proves that forcible PNA's necessity for the accomplishment of states' national interests. In this regard, the doctrine's historical, doctrinal and practical analysis is fundamental for the shape of its content.

The preceding chapters bring forward several criteria that would possibly help in the doctrine's configuration and better understanding. Except for the general interpretative principles which govern all use of force doctrines, *id est* necessity, imminence and proportionality, the analysis has further explored the doctrine's constituents. Concepts like "peril", or "nationals" have been examined, in order to reach an objective conclusion as to the doctrine's content and thus its legality under international law. In addition, the analysis was not confined to strict theoretical limits. Rather, it explored the doctrine's practical implications and operational limitations. In this context, the number of people in peril, the type of the operation designed, as well as hostility of the environment, hold a crucial part in the doctrine's understanding.

The above is indicative of the difficulty to set clear lines regarding forcible PNA's legality. However, the above cannot offer complete answers as to the key question, which is how forcible PNA affects state sovereignty. International legal discourse adheres to the proposition that forcible PNA is not tolerated by the law of the use of force, since it trespasses its key prohibition and infringes state sovereignty and in particular territorial integrity. For this reason, the invocation of forcible PNA always met the international community's suspicion. Yet, if one is to offer a solid reading of the doctrine and bridge the gap between use of force theory and state practice, then

© The Author(s), under exclusive license to Springer Nature Switzerland AG 2025

I. Pervou, *Protecting Nationals Abroad and the Reconceptualization of Sovereignty*, Studies in the History of Law and Justice 32,
https://doi.org/10.1007/978-3-032-05231-5_6

forcible PNA cannot be erased from the *jus ad bello* catalogue. In this context, the key to the doctrine's assessment is the current perceptions over the notion of state sovereignty. State sovereignty is one of the pillars of the international community. The term's substance seems familiar, but it is far from specific or tangible.

In the post-Charter era, the formation of states that would adhere to the use of force prohibition and guarantee safety of borders became a synonym of state sovereignty. Sovereignty was seen mostly through the lens of territorial integrity (and subsequently political independence). This was well expected, considering the broader historical context. Nevertheless, state sovereignty is not exhausted in these elements. Nationality is also an uncontested tenet of state sovereignty, in the sense that sovereignty cannot exist without national populations. The exercise of sovereignty over a state's nationals is also a central feature of the international legal order, as well as national jurisdictions. Thus, the protection of a state's population is an inherent right in all its aspects.

Having this in mind, forcible PNA is of certain value for states, which always hold the right to exercise sovereignty over their citizens. This idea is not far from the Vattelian perception of sovereignty and its extraterritorial nuance. However, it would be more concise to speak of the human aspect of sovereignty, which may be exercised extraterritorially. This course of thinking was commonplace in the pre-Charter era and was vehemently rejected after the end of WWII. As a result, if a more human-centric, or extraterritorial, understanding of state sovereignty is proposed, then the last remaining question is whether there is a shift in the underpinnings of the international community, and if such a shift is acceptable, or even welcome today. The historical part of the preceding analysis reflects a shift from the after the UN Charter came into place. After the end of WWII and as soon as decolonization turned into flesh and blood, territoriality was not anymore, the epicenter of attention, or states' point of concern. This explains why the international community demonstrated an interest in the conditions within states, the level of democracy, rule of law and human rights protection. The institutionalization and stability of territoriality over time allowed states to look beyond the strict limits of borders. State practice from 1945 onwards is apt proof that military interventions of states became a normalized exception.

Invocations of the forcible PNA doctrine were few, but did not cease, confirming that states' interpretation of the Charter did not outlaw forcible PNA, or at least that the doctrine was tolerated. In turn, forcible PNA was adjusted to the parameters set by the Charter and its legality was bound by them. However, the doctrine's standardization is not yet given. Forcible PNA covers a wide range of operations, from raids to full scale military operations. The mere common element between them all, is that force is used in the name of a state's nationals. This is what signifies the turn to a more human centric perception of state sovereignty.

So far, it is argued that there is a gap between the legal domains of use of force and the international human rights regime, which is occasionally covered by forcible PNA. However, it is more than the legal approach to forcible PNA and whether the perils faced by nationals abroad are a matter relating mostly to human rights or recourse to force. A humancentric approach of sovereignty comprises of both, after all a sovereign's cause cannot focus only on the protection of territorial integrity and leave aside their nationals. This reading of state sovereignty rectifies the falsified perception on the legality of forcible PNA which has existed over the last decades.

If this view is apprehended, then the content and limits of forcible PNA become the focus of interest. Many theoretical approaches are submitted to this debate, each one proposing particular criteria, that would prevent the doctrine from becoming a means of "intrastate bullying". Taking as a starting point that forcible PNA necessarily entails the trespassing of another state's territorial integrity, then the doctrine's limits are related to ensuring territorial integrity. That is, while the doctrine implies by definition a breach of territorial integrity, this cannot amount to territorial claims. This view distinguishes forcible PNA invocations which led to full-scale warfare, or annexation of a third state's territories, from raids, or military operations which targeted on the protection of nationals' groups.